Praise for
GLIMPSES

"THIS BOOK is a braid of stories, about family, a huge career, and God. It utterly charmed me. These stories are sometimes funny, sometimes tender and spiritually uplifting, sometimes all at once."

—ANNE LAMOTT, *New York Times* bestselling author of *Help, Thanks, Wow; Some Assembly Required; Bird By Bird*

"MATT WILLIAMS, one of the greatest comedy writers of all time, tells the story of his life in *Glimpses*. Incandescent, emotional, and real, this collection is a primer in how to get the most out of life, love, and work by a master craftsman who has lived it."

—ADRIANA TRIGIANI, *New York Times* bestselling author of *The Good Left Undone*

"MATT WILLIAMS has done something extraordinary in this book: he has revealed his flawed humanity so that we may see ourselves more honestly—and more hopefully. I finished *Glimpses* inspired to notice more, savor more, and, most importantly—love more. Not many books do that."

—FATHER EDWARD BECK, author, on-air contributor for CNN

"I COULDN'T PUT this book down! Matt Williams's authentic voice shines brightly in stories that take you through his journey as a creator, father, and husband. *Glimpses* will fill you with joy, wonder, and hope. A feel-great book."

—DETE MESERVE, bestselling author of *Good Sam*

"AN EASY WINNER! Matt Williams looks back on his legendary life with wit, warmth, and wisdom. It's one of those books you'll find yourself rereading again and again."

—ALFRED UHRY, Academy Award–, Tony Award–, Pulitzer Prize– winning playwright of *Driving Miss Daisy, Parade*

"IN THESE TIMES that try our souls, Matt Williams offers the proverbial 'balm in Gilead' stories from an epic life odyssey that will resonate with anyone who has ever loved, lost, dreamed an impossible dream, or sought to put together the pieces of their shattered heart. The tales in *Glimpses* will make you laugh, cry, and inspire you to be a better human being."

—SUSAN FALES-HILL, television writer, producer, author of *Always Wear Joy, A Different World*

"MATT TOOK THE seemingly mundane moments of everyday life, presented them in a new light, and elevated them into meaningful moments of sheer joy and wonder. After reading *Glimpses,* a remarkably witty, funny, and poignant series of essays, I now see the world filled with that light, giving me a new sense of hope, appreciation, and love for all that's around me. It's a beautiful piece of work."

—JAMES MANOS, JR., Emmy Award–winning writer of *The Sopranos, Dexter*

"*GLIMPSES* OPENED my hardened heart to hope again. I laughed myself to tears and felt deeply moved to remember the long arc of life. Our pain has a purpose, and if we look up and around, we can catch little glimmers of goodness in the people and places we encounter daily. Matt Williams is a steadfast spiritual guide in the wilderness, and you'll want to buy this book for everyone you know who needs laughter and joy on their journey."

—ASHLEY ABERCROMBIE, author of *Rise of the Truth Teller, Love Is the Resistance*

"*GLIMPSES: A COMEDY Writer's Take on Life, Love, and All That Spiritual Stuff* made me examine my own life and explore the choices and events that have shaped my journey. I could not put it down. It's an outstanding piece of work."

—DAVID ZAYAS, Tony–nominated actor, *Between Riverside and Crazy, Dexter, Oz*

"MATT WILLIAMS cherishes the still, small voice within, and it has guided him through a fascinating life. By turns funny, full of heart, and sharp observation, *Glimpses* details the sweet without dodging the tough emotions in every human life. You'll be inspired by this very personal and creative approach to what Williams calls 'that spiritual stuff!'"

—IRENE O'GARDEN, poet, playwright,
author of *Fulcrum, Women on Fire*

"HEARTFELT, WISE, often hilarious, and, yes, inspirational. Reading *Glimpses* is like hanging out with a longtime friend who has a good soul and also happens to have created some of television's most beloved shows. I'm certain this book will also put smiles on faces and touch many hearts."

—DAVID HENRY HWANG, Obie Award–winning playwright,
librettist, screenwriter, *M. Butterfly, Yellow Face*

"IN A DARK TIME, Matt Williams throws some light."

—TOM FONTANA, Emmy Award–winning
writer and producer, *Oz, Homicide: Life on the Streets*

"IN THE MIDST of so much uncertainty and pain in the world, we all need to be reminded of the glimpses of goodness that are happening all around us—if only we would take the time to recognize them."

—ARIEL CURRY, ghostwriter, editor, coauthor of *Hungry Authors*

"TO CALL THESE beautifully written pieces 'essays' is far too limiting. These are must-read, real-life experiences that will lift your heart, restore your spirits, and nourish your soul with joy. A captivating celebration of goodness!"

—DAVID MCFADZEAN, television writer, producer,
playwright, cocreator of *Home Improvement*

"MATT WILLIAMS has written a wonderful memoir filled with humor, honesty, and insight about his spiritual journey and how the memorable and unique personalities of his wife, children, siblings, parents, and friends touched his life and career in poignant, sometimes tragic, and often hilarious ways. The lessons he learned in trying to find glimpses of God in himself and others will resonate with you long after you finish the book."

—CARMEN FINESTRA, television writer, producer,
The Cosby Show, Home Improvement

"MATT WILLIAMS gives us something extraordinary in *Glimpses*. The stories range from uplifting to raw, heartbreaking to hilarious, and together they absolutely delight. *Glimpses* is a book to read again and again for inspiration, for beauty, and for deep, whole-body laughter."

—TREY ELLIS, screenwriter, playwright, essayist,
*Platitudes, Bedtime Stories: Adventures
in the Land of Single Fatherhood*

"IN *GLIMPSES*, Matt Williams has woven a tapestry of Faith with golden threads of Hope and bound together with cross-stitchings of Love. Enjoy!"

—JOHN PIELMEIER, playwright, screenwriter,
novelist, *Hook, Agnes of God*

"*GLIMPSES* MADE ME laugh, it made me think, and, best of all—it gave me hope."

—RICHARD KARN, actor, *Home Improvement*

GLIMPSES

GLIMPSES

A COMEDY WRITER'S TAKE ON LIFE, LOVE,
AND ALL THAT SPIRITUAL STUFF

MATT WILLIAMS
THE CREATOR OF *ROSEANNE* AND *HOME IMPROVEMENT*

Forefront
BOOKS

Published by Forefront Books, Nashville, Tennessee.
Distributed by Simon & Schuster.

Library of Congress Control Number: 2023921837

Print ISBN: 978-1-63763-249-9
E-book ISBN: 978-1-63763-250-5

Cover Design by Bruce Gore, Gore Studio, Inc.
Interior Design by Mary Susan Oleson, BLU Design Concepts

Printed in the United States of America

FOR ANGELINA

Evil has a blockbuster audience,
while goodness lurks backstage.
—TONI MORRISON

I think it is time for goodness
to step up to center stage,
take a bow, and bask in the spotlight.

AUTHOR'S NOTE

Love. Create. Serve.

The author's profits from this work
are donated to charitable organizations
to help children in need around the globe.

CONTENTS

INTRODUCTION

Chances are you grabbed this book because you watched *Roseanne* or *Home Improvement*. Or maybe you're curious about *all that spiritual stuff*. Why would a guy who created sitcoms write a faith-inspired book? Good question. I'll tell you why. We all need to be uplifted. In this age of chaos, conflict, and enmity, there are some things that everyone would have a hard time opposing. For example, we need more love, kindness, and compassion. We need more empathy and less hatred. We need more inclusiveness and acceptance, less divisiveness and intolerance. I think we can agree on that, right?

Like many people, I had grown weary of all the bitterness in the world, the anger, and the frustration. I got tired of the constant algorithms of fear popping up on my cell phone, the horrible headlines, the bad news blasting through my television, the outraged, indignant newscasters determined to inflame rather than inform. So many horrors, atrocities, and woes made me enraged, then tired, then numb. Fight, flight, or freeze. I was frozen.

One day during one of these downward spirals, I heard the term *compassion fatigue*. I went online and found this definition: "Compassion fatigue is a broadly defined concept that can include emotional, physical, and spiritual distress."[1] The symptoms are apparent: chronic physical fatigue, emotional exhaustion, irritability, feelings of self-contempt and inadequacy, and difficulty sleeping. That was me. I had been beaten down, become bitter, and stopped caring about the suffering of others.

And then, at my lowest, I saw something while riding the subway in New York City. I was on my way to Columbia University to teach a class, and across from me I watched a five-year-old child sitting next to his grandfather. The boy, bursting with pride, told his grandfather, "I learned to write my name in cursive today!" The grandfather kissed the top of the boy's head and whispered, "That is remarkable. I am so proud of you." The boy beamed. I smiled and thought, *I just saw a little glimpse of God.*

That simple moment calmed my worries, eased my numbness, and helped me to thaw a bit. And I realized that if I was to counter feelings of despair and overcome the headlines of fear, anxiety, and conflict, then I had to do a better job of noticing the "glimpses" of goodness that God sends my way. My job is to pay attention and be on the lookout for them.

This book tells my story but don't expect a typical Hollywood memoir in which I dish gossip while I explain how I wrote for *The Cosby Show*, created top-ten television

---

[1] "Compassion Fatigue," Spectrum Health Lakeland, accessed August 16, 2023, www.spectrumhealthlakeland.org/employee-assistance-program /compassion-fatigue.

programs, produced successful movies, and wrote plays. Yes, those things are in here, but they are not what this book is about. They serve as the backdrop.

When I look back on my life, I don't see some grand story with me at the center. What jumps out at me is how consistently I have experienced glimpses of grace, goodness, and God. These are what have brought meaning to my life, serving as life vests when I felt I was drowning or as unexpected gifts of joy that have brightened and sustained my world. In the following stories I try to describe what I have learned and perhaps inspire others to spot their own glimpses.

I should explain that, for me, the source of these glimpses is God, and that their essence or source is love. I also believe Jesus Christ is the embodiment of that love. That's right, I am a Christian. But don't let that scare you off. I know Christians are perceived by some people as intolerant, judgmental, self-righteous, and closed-minded, with many public figures fulfilling those expectations. They're thought of as hair-sprayed television evangelists, thumping a Bible and raging about God's wrath while soliciting donations to buy another private jet. Being a Christian in many people's minds means being white, tight, and headed toward the light. It means being closed off to any new ideas, any theologies that challenge or differ from a literal interpretation of the Bible. It means thinking that God is an old white guy with a beard sitting on a cloud with a thunderbolt in hand, waiting to flash-fry your ass if you step out of line.

That was never my image of God.

And I am not blind, nor do I dismiss the barbarity, the senseless cruelty that has been perpetrated in the name of God. Organized religions have a bloody history, a red-soaked path of slaughter and unimaginable cruelty. But, for me, that is not God. That is not Jesus. That is corrupt humankind using the name of God for selfish purposes.

All my years in Hollywood, I never mentioned my faith. I didn't feel I had to. I tried to live my Christian beliefs by treating others how I wanted to be treated and practicing patience, kindness, and tolerance. With every new film or television series, I tried to treat the staff and production crew respectfully and show appreciation to all, from the network executive to the craft-service person serving bagels and coffee. I tried to be Christlike in all my encounters, humble in success, and gracious in failure. The operative word for living by these ideals is *tried*. I didn't always succeed. I used to have a terrible temper. And I was racked with crippling insecurity. I was competitive, seeking to defeat and crush the opposition but still have them love and adore me.

Instead of calling myself a Christian, I said, "I am a follower of Christ." That may not sound too different, but for me it is. I tell you this not to convince anyone to become a

Christian. I don't think the efficacy of noticing glimpses of goodness is dependent on being a Christian or even on being religious. Still, you will see that this is the language or context I use for understanding these glimpses. Feel free to ignore my religious language. The power of noticing glimpses still works.

When I started my current quest to find little glimpses of God in everyday life, the clouds didn't open, and a voice like rolling thunder didn't call down to me; there were no angels, no harps, not even one chubby cherub. But I started noticing simple acts of kindness, moments of grace that reflected God's loving presence in the world. They could be family events or memories seen in a new light, or they could have nothing to do with me directly. This practice or habit of taking the time to notice these glimpses changed my life.

Instead of blasting my way through the week—competing, hurrying and scurrying, fighting for my personal space, my necessary self-care, and my ego-based impulses—I started consciously looking for God's goodness. And I found it everywhere. I watched a teenager wearing a faded Hollister T-shirt hold the door open for an older woman, smiling at her. She smiled back, a radiant smile. That was a little glimpse of God. I believe holding the door open for a stranger is, in some small way, a holy act.

My wife tripped on a piece of broken sidewalk in New York City and fell. She landed hard. Instantly, three strangers hovered over her making sure she wasn't hurt. They gathered her belongings and helped her to her feet. I watched a man dressed in an expensive charcoal-gray pin-striped suit stop, turn around, and help a young mother carry her baby stroller up the steps out of the subway. There is a softball field in our neighborhood in the West Village. One day, I saw a young boy sitting near third base crying. Two other children were bent over whispering soothing words, encouraging him to keep playing. They were kind. They were caring. They were gentle. Another glimpse.

The Bible says that the measure you give is the measure you get.[2] Kindness is rewarded with more kindness. It grows and expands. Kindness is contagious.

Not only did I look for and find those glimpses of divinity, but I also started practicing what I preached. I was reminded of Dr. Norman Vincent Peale, the famous pastor and author of the perennial bestseller *The Power of Positive Thinking*. The first year I moved to New York City, in the late seventies, I attended his church, Marble Collegiate Church on Fifth Avenue. Dr. Peale was still alive and preaching, telling his magnificent stories with passion and zeal. The man, his simple message, captivated me. I bought his bestselling book, and it changed my life. Cynics today may roll their eyes at the seemingly idealistic message of Dr. Peale's book, but his words are truthful and still resonate. Look for positivity and you are more likely to find it.

In one chapter, Dr. Peale references Dr. Frank Laubach,

---

[2] Matthew 7:2.

who talked about how he would "shoot" prayers at people. Dr. Laubach called this kind of praying "flash prayers." It's a simple concept: as you pass a person on the sidewalk, sit across from someone in the subway, or dine near someone in a restaurant, you pray for that individual, flash him a blessing, surround her with light, or send him good thoughts. That person will often look up, smile, shift a little, and look around as if tapped on the shoulder. The vibrational energy of a simple prayer stirs souls and awakens the consciousness. I started praying for others, blessing people on the street, patrons in restaurants, and strangers hurrying out of a deli. Those flash prayers may not have affected others, but they certainly influenced me. I found myself less bitter, more empathetic, more energized, and more aware of my connectedness to other people. In short, I felt more human.

And this quest to find glimpses of God in the quotidian motivated me to look back at my life and spiritual journey and identify how God has touched my life with moments of grace, goodness, insight, and inspiration. The more I recalled that journey, the more I realized how a divine spirit protected me through my tumultuous teenage years, guided my roller coaster of a career from starving actor to creator of number one television programs, comforted me through heartbreaks, and blessed me with a loving wife and wonderful family.

All of this brings me to why I decided to write this book. *Glimpses* is a collection of personal essays and spiritual musings. Some are short and some are long; some are memories and thoughts; some are questions about the cosmos and the nature of God. I don't pretend to have answers. I am no preacher, no rabbi, and no imam. I do not have a degree in theology. I am not a scholar. I am a simple, flawed individual who has stumbled upon a way to find solace in a tumultuous world. Instead of drowning in an ocean of despair, I want to pass along the habit of paying attention to one's life in order to see the many glimpses of grace and goodness all around us. These glimpses can become tiny islands of hope where we can stop for a few minutes and think about the goodness that still exists in the world.

Regardless of your beliefs, culture, or orthodoxy, I hope this book will inspire you to look for and find little glimpses of God in your daily life.

1

MASKS

Three things in human life are important:
the first is to be kind; the second is to be kind;
the third is to be kind.
—HENRY JAMES

Something happened to me at the grocery store this morning.

I selected a cart with wheels that didn't wobble and worked my way down the produce aisle, but my glasses kept fogging up. I was shopping for the family, had my list, my reusable bags, hand sanitizer, and, of course, my mask—a KN95 face mask to be exact. But with each breath, a moist mist fanned across the lenses. We're talking dense fog, a San Francisco fog, a London fog. I tugged at my mask, pinched the noseband, and adjusted my glasses, but nothing worked. Finally, I took off my glasses and jammed one stem into the open collar of my shirt. I double-checked to make sure the frame was secure because designer bifocals are expensive. The store appeared fuzzy but navigable, so I made my way to the deli counter.

I asked for a half pound of sliced turkey breast.

"Boar's Head?" the woman behind the counter asked.

"That will do," I said. She went to work cutting the turkey. Her ash-blonde hair was tucked inside a hairnet, and she also wore a mask and glasses. I watched her work and asked, "How do you keep your glasses from fogging up?"

"Oh, they fog up all the time," she answered, flopping the turkey slices onto the scale. I assumed she was smiling because the skin around her eyes was crinkly. "I'm surprised I haven't cut my thumb off. I spend half my day fiddling with my glasses," she said, handing me the wrapped turkey.

"Well, you're doing better than me." I tugged on my shirt collar, showing her my glasses. I thanked her, pushed my cart down the aisle, and parked it by the cheese section. I grabbed a couple of containers of olive tapenade hummus, kalamata olives, and a bag of crumbled feta, and then I remembered the crackers. I left the cart and walked to another aisle, grabbed Mary's Gone Crackers, my wife's favorite, and a box of original Triscuits.

When I came back, a woman was going through my cart, handling items. I thought, *Is she stealing my olive tapenade hummus?* And then I noticed the hairnet. The deli lady turned around and held up a sealed plastic bag. Inside the bag was a face mask.

"I bought a bunch of these. They work better than the

other masks I found, you know, to keep your glasses from fogging up," she said, handing me the mask. "I was going to leave it in your cart. But here, you can have it, I mean, for free."

"Why, thank you," I said, a little surprised. She waved a dismissive hand. "Have a good day."

At home, my daughter, Matisse, helped me unpack and put away the groceries. When I showed her the sealed mask the deli lady gave me, she said, "Oh, that is so sweet." Matisse put the hummus and olives in the refrigerator. Then my sophisticated thirty-two-year-old daughter got teary-eyed. "I mean, really, that is sweet."

I thought about it for the rest of the day. I knew this brief encounter was definitely an example of a glimpse of grace. Still, this one moved me since I was the recipient of her generosity. I wondered if that woman had felt the gentle promptings of Spirit—the same spirit who has guided me and watched over me throughout my life, the same spirit that connects all humankind.

A Jean-Jacques Rousseau quote appears beneath the signature at the bottom of my emails: "What wisdom can you find that is greater than kindness?" If everyone on the planet took the time to perform a simple act of kindness, we could change the world.

2
NOVA

Nova came crashing into our life the day before Thanksgiving, ten weeks old, with jet-black fur, floppy ears, and paws the size of small dinner plates. My wife had bought a Labrador puppy. I thought about taking the leash and strangling her—my wife, not the dog. Chaos reigned. This black streak tore through our house, slamming into furniture, pulling dish towels off the rack, and knocking over her water bowl; it was like inviting a Tasmanian devil to a tea party. Angelina sighed, "Oh, I just love her so much," as the dog pissed a puddle the size of Lake Erie on our kitchen floor.

We put up wooden gates, cordoning off the mudroom and kitchen area. The house turned into a kennel; we were prisoners in our own home. Our daily life quickly revolved around poop: where did Nova poop, when did she poop, and when should we feed Nova so she poops on a schedule? And, of course, no more walking around the house in stocking feet because of all the pee puddles. Dante didn't know a thing about hell. Hell is a ten-week-old Lab puppy.

31

My wife and I had the same argument week after week.

"We are not getting a dog," I had said.

"Why not?"

"We are old. The kids have moved out of the house. We are alone and can enjoy our time together."

"We can enjoy our time together with a puppy."

"No!"

This argument went on for about three years. I flatly refused to get a dog, but Angelina is like water on sandstone; she wears you down. Then the coronavirus swept the planet, killing millions and isolating even more. We both got very ill during the early months of the pandemic. But we survived. And now we were quarantined, separated from family and friends. Angelina was restless, so one day she pulled up pictures of puppies on the Internet. She had inquired about adopting a dog from a shelter, but the shelter was empty. It seemed everyone was adopting a dog during the pandemic. She called local breeders with the same result. Every dog was spoken for; every dog had a new home. That's why she sat at her desktop scrolling through photographs of big-eyed, adorable puppies.

"Come over here and just look," she said.

"No."

"Just look."

"I don't want to look. I'd rather you pulled up pictures of alligators. In fact, if you want a companion, let's adopt an alligator."

"Oh, be quiet. Come over here."

I could feel the waves of Angelina's strong will lapping away at my resolve, breaking me down, and, like an idiot, I walked over and looked at the computer screen. And there was Nova. Adorable. Sweet. Angelic. You could see the tenderness of the dog's soul reflected in her watery brown eyes as she stared into the camera lens. Angelina looked up at me with her own watery brown eyes and softly sang, "She's very cute."

I must have been drunk or high on mushrooms because I said, "OK."

"Really?!"

"Yes."

"Thank you, thank you, thank you!"

"But," I said, with a pause for emphasis, "*you* are going to watch this dog. You will walk it and feed it and clean up after it. I am not doing any of that. You understand?"

"I'll take care of her. We're quarantined. I'll have all day to train her."

"For the next twelve weeks, training this dog is your full-time job."

"Of course, it'll be perfect," she said, clicking through several more photos of Nova's precious face.

Crash! Nova pushed through the gate that divided the kitchen from the living room. We had put up our Christmas tree and all the decorations. Nova was eating every ornament off the lower half of the tree. I chased her away, and she jumped up onto the coffee table and started chewing on the papier-mâché nativity from Spain. I rushed over, stumbling on the rug, determined to save the nativity. She ate two wise men and a shepherd before I could stop her. By some miracle, baby Jesus was still in the manger. I had this horrible nightmare of Nova eating the manger and pooping out the Son of God.

Eventually, things settled down into a routine; there was a rhythm to the chaos. We were up on our farm and had easy access to the outdoors, which made housebreaking Nova much easier. There were a few accidents, but for the most part all the toilet stuff was outside in the grass, not on the floor. But then we had to go to the city.

Angelina was cast in a play reading on Zoom. She was "safe distance" rehearsing in the city for most of the day, so I had the dog. It was bitterly cold, about twelve degrees, the sidewalks of New York slick with ice. I noticed Nova walking in a circle sniffing by the front door, a sure sign she needed to go out. I threw on a coat, put on my mask, and rushed out of the house. I didn't have time to get a plastic poop bag, so I grabbed a handful of tissues as Nova yanked me out the door. Nova is amazingly strong for a puppy, the Arnold Schwarzenegger of dogs. I am convinced that while Angelina and I sleep at night, Nova bench-presses fifty-pound bags of puppy chow.

Hitting the cold air, huffing and puffing into my mask, my glasses instantly fogged up as Nova pulled me along the frozen sidewalk. She jumped off the curb, dragged me into the middle of Commerce Street, and took a big dump. I couldn't see the poop because of the fogged glasses. A car honked. I waved them off as I searched for the turd. More honking. Nova kept yanking on the leash. My glasses slipped down on my nose. I nudged them in place, but now they were completely fogged over. I couldn't see a thing. Honk, honk! I ignored the idling car, aimed the wad of tissues, guessing where the turd had landed, and jammed my hand into the center of the warm goo. *Honk!* "Shut up!" I politely yelled to the driver as he flipped me off.

I dragged the dog back to the curb. No trash cans. Anywhere. They had all been removed for some reason. So I headed back to the house, leash in my left hand, my right hand smeared in poop, clutching a soggy tissue. As I got to the front door, I realized that I had a bigger problem: my house key was in the right front pocket of my pants. The dog was yanking. I'm gagging. I don't know how to get the key out of my pocket without smearing crap all over my pants. I tossed the dog turd into a nearby planter—shameful, I know. I hate when people do that. I plunged my hand into my pocket and dug out the key.

But my glasses were still fogged, so I couldn't find the keyhole. I kept stabbing, peering over the glasses, looking for an opening. Finally, I unlocked the door and stumbled into the house, the leash tangled around my ankles, the dog barking, just as Angelina came home and cried out, "There's my sweet baby!"

I knew she wasn't talking to me. She hugged the dog while I ran to the bathroom to wash my hands. As hot water scalded my fingers, I had an epiphany: Nova had complete control of our lives. Every minute of every day revolved around her. Our home was a kennel, the floors littered with chew toys, rawhide strips, and cow bones. I dreamed about piles of poop. I had to do something.

I got on my computer and researched the life expectancy of Labrador retrievers: ten to twelve years. Son of a bitch! I was turning seventy years old in a few months. This dog could outlive me. We are in a race to the death. I did the math. If I outlive Nova, I will be eighty-two when the dog croaks. If Nova dies before I do, Angelina will buy another puppy, and that will definitely kill me. There's no doubt the dog is sweet, but enough is enough. I decided to confront Angelina and tell her "You must decide. It's either the dog or me." But I didn't say anything because I didn't feel like moving out.

The winter days got shorter and colder. One morning, I was in my study, attempting to write something halfway coherent, but it was difficult because of the barking and the squeaking of toys. Angelina eventually took Nova outside, so things quieted down.

I sat at my desk, looked out the window, and saw a halo of gray hair curling out from under the hood of Angelina's puffy winter coat. It had snowed. The sun had come out. Angelina and Nova were playing catch with an old tennis ball. They were far enough away that I couldn't hear them, but I could see everything. Nova raced after the ball, slipping and sliding on the snow, dug it out of the cold powder, and raced back to Angelina; she threw herself at Angelina's feet, rolled onto her back, and spit out the ball.

Angelina laughed—threw her head back and laughed a laugh of pure joy. She was radiant, as if God had just kissed her on the forehead. The past year flashed through my mind: how we battled COVID, forced quarantine, and months of isolation, cut off from family and friends. And yet Angelina was laughing. I thought, *This is the woman I have loved for more than thirty-six years.* We have fought and argued, made love and made babies, built homes, and built a life together. We struggled to balance our family life and our careers, sometimes successfully and sometimes not. We have raised children and buried parents. Our lives are entwined, the weft and warp of our souls woven tightly together to make the tapestry of our marriage. If this little creature can bring my wife that kind of joy, then the least I can do is pick up a few turds. All I have to do is outlive the dog.

3

ALONE WITH GOD

My friend Jim Manos came up to our farm in the Hudson Valley to escape the city for a few days. Jim, who won an Emmy writing for *The Sopranos* and created the series *Dexter*, is one of the most intelligent people I know. I like him because he challenges me. Jim describes himself as "a hypochondriacal pessimist who is surprised that he wakes up on any given morning." And he is the only person on the planet who calls me *Matty*. We sat on the back porch and watched the setting sun streak the river with slashes of pink. As we sipped wine, Jim asked something I had never considered before.

"When did you first feel God in your life?"

"The first time?"

"Yeah."

"I always sensed God was in my life."

"But was there a moment? Did something happen? How did you know?"

I realized his writer's mind was looking for an inciting incident, a specific moment when—*bam!*—I knew there was a God. I told Jim that I didn't have an epiphany. There was no Damascus-road experience. "Even as a young child," I explained, "I always felt there was a presence in my life. I knew I was alone in this world with God."

"Alone with God? I don't understand that."

"When I was three years old, I was aware that I was small, but I sensed that I was a part of something bigger than myself. I wasn't sure what that 'something' was, but I knew it surrounded, protected, and guided me. My mother used to brag that her firstborn son cooked his own breakfast when he was three."

"Three? Really?"

"It's true. I did that. I'd wake up before my parents, wearing my Roy Rogers pajamas, scurry into our kitchen on Read Street, pull a chair over to the gas stove, stand on it, and cook breakfast. I'd fry two strips of bacon in the cast-iron skillet, then fry one egg in the bacon grease while the bread toasted in the toaster. I carried the food to the table, dragged the chair back over, sat down, and ate alone. I somehow sensed that I shouldn't depend on anyone, even at that young age. It wasn't that my parents were neglectful. I loved and trusted them, but deep down I knew I had to be self-reliant and that, ultimately, I was alone with God."

"But, Matty, when did it happen? When did you know there was this God presence—Yahweh, Jehovah, I Am Who I Am, whatever? By the way, *I Am Who I Am* sounds like Popeye to me."

I thought about it for a moment, then told him this story.

When I turned five and started kindergarten, I walked to and from school every day along Virginia Street, crossing a major thoroughfare, unaccompanied. Can you imagine? But it was 1956, a different world from today. My mother walked me on the first day of school, and I observed all the landmarks and memorized the street signs. I was never afraid. I knew that I could live on my own if necessary. I knew how to cook meals, dress, and bathe myself. I didn't need anyone because God was with me. It was a feeling, a sensation. My image of God was shaped by what I heard in church.

Every week, I attended Sunday School and services at Saint Paul's Lutheran Church with my family. I was usually wedged between my mother, Lillian, and my maternal grandmother, Hedwig. All the grandchildren called her Momo. My mother always looked tired as she cradled my baby sister, Beth, in her arms. My three-year-old brother, Randy, fidgeted in the pew next to my father. Momo wrapped an arm around me, stroking my hair as we listened to the pastor. Reverend Dobelstein loomed above us from the pulpit. I was fascinated by his large hands, massive head, and the dark mole protruding from his chin. As he preached, my five-year-old brain struggled to comprehend the mystery of a triune God: Father, Son, and Holy Ghost.

The Father was the angry one. He lived in burning bushes and handed out commandments on stone tablets. I was supposed to fear him. And tremble. The Father had white hair and a beard, like Santa Claus. I imagined he had a list that he checked twice to see if I was naughty or nice. If I were good, I'd get a checkmark by my name, and he would answer my prayers and give me a new toy or a puppy. If I were naughty, the Father would slash a big *X* through the list and cast me into the fiery pits of hell, where Satan and his demons would poke me with pitchforks.

The Son was the dead one. He was very skinny. Someone stuck a crown of thorns on his head and hung him on a cross. His name was Jesus. He was sometimes called the Lamb of God, but that didn't make sense to me. He wasn't a sheep. Jesus was the only Son of the angry Father. And the Father let his Son die to save the world from sin. From the stories I heard in Sunday School, Jesus liked children and men who caught fish. I thought the Son was probably a nice person, but he seemed sad.

And there was the Holy Ghost. But he wasn't a scary ghost; he was more like Casper, the friendly ghost. Like all ghosts, he could fly around the room or stick his head through walls. And Reverend Dobelstein explained how the Holy Ghost came down and appeared as tongues of fire on top of the disciples' heads. That was confusing. The tongues were on fire? And how did they get on top of people's heads? You couldn't see this friendly ghost, but you could feel him. Maybe the "something" I felt was the Holy Ghost.

What really confused me was that all three people in the

Trinity were men: Father. Son. Holy Ghost. There were no women. How could that be? No mother, grandmother, sister? How did the Father have a son without a wife? Why wasn't a mother a part of the triangle? I always noticed that the angels in the stained-glass windows at Saint Paul's looked like girls. They had long hair and wore white gowns. I could imagine angels tucking children into bed or watching over them while they slept. But who protected me? Was it angels or the Holy Ghost?

One afternoon as I walked home from kindergarten, I saw flashing lights. There was an ambulance and a police car. Traffic was stopped, and people were gathered on the sidewalk. A boy was lying in the middle of Virginia Street. He was older than me, maybe eight or nine. His head was bleeding. He was moaning. Someone ran from the back of the ambulance and put a napkin on his head. The police officer told everyone, "Please step back."

When I stepped back, I saw a can of corn. It was dented and had a green giant on the label. It must have rolled across the street and bumped into the curb. Then I saw two more cans, a loaf of bread, and a ripped brown paper bag. A car was parked sideways in the street. A police officer talked to a woman who stood by the car's open door, crying and shaking her head. I watched as the boy, now on a rolling bed, was placed into the back of the ambulance. As the ambulance drove away, I started to pick up the can with the green giant but stopped. I didn't want the policeman to think I was stealing the boy's corn. The officer walked over to the sidewalk, waving his arms, and said, "Move along. Everyone, please move along."

As I walked home, I wondered why this happened. Why did the boy with the grocery bag get hit by a car? Maybe he didn't look both ways. Maybe he crossed in the middle of the street and didn't wait for the light. Did the triune God do this? Did the boy break one of the commandments? Did he steal the corn? He must have done something terrible to make the Father so angry. And then I realized the boy might die. Would he go to hell and be tortured by demons with pitchforks? The sad Son had died for his sins. If the boy believed in Jesus, he would go to heaven to be with the Father. But what if the Father was still angry with him? And where was the Holy Ghost? Why didn't the angels protect him—like the angel in the picture hanging on the wall in Momo's bedroom? Two young children cross a broken bridge at night. An angel walks behind them, arms outstretched, protecting them.

I grabbed the wine bottle and held it up. Jim nodded, so I refilled his glass.

"Thank you," Jim said. "Did the kid die?"

"I have no idea. At five years old, I understood that I could die. My life could be snuffed out in a moment. But I was never afraid. I knew I wouldn't get hit by a car."

"How would you possibly know that?" Jim asked.

"Call it instinct or a hunch. I knew I was here for a

purpose. I sensed I was a part of something. Something bigger, some kind of plan."

"Sounds like you're talking about destiny."

"*Destiny* is too grand of a word. This felt more intimate. Like there was something protecting and guiding me on my journey. A white light, vibrating energy, a loving force, something. I call that something 'Spirit.'"

The sun had set. Shadows darkened the porch. I poured myself another glass of wine. "So, there was no single moment that I felt God. But I guess that day, the day of the accident, I started questioning—who is God? What is the nature of God? What is my relationship with God? I am still on a quest to penetrate and understand the mystery."

"And by mystery, you mean the ineffable cosmic creator thing?"

"Yes."

"And you still feel alone?"

"Absolutely. I love my family and friends, but only God knows my heart. I believe our one essential, abiding, and authentic relationship is with Divine Spirit."

"OK, all right. I'm not sure how you have a relationship with a spirit." Jim leaned back, processing that thought.

I didn't tell him that the following year, while I was in the first grade, Spirit became more than a feeling. I heard my spirit's voice.

4

SPIRIT VOICE

The first time I heard my spirit voice, I was six years old, frightened, sitting in the cold, waiting for my grand-mother to come home. I attended the first grade at Saint Paul's grade school. Every day, I walked to and from school, crossing major thoroughfares, unaccompanied. Saint Paul's was located midway between my parent's house on Read Street and my maternal grandmother's house on Michigan Street. Given a choice, I always rushed to Momo's house, which smelled of baking kuchen, which is German for cake: flour, cinnamon, sugar, and melted butter. If angels came down and opened a bakery, it would smell like Momo's kitchen.

Hedwig Schmitt had survived the Great Depression. Nothing was wasted. She saved everything. After using aluminum foil, she washed it, pressed it flat with a cold iron, folded it, and placed it in a drawer to reuse. I swear she had only one tissue that she carried throughout my childhood. She dried my tears with that one tissue, helped me blow my nose, cleaned smudges off my face, wiped down the kitchen counters, washed windows, and waxed the car. It was a miracle tissue. I suspected Momo cupped the tissue in her calloused hands every night and prayed over it.

There were a few raspberry bushes along the fence in Momo's tiny patch of yard between the house and the detached garage. When I was a toddler, she would take my hand and lead me to the bushes. She plucked the raspberries, warmed by the sun, and fed them to me. I tilted my head back like a baby bird, and she placed berries in my mouth, one at a time. She would use the last piece of toast at breakfast to scrape the egg yolk off the plate, then offer it to me like a Communion wafer.

When I spent the night at Momo's house, she lulled me to sleep rubbing Jergens lotion on my back as she sang German lullabies. I was always terrified of the dark, so Momo found a small, plastic glow-in-the-dark cross for me. She held up the plastic cross to a hundred-watt light bulb and then propped it up on the nightstand. After saying our prayers, she kissed my cheek and whispered, "If you get scared, look at the cross. And don't worry. I am always here." She clicked off the light and closed the door. I stared at the glowing cross through sleepy eyes as her scent lingered in the darkness— warm kitchen smells, Ivory soap, and a hint of lavender.

Momo was an excellent listener. After school, I'd slam the back door open and run into her kitchen. She would stop whatever she was doing, wrap me in a hug, plop me on a chair, and give me snacks. I munched on carrots, crackers, and cheese cubes and told her about my day at school and how I missed two spelling words. And how the girl next to me smelled terrible. And how we found a baby robin that fell out of the nest. Its mother chirped and flew over our heads. My teacher wrapped the bird in a dish towel and gave it to the janitor. The class watched as he crawled up a ladder with the towel and placed the baby bird back in the nest wedged in the roof of Saint Paul's Church. As I chattered on and on, Momo wiped the crumbs from my face with her miracle tissue.

One day after school, I left Saint Paul's and headed east toward Michigan Street instead of west toward home. I remember it was autumn because I played hopscotch with the red and gold leaves scraping along the sidewalk. When I got to Momo's house, I ran up the back porch steps and turned the knob, but the back door was locked. The lights were off. No one was home. This was impossible. Momo never left the house. She was as constant as gravity or the rising sun. How could she not be home? It was late October. The sun was already setting. I had no idea what to do, so I sat on the concrete steps and waited. I stared at the raspberry bushes. The branches were bare, except for a few dead leaves. It started to get cold.

My imagination flashed to possible scenarios. Did Momo run away from home? Did she die? Did someone kidnap her? I decided to walk home, but when I stood up, I saw that shadows had crept across the yard. I would have to walk home in the dark. I sat back down with my hands in

49

my lap and fretted. Then I recalled what we talked about in Sunday School. *God answers prayers. God listens.* So I prayed. I didn't say the words out loud. I prayed silently in my mind, *God, I am scared. I don't know what to do. Where are you? Tell me what to do.*

And from deep within me, I heard my spirit voice for the first time. My inner voice, my true voice, was clear and distinct and said, *Stand up. Stand up now and walk to the front of the house.* My six-year-old mind knew this wasn't a human voice in the real world but a voice coming from within me.

I felt the words vibrate inside me, and the voice repeated, *Stand up and walk to the front of the house.*

I obeyed the voice's instructions. I jumped up and ran through the shadows between Momo's and the neighbor's house. I turned the corner and arrived at the front stoop just as my mother drove up in our green Chevy. She pulled to the curb and called out the open window, "There you are." She got out and said, "I was so worried. Are you all right?"

"Momo's not home," I told her. "She's not here."

"Come on, get in the car."

My mother explained that Momo had visited a friend from church, someone who was sick. She would be home later that night. I listened to my mother without really hearing what she was saying. I kept thinking about the voice I had heard, the voice that lived inside me. How did it know I should walk to the front of the house at that moment? I had said a silent prayer, and the spirit voice answered and gave me clear instructions. I didn't tell my mother about hearing voices on the car ride home. It was my secret.

Here is what I have learned about listening to this voice within. When we pray without words, we settle into the presence of God. The silence draws us deeper and deeper into the mystery and majesty of divinity. When spirit voices converse, there is a deep knowing. Call it instinct, gut, hunch, intuition, mystery, whatever. There is an aliveness of being, a vibrancy that connects us directly to divine intelligence. God listens and speaks to us through Spirit and sometimes feeds us fresh-picked raspberries warmed by the sun. Our job is to listen and notice these small moments of grace.

5

RICH MAN

I gave a light knock on the door. Nothing. So I pushed the button on the metal box. It buzzed.

A voice crackled through the speaker. "Yes, may I help you?"

"I'd like to drop off my headshot and résumé," I said to the metal box.

"Leave it under the door."

"I'm sorry. Do what?"

"Slide it under the door."

"Under the ... Oh, OK."

I kneeled down and slid a photograph with my résumé stapled to the back of it under the door. Then I bent over, my head touching the floor, and yelled "Thank you!" through the gap between the locked door and the linoleum floor. I brushed off the knees of my slacks and continued my rounds to all the talent agencies and casting directors in the city.

Fresh out of graduate school, armed with a BFA in acting and an MFA in directing, convinced that fame and fortune awaited me, I moved to New York City in October 1976. At the time, New York City had one of the highest murder rates in the world. Times Square was filled with pimps, whores, peep shows, derelicts, and drug addicts. You didn't leave your apartment without mug money, at least twenty dollars to keep from getting stabbed or shot by an impatient street thief. I was living in a single room, a twelve-by-fourteen studio apartment with my wife at the time. The cold blade of indifference had separated us and shredded our relationship. Peggy and I never argued or fought. We were respectful roommates. She worked as a personal assistant to a high-powered bond trader on Wall Street. I was unemployed. My only income came from working part-time at night as a moderator on conference calls for companies that sold pharmaceuticals to doctors and fertilizer to farmers. I usually got off work around midnight. I took the subway back to our apartment, patted my pocket to make sure I had mug money, walked past clusters of hookers who winked and asked, "You want to date me?"

"Uh, no, thank you," I mumbled.

"Hey, honey, you steppin' out tonight?" asked one particularly tall hooker, wearing a faux-fur coat.

Steppin' out? I'm from Indiana. I don't *step out*. But I didn't say anything. I flipped up my collar and picked up my pace. The tall hooker laughed and flicked her cigarette butt into the street. When I'd wake up in the morning, Peggy would already be at work, not returning until late at night. So I would sit alone in our one-room apartment, contemplating sticking my head in the toilet and flushing it a few times.

But I refused to play the victim. I decided to take control of my pathetic career. After all, it was called show *business*. I would treat it like a business. Every morning I showered, shaved, put on slacks, a shirt, and a tie, and sat at the wobbly table we'd found discarded on the sidewalk to mail out my headshots and résumés to agencies and casting directors. Then I waited three days and mailed out postcards with my picture and the phone number of my answering service printed on them. Keep in mind that this was the 1970s, so there were no computers, no cell phones. Back then, actors used answering services. I paid a monthly fee for someone to take messages, and then I would call in throughout the day to find out if I had an audition. I didn't receive a single message for a year, other than the chirpy guy at the answering service reminding me to pay the monthly fee. No one responded to my mailouts or postcards, so I decided to walk the streets of Manhattan and hit every agency and casting director's office, sliding my smiling face under doors all over the city. Nothing. No one responded. Doors literally did not open for me.

Then, after months of pounding the pavement, I got a call: my very first interview, an appointment with a talent agency that represented actors, models, and spokespersons. The chirpy guy from the answering service seemed surprised I had an actual interview. He read the message. Someone at the agency saw my postcard and thought I might be right for them.

I got my portfolio in order, stapled résumés to the backs of fifty headshots, and got a haircut. On the day of the interview, I brushed my teeth until they bled, combed and recombed my hair, and changed my clothes a hundred times. I didn't have that many clothes; I just kept mixing and matching before deciding on a sports jacket and a tie. Then I decided the tie was too much, just a sports jacket. I ran through the two monologues I always had prepared—one comedic, the other dramatic—in case they asked me to perform something. I was pumped and ready and rode the subway to an office building at Broadway and Fifty-Fifth Street, just north of Times Square. I pushed the button and blurted out my name. Someone buzzed me in. A sleek receptionist sat with her elbows resting on a sprawling glass-topped desk. Her hands were folded. She looked like an attractive praying mantis. I smiled and said, "Hi, my name—"

And she said, "No."

"What?" I stammered.

"No," she said, not unkindly.

"But I have an appointment."

"No."

"But I sent you a postcard. You called me—"

The praying mantis cut me off. She flipped her bangs off her tortoiseshell glasses and said, "You are not right. You are not the type we represent at this agency."

"But I have an appointment."

"Look, it would be a waste of your time and our time. So, no."

I realized my mouth was hanging open, so I closed it. I must have looked pathetic, because she sighed and explained, "We have a very specific type that we represent at this agency, a certain look. And you are not it."

"Then why did someone call me in?"

"I don't know."

I nodded. "OK. Can I leave a photo and rés—"

"No!"

The thing you are never taught in college when getting a degree in theater arts is how to deal with rejection. Talent agencies aren't rejecting a product, such as a vacuum cleaner or a hairbrush. They are rejecting a person, a human being— *me*. I am not right. I am not good enough. They don't want *me*. I sat in the apartment for three days berating myself. What was I doing? Why did I ever move to New York?

And then, about a week later, my answering service got a call from the office of Mari Lyn Henry, director of casting, East Coast, for ABC/NY. She supervised the casting of all soap operas in New York City and many of the television series on ABC. The chirpy guy at the answering service was more excited than I was, and he informed me that Mari Lyn Henry was a rock star, the Tina Turner of casting directors. I called the office, and the receptionist explained that Ms. Henry responded to my photo and thought I might be the right type for them, so she requested that I come in for an interview.

I shaved, brushed my teeth, and changed clothes a few times, deciding on jeans and a casual shirt since the sports jacket didn't work out at the last interview. I arrived at ABC off Columbus Avenue on Sixty-Sixth Street and was greeted by the perky receptionist. She asked me to take a seat and explained that it would only be a couple of minutes. Before my butt cheeks had settled into the cushions of the couch, my name was called, and I was escorted into Mari Lyn Henry's office. I was meeting the goddess who held the keys to the television kingdom. Mari Lyn Henry was warm, businesslike, and focused. After some introductory small talk, she pulled out a scene from one of the soaps and had me read it with her. I don't remember the details of the scene, but it involved a car wreck, someone in a coma, and lots of talk about a conniving woman named Erica. I read the scene, knowing not to push or get too big or theatrical. After all, this was for the small screen; I wasn't filling a theater. I endowed each moment, actively listened, and layered in subtext. I finished and felt good. Mari Lyn Henry thanked me for reading. I sat and waited. She stared down at her desk, rolling a pencil between her fingers.

"Should I read another scene?" I asked.

She shook her head no. She stopped rolling the pencil and set it on her desk. "I don't know how I could ever cast you," she said, "unless it was a hillbilly cousin."

I was too stunned to speak. She continued, "Your accent is awful. I mean, that twang. What is that—Southern? Appalachian?"

"Southern Indiana," I murmured.

"Well, it's just awful. I would like to use you, but there is no way."

Mari Lyn Henry wasn't being harsh or mean spirited; she was being honest. A little blunt, maybe, but honest. She thanked me for taking the time to come in for the interview, but all I heard was "You are a worthless piece of shit, an untalented, untrained, degenerate waste of human flesh who has no business attempting to work in show business. Go back to Indiana and drive a truck, lay bricks, or, better yet, get a shovel, dig a hole, and bury yourself alive."

It was three more days of despondency and despair in that tiny apartment. There was only one window, located in the very back of the building, looking out onto a rusted fire escape. Sunlight bounced off the building across the littered courtyard and shined through the dirt-streaked window for about eight minutes a day, then disappeared in the gray shadows of the other buildings. *Hillbilly cousin?* Mari Lyn Henry had heard my twang and discerned the truth: I was a hick, an ignorant, working-class redneck from a blue-collar family. I was nothing, a poser, an impostor, an ambitious twenty-six-year-old with two useless college degrees and no talent. I flagellated myself with the lash of self-loathing.

Miserable wasn't the right word, because being miserable implied some kind of feeling. I was numb, empty, devoid of life, sitting in the dark, waiting for eight minutes of sunlight. And, of course, when things are truly bleak, and you bottom out, when you are broken and have no idea what to do, you think: *Maybe I should consult a higher power. Maybe I should try praying.* I sat at the wobbly table with a yellow pad and pencil and prayed for the first time in a long time. I don't remember the exact words, but I said something like "I am lost. I don't know what to do. My marriage is dying. I have no career. I am a hillbilly cousin. Can I ever earn a living in this industry? Was this all a mistake?"

Then I heard a voice, or, more correctly, intuited a voice, from deep inside me that said, *I will prosper you in ways you can't even imagine.*

Hold on, *what?* I was afraid to move, scared the voice would stop speaking. I waited and clearly heard the spirit voice inside me repeat, *I will prosper you in ways you can't even imagine.* I scribbled down and underlined words on the yellow pad: *Faith. Trust. Promise.* I knew I wasn't talking to myself. I knew, or at least thought, I was not going insane. I knew I heard a voice from deep within my soul. A promise had been made.

I didn't say anything to my roommate wife or anyone else. I felt that I would be betraying a secret, breaking a covenant. During the next few days, I thought about my situation. If the only thing holding me back was my accent, then all I had to do was get rid of my southern Indiana twang. I called a friend and a few actors and inquired about voice coaches. I did some research and discovered that the best vocal coach in the city was a man named Tim Monich at The Juilliard School. I set up an appointment. Tim was patient and kind, and he took me on as a private student. I don't remember the cost per lesson, but it was something like fifty dollars an hour, an astronomical amount of money for me at the time, but it was worth it. I met with Tim weekly and worked on eradicating my accent every day. I read poetry and Shakespeare aloud, articles from magazines and newspapers. I wasn't making a penny, but I was spending hundreds of dollars a month not to sound like a hillbilly.

Then I got a call from a nonunion agency in Midtown near the Forty-Second Street Library, the library with the iconic lions out front. I didn't brush my teeth obsessively or fuss with my clothes. I dressed comfortably and arrived at the agency a few minutes early. I was buzzed in. There was no receptionist, only a small waiting area with a couple of chairs and a coffee table with stained copies of *Variety* stacked on it. I could see through the glass partition into the office of the former model who ran the agency. She blew smoke, waved her cigarette, and mouthed, "Be with you in a minute." She turned back to the man sitting opposite her desk. I couldn't hear what they were saying, but she seemed enraptured, captivated by his every word. The man was tall, angular, and cadaverlike, his thinning hair combed straight back. He reminded me of Peter Cushing, the British actor who played the mad scientist or demented doctor in all of those B-level horror movies I had watched at the Evansville drive-in theater.

Peter—I decided his name was Peter—shook hands with the former model and stepped out the door. For some reason,

I stood up. I don't know why. Was it an impulse, nervousness, or manners? As I stood there, Peter locked eyes with me, walked up, and said, "You are going to be a very rich man."

"Yeah, well, I wish," I shrugged.

"I am very serious," Peter said. "You are going to make a lot of money in this business."

I didn't know what to say, so I said nothing. Peter continued to stare at me. He was close enough that I could see my face reflected in his pupils. His eyes crinkled as he smiled and said, "You will be very successful." And he turned and walked out the door. I stood there for a moment and noticed the former model waving me into her office.

I settled into the chair opposite her desk. She still had chiseled cheekbones, but her blonde hair was brittle, and her skin looked like worn sandpaper. Maybe it was too many cigarettes, too many drugs, or too many late nights at Studio 54 with Halston or Warhol. She stubbed out her cigarette and studied my résumé. I realized that I must have mailed it to her office months ago. I couldn't remember. As she perused the résumé, I asked her, "Excuse me?"

"Yes?"

"Who was that man, the one who just left?"

"He's my psychic."

"I'm sorry—your what?"

"Psychic. He is a gifted clairvoyant, very intuitive. I consult with him before making any decision, business or personal." The former model studied my photo, then looked at me, wrinkled her brow, and asked, "Would you be willing to dye your hair?"

I thought, *Hell, woman, I'll set my hair on fire to get this job.* But instead I said, "Of course. I have no problem dying my hair."

"I think you are perfect for a role I'm casting."

"Is there copy, anything you want me to read?" I asked, parading my newly found neutral Mid-Atlantic accent, thanks to Mr. Tim Monich of Juilliard. I rounded my vowels and clipped my consonants without a hint of hillbilly twang.

"No, there is nothing to read. I am looking for a type, a certain look, and I think you would be just right. If you are willing to dye your hair black."

"Of course," I said, "no problem."

It was a commercial for hair pomade that would air on the Spanish-speaking stations in the New York area and Puerto Rico.

OK, I have to stop here. I am Caucasian, an Irish-German mixed-breed mutt from the Midwest. Today, because of societal sensitivity and cultural appropriation, no one would ever cast an Irish-German mixed-breed mutt from the Midwest to play a Puerto Rican with a head full of black pomaded hair. *Never. It's ludicrous.* But this was the late 1970s; cultural sensitivity was practically nonexistent. So I was cast and booked the commercial.

I went through two boxes of Miss Clairol Blackest Black to get my hair as shiny and inky as a matador's. When I arrived at the studio for the shoot, the makeup artist was pleased with my dye job, but my eyebrows were a problem. They had to be darkened with a pencil. A little makeup was applied to cut the shine on my nose and forehead. I went to wardrobe, where they stuffed me into the tightest pants imaginable. My thighs went numb, and my toes tingled from lack of circulation. Then the wardrobe assistant draped a silky shirt over my body. The shirt was unbuttoned down to my navel, and they hung a gold chain with a medallion around my exposed neck. The director was pleasant and professional and told me to stand in front of a vanity with an ornately carved mirror. If I remember correctly, two lit candles flickered on each side of the vanity.

We rehearsed the commercial and got ready for the first take. The director played a tape recording of a slow, sexy samba. I thought of it as baby-making music. As the melody set the mood, a recorded voice-over artist with a rich baritone whispered Spanish words, words I didn't understand. My job was to begin buttoning up my shirt, then look into the mirror and stop when I noticed a sultry Spanish siren slinking her way toward me. The sultry siren was dressed in a low-cut gown that caressed her cleavage and hugged her hips. She sashayed up behind me, draped her arm over my shoulder, and ran her long, slender fingers into the open shirt, caressing my pectoral muscle. Then we both looked into the mirror at our reflections and locked eyes, a smoldering gaze that promised a night of *amor*. Fade to black . . .

That was the commercial. I didn't understand one word of the voice-over, but the baritone guy seemed to be saying that if you used this particular brand of pomade, a beautiful woman would run her lacquered nails through the hair on your chest and fondle your gold medallion. I never saw the finished commercial. Being nonunion, I didn't collect residuals, so I had no idea how often the commercial played or if it ever aired. But I got paid. I received a check with my name on it for dying my hair black and casting smoldering glances into a mirror. Was this an answer to prayer? Was this what the spirit voice inside my soul meant when it said, "I will prosper you in ways you can't even imagine"?

Believe it or not, that nonunion commercial was like the first olive out of the jar because other commercials followed. I joined all the unions. There was already a Mark Williams in Actors' Equity, so I changed my professional name from Mark Williams to Matt Williams. I spent three years acting on a soap opera, acting on the stage, as well as directing and writing plays, eventually landing a job writing for *The Cosby Show*. Peggy and I divorced, which was the right thing to do. Our marriage had worn out, the final tattered threads pulled apart. I met and married the love of my life, Angelina Fiordellisi, my partner and mother of our two beautiful children.

Many years later, Angelina sponsored a benefit for the League of Professional Theatre Women to honor the brilliant actress and director Billie Allen. Phylicia Rashad was the moderator and interviewed Billie, which was filmed for the archives at Lincoln Center. In the lobby after the event, I bumped into Mari Lyn Henry. We were both shocked, both a little more wrinkled, both a little mellower and more relaxed. Mari Lyn Henry was amiable and gracious. We caught up with small talk, and then she said, "Do you remember when you came in and auditioned for me?"

"Remember?" I said. "It is seared in my memory forever. With a branding iron."

She laughed. What I didn't tell her is that moment of scorching humiliation had been a blessing. It was the kick in the ass that I needed, the catalyst that started me praying and listening to and trusting the spirit voice inside me.

Before we said our goodbyes, Mari Lyn Henry turned to me and said, "Look at your life, all you've achieved, acting and directing, producing movies, and creating television series. You have had an amazing career."

"I've been very blessed," I said.

Mari Lyn smiled. "Who knew?"

6

KNEE-SLAPPER

Laughter is the closest thing to the grace of God.
—Karl Barth

As a young child, my greatest joy in life was making my mother cry—from laughter. She would sit with her elbow resting on our new kitchen table with the chrome legs and cream-colored Formica top, chin in hand, with a cup of coffee while I entertained her. I told her knock-knock jokes and did pratfalls or impersonations. I imitated my grandfather smoking his pipe and flipping the pages of the newspaper. She laughed hardest when I imitated the three winos who lived next door.

Our little white house at 417 Read Street was wedged between a corner tavern and a dilapidated gray house where the winos lived. (I only ever heard our neighbors referred to as *the winos*.) There was Herb. He was round, avuncular, and he wore a brown fedora hat. Gladys had bags under her eyes and painted her lips bright red. She was what my mother called

67

a "peroxide blonde." And there was the emaciated one with the protruding Adam's apple. I think his name was Dale. He always wore baggy work pants and a dirt-streaked undershirt. From my sandbox in our backyard, I watched the winos come and go. They seemed happy, except when arguing or yelling at squirrels. Herb had a garden that consisted of three withered tomato plants. For some reason, the squirrels couldn't resist those sad-looking tomatoes.

So while my mother sipped coffee, I impersonated Herb. I waved my imaginary fedora and yelled, "Get away from there! Get!" I staggered the way Herb walked around the yard and threw my imaginary hat at the imaginary squirrels. "Get away, you fuzzy little bastards!"

My mother slapped her knee and bent over, laughing. I knew I had her when I made Mom laugh so hard she had to wipe away tears and blow her nose. I lived for those moments, the moments she saw me and appreciated me.

"Want me to do Aunt Mouse?" I asked.

My mother wiped her cheeks, then waved a hand at me. "No. That's enough. I can't take it."

I launched into an impersonation of my great-aunt Mouse. Her real name was Mary Alice, but the two words had blended over the years and became her nickname: Mouse. Ironically, her sister was named Kitty. But that's another story. I grabbed a pencil from the basket on the table and puffed it like a cigarette. I stammered, twitched my right eye, and jerked my head to the side like Aunt Mouse did when she got angry.

"D-d-d-damn him. He's c-c-c-cheating at cards again!" Aunt Mouse cussed like a sailor, smoked like a chimney, and hated cheaters. I'd flick my pencil in the general direction of the ashtray, the way Aunt Mouse did, and fume, "I am going to r-r-r-rip him a n-n-n-new asshole if he doesn't stop that cheating." Mom doubled over laughing, struggling to catch her breath. I wanted that moment to last forever. To me, her laughter was her love. It doesn't take a boatload of psychotherapists to figure out why I ended up working in television as a comedy writer.

But when I misbehaved, my mother's punishment was to ignore me. She pretended I wasn't in the room. I didn't exist. She would walk right past me without acknowledging my presence. It drove me insane. At five, I thought I was self-sufficient and didn't need anyone, but I longed for my mother's approval. I wanted her to laugh and notice me. I went to extremes to get her attention, such as catching the kitchen table on fire.

I was at home sick from school with the measles and more or less getting on my mother's last nerve. My red-faced, screaming baby sister, Beth, cried constantly, and my mother changed about a thousand diapers a day. When Mom wasn't changing diapers, she was wrangling my younger brother, Randy, who pulled everything out from under the kitchen sink—detergent boxes, sponges, old rags, Brillo pads. He was determined to drink the can of Drano. Pots boiled on the stove. Dirty dishes piled up in the sink. Trash spilled out of the can. My mother was overwhelmed, so I didn't exist. Despite sitting at the kitchen table in my pajamas with measles dotting my face, I was invisible to her.

When my mother finally got the baby to sleep and put Randy down for a nap, she returned to her chores. Mom wiped down the stove, washed the dishes, and stacked them in the rack beside the sink. She carried two bags of garbage out to the trash can in the alley. Through the screen door, I saw her stop to talk with Gladys, the peroxide-blonde wino.

I was bored. And lonely. I sat at the kitchen table playing with my collection of plastic animals. They were the characters from the animated film *Bambi*. It was my favorite movie, even though Bambi's mother got shot by a hunter. Bambi was very sad and went to live with his father in the forest. Then I remembered the forest fire in *Bambi*. I had an idea: I circled all the plastic animals around a nub of a candle I found in the basket on the table. I dug a box of wooden kitchen matches out of a drawer and lit the candle. I pulled paper napkins out of the silver holder and tore them into shreds. Then I placed each piece of paper on top of the candle flame. The forest fire grew. I put Flower, the skunk, Thumper, the rabbit, Bambi, and the other animals in a circle around the forest fire so they could watch from a safe distance. The flames grew higher, the heat forcing me to scoot my chair back. I added more paper, and the fire spread across the table. I grabbed Bambi and Thumper and pretended they were running away from the burning forest. "Run, Thumper, run!"

70

My mother opened the back door, screamed "Oh, dear God!" and ran to the sink. She turned on the faucet, grabbed a pot off the stove, and filled it with water. She stumbled to the table and sloshed water onto the flames. The water splashed on me and washed the candle and all the plastic animals off the table—it puddled on the floor, along with the cartoon characters and pieces of burnt napkins. I expected my mother to go berserk, yell at me, spank me, or send me to another room. Instead, she crumpled into a chair at the end of the table, put her face in her hands, and cried.

I sat there, worried. Would she spank me? Would she call my father at work? Would she ask one of the winos to help her clean up the mess? Finally, my mother stood up, and without looking at me, without saying a word, she grabbed a bucket and a mop from the pantry and started cleaning the kitchen. I didn't know what to do. Should I help her clean up the water? Would I be in her way? The wooden mop handle clunked against the chrome leg of the table, splashing ashy water on my pajama bottoms. I gathered Bambi, Thumper, and the rest of the animals and went into the next room. I sat on the white plastic couch and waited. For what, I didn't know.

Our relationship with our parents often defines our perception of God. Throughout most of my childhood I sensed that God loved me, like my mother did, but he was occasionally distant and detached, like my mother was. But I thought if I prayed hard enough, I might get God's attention. Pray or be a good boy. I tried desperately to be a good boy for

71

the triune God—Father, Son, and Holy Ghost—and for my mother. I wanted all of them to love me and laugh at me. But sometimes they felt so far away. I berated myself for not being good enough. I wanted to be worthy of love, but I always fell short. How could a perfect God love me when I was so flawed and imperfect?

It wasn't until I married Angelina and had children that I understood unconditional love. Matisse and Fred, two angels from heaven, came along and wrecked our lives. They spilled juice on Angelina's new rug and broke my favorite coffee cup. While potty training, Fred tried to see how far up the bathroom wall he could pee. Matisse cut her bangs with pinking shears and painted the dog with her mother's lipstick. Our home was cluttered with cribs, strollers, high chairs, and sticky toys. The living room looked as though a deranged elf had set off a bomb inside Santa's toy factory. It didn't matter. I loved them both. I loved our babies so much that I wanted to swallow them and carry them inside me.

Eventually, I realized God must love us that way as well. I don't know if I exist inside God, but I sense God lives inside me. I carry a spark of divine spirit inside this fleshy form as I bumble and stumble around, trying to figure things out. It's OK. I am not perfect. I am loved. Unconditionally. I don't have to make God laugh. I don't have to do pratfalls or imitate my Aunt Mouse. God loves us even if we are winos who yell at squirrels. Even if we catch kitchen tables on fire. God's love is pure, constant, and unwavering. That's why it's called grace:

unmerited favor, love that is not earned but freely given by a caring Creator.

I don't know when I fell asleep on the white couch or how long I slept. I was awakened by a cool hand on my forehead and my mother's voice, "You don't have a fever." I blinked my eyes open and sat up. I was still holding Thumper. My mother patted the spot on the couch next to her. I scooted over. She put her arm around me. "Do you want a drink of water?"

"Yes," I said, wiping the sleep from my eyes.

My mother rubbed my shoulder, staring out the window at the gray house next door. She never got me the glass of water.

7

THE LANTERN

There are a number of recreational activities that I aggressively avoid. First on the list is parachuting. Plunging through the sky toward my probable death, with only a piece of cloth stopping me from splattering on the ground, doesn't sound like a lot of fun. I feel the same way about racing dirt bikes, floating on a surfboard in shark-infested waters, or skiing down a frozen mountain at breakneck speed, dodging tree branches and boulders. No thanks. Fifth on my list is camping. Something I did only a few times when our children were very young. Call me crazy, but I don't relish sleeping on the cold, lumpy ground or on a blow-up mattress that deflates halfway through the night, about the same time the tent collapses on my head. Not to mention insect bites and poison ivy, and stumbling in the dark, stepping on snakes to take a pee.

What triggered this anti-camping tirade? I recently came across an old lantern. About six months ago, I dug a Coleman lantern out of storage from the depths of our basement. It was filthy and covered with grime, but under all that dirt was a perfectly good lantern, so I cleaned it with soap and water and Windex. It sparkled. And it worked. The light inside shined bright and brilliant, and I recalled the phrase "Let your light shine before others . . ."[1] Let your light shine.

According to the Bible, God started the whole big bang of creation with a simple statement: "Let there be light."[2] In almost every wisdom tradition, light represents spiritual illumination and intelligence and is a metaphor for truth. I read somewhere that our souls may be composed of trapped particles of light. Is the soul made up of photons? I don't know. But if one's soul, one's very essence, is made up of photons, then that means we are all beings of light. We possess divine radiance, and that radiance spills out into the world when we are loving, kind, and compassionate.

And that got me thinking: if we are like lanterns, with light living inside us, then sin is anything that dirties the glass and dims the light: greed, rage, theft, murder, infidelity, and cruelty, anything that hurts another, smudges the glass and imprisons the radiance. We are encouraged not to hide our light under a basket. We are told to let our light shine. But how do we stay clear so our light can radiate out into the world? I believe prayer, supplication, praise, and deep silence help keep the glass clean so our inner light shines forth. And, especially now, our dark world needs light to survive.

---

[1] Matthew 5:16.
[2] Genesis 1:3.

THE LANTERN

Years ago, my father took me to Cave-in-Rock, an infamous cavern in southern Illinois that overlooks the Ohio River. In the 1800s it was a tavern and lair for the Mason gang, who pillaged, robbed, raped, and killed unsuspecting travelers coming down the river. Later the Harpe brothers continued the treachery before enough law-abiding citizens moved into the area and drove the river pirates away. The cave was, literally and metaphorically, a dark place. My father and I walked deep inside the cave, and the tour guide turned off the flashlight. We were instantly plunged into complete and total darkness. I could not see my ten-year-old hand in front of my face. Fear crept in. Then the guide lit one match, a wooden kitchen match, and the tiny flame pushed back the darkness, gradually illuminating the space around us, revealing faces and hands, stalactites and rivulets of water trickling down the stone walls—all of that from one match.

I am too old and cranky to go camping anymore, but I keep that Coleman lantern on a shelf in my study. When dark thoughts cloud my consciousness, when anger or negativity, fear or doubt creep in and start to dim my spirit, I look at the lantern. It's a reminder to keep the glass clean and the flame alive.

8

THE EWE

*Humankind has not woven the web of life. We are but one
thread within it. Whatever we do to the web, we do to ourselves.
All things are bound together. All things connect.*
—CHIEF SEATTLE

I was sitting on the porch with a cup of coffee, a yellow
pad, and a pen, and I saw a spider on the table. It was
jet black, about the size of a dime, and was scurrying across
the wood, looking for something—food, a mate, a place to
hide? Without thinking, I smacked it with the yellow pad.
The spider was now a smudge embedded in the grain of the
wood. Nothing. No life. No movement. Only a wet smear. I
felt remorse. I had just snuffed out the very life of that creature without hesitation. So what happened to the energy
that animated the spider? What happened to the life force
that lived inside that tiny insect just moments ago? Did that
energy—ka, chi, prana, anima, whatever—just disappear?
Did it return to a source, the creative force that is God? Or

was it simply tissue and tiny brain, smashed eyes, and twisted legs? Was there some divine intelligence living inside that creature? Does a spider have a soul? Or did I just have too much time on my hands to sit around on my porch, drink coffee, and ask unanswerable questions?

The law of conservation of energy says that energy cannot be created or destroyed; it can only be changed from one form to another. If that is true, did the energy that lived inside the spider transform? I went to my computer and researched various wisdom traditions. I am not a scholar, a theologian, or a scientist. But I was curious. Is the universe alive, sentient, and is everything connected by spirit? After chasing the rabbit down the hole for several hours, my eyes started to cross, and my brain cells sizzled, so I took a break. I made myself a cup of green tea, ate a big spoonful of Häagen-Dazs Vanilla Swiss Almond, and watched the birds flutter around the feeder. Saint Francis preached to the birds. Do they have souls? Does an eternal spirit live inside their hollow bones and feathers?

I kept wrestling with this concept of soul versus spirit and whether animals had either, and talked to Angelina about it incessantly until she finally suggested that I sit down, shut up, and watch *The Voice*. We went to bed that night, and, as I was drifting off to sleep, I saw faces. Does that ever happen to you? Sometimes when I am in that twilight sleep, just before going completely under, faces materialize and morph in my mind's eye. I see all sorts of faces, male and female, all ethnicities, some young, some old. I've always wondered if the faces are reincarnated souls, spirit guides, angels, or simply my imagination, synapses firing before drifting off to sleep. This night, my father's face appeared, and I heard his voice.

"Wake up. Son, wake up." I felt the bed shake. I knew I wasn't dreaming. I knew I was lying in bed, under the sheets, beside my sleeping wife.

"I need your help. Get dressed," my father said. I realized it wasn't a dream but a vivid memory from when I was eleven years old.

I crawled out of bed, careful not to disturb Angelina, threw on a robe, went down to my study, and opened my computer to record the memory. I recalled it was freezing that night, the wind was blowing, and I remember my father's voice whispering, "I need your help." I forced my sleepy eyes open and saw my father leaning over the bed, fully dressed in a winter coat and wool stocking cap.

"What . . .?" I said, wiggling out from under the covers. "What is it?"

"Shh, don't wake your brother," Dad said, nodding at the other bed. Randy was buried under the quilt, arm over his head, breathing steadily.

"What time is it?" I asked.

"It's late. I need you. Get dressed," Dad said. He patted the blankets and disappeared down the stairs.

I tossed off the covers and stood up. The wooden floor felt like a frozen pond, numbing my feet. I plopped onto the edge of the bed and quickly pulled on my wool socks, then put on layers of clothes over my flannel pajamas and headed downstairs. Wind rattled the shutters.

Dad was at the kitchen sink, filling two five-gallon buckets with hot water. "What's going on?" I asked, rubbing sleep from my eyes. I went to the coatrack and grabbed my coat.

"That one ewe, she's in labor. Twins. She's having a rough time," Dad said, setting the full bucket on the floor. He grabbed the other bucket and placed it under the faucet.

I zipped up my coat and pulled on my hat with the fuzzy ear flaps. Dad handed me a stack of tattered towels from under the sink. "Here, bring these," he said, adding a bar of soap and a pair of yellow rubber gloves, the gloves my mother used when washing dishes. He grabbed a first-aid kit with a red cross stamped on the lid, stuffed it in his pocket, and then lifted the buckets.

The wind slashed our faces as we stepped outside. I held the door open with my back so that Dad could pass by with the buckets. Snowdrifts had formed on tree trunks and up the side of the house. The night was cloudy. No stars. The only light came from the dusk-to-dawn light above the barn. The snow was up to my thighs, so I had to trudge my way through the damp powder, clutching the soap and rags, trying not to fall over. As Dad walked ahead of me, hot water splashed out of the buckets, melting the snow and sending up wisps of steam. Ice crystals formed in my nostrils. With each breath, a small vaporous cloud hung in the air briefly and then vanished. I hated the cold, but I loved the snow because it had meant no school for the past two days. I realized all the roads were still closed, which was why Dad hadn't called the veterinarian. He set the buckets down, flipped the wooden latch, and pushed the barn door open. We stepped inside and were instantly enveloped by the familiar warmth of hay and straw, dust and grain, and sweet animal smells.

Dad flicked the light switch on. The ewe was on her side. Her breathing was labored and shallow, her massive belly swollen with life. She lifted her head but didn't try to stand. Dad set the buckets down and kneeled in the straw. He examined her and explained, "I had a feeling. I came out earlier to check on her. I saw she was in trouble." He dipped one of the rags into a bucket, soaked it, and wrung it out. "The first one is turned around, a breech birth. It's twisted backward and blocking the birth canal."

Dad touched the ewe with the warm rag; she snorted and jerked her head. "Hold her," Dad said. "I need you to hold her down and stroke her head." I knelt beside her. "Talk to her, keep her calm," Dad said. He dipped the rag into the bucket and washed the ewe's hind end with warm water and soap. He finished cleaning her and then put on the yellow Playtex gloves. They were too tight for his hands, but he stretched, squeezed, and wiggled his fingers into them. He soaked another rag and held the warm cloth just below her tail.

"Her water has already broken. This will relax her, help with the contractions."

I leaned over and whispered in her ear, "You're going to

be all right. You're doing great." I stroked her black forehead, rubbed between her eyes. Dad taught me that massaging an animal between the eyes usually relaxes them. When I was little and couldn't sleep, he would do that to me, rubbing between my eyes until my eyelids fluttered shut and I drifted off.

The ewe suddenly moaned, tossing her head. "Hold her down," Dad said. "Don't let her stand up. Keep her down." I put one hand on her neck and the other on her shoulder and said, "You're fine. It's OK. It'll be OK." I watched as my father folded his fingers and thumb into a kind of cone shape, then he reached his hand inside her body, feeling for the baby.

My Irish soul may be romanticizing this part of the story, but this is how I remember it: There was a hundred-watt light bulb hanging from the rafters on an electric wire. The light bulb cast a perfect halo around us. The sheep, my father, and I were inside the halo. The corners of the stall were shadowed, with spiderwebs catching the light. I couldn't see the other animals, the donkey, the two horses, and the other sheep, but I could hear them breathing.

The barn creaked in the cold. The ewe let out a low groan. I stroked her head. My dad's hand was inside her body, feeling the contours of the unborn lamb. He twisted his arm, but he couldn't get a grip. He withdrew his hand and stripped off his coat, and I saw that he had sweat through his sweater. Dad washed his gloved hands again. "I can't turn the baby around. I need to get the hind feet. Keep talking to her."

I leaned close to her ear, whispering, "You will be all

right. Everything is fine. Good girl, good girl." I watched his gloved hand disappear inside again. Dad bit his lower lip, which he always did when driving a nail or changing a diaper. He moved his hand inside, stopped momentarily, and slowly pulled the lamb out. There was a moment of tension, but the hind legs appeared, and the lamb slipped out the birth canal.

Dad wiped the mucus from the baby's nose with a dry rag, then lifted the lamb toward the light. He put his finger inside the lamb's mouth and blew into its nostrils, once, twice, three times. The lamb gasped and then sneezed a tiny, squeaky sneeze and started to breathe. Dad placed the baby in the straw near the mother so she could lick its face and neck. Dad checked her hindquarters. The second lamb wasn't coming out. He reached inside again, feeling for the other baby. It didn't take long. The second lamb came out fast, headfirst. Dad snatched it up and wiped the nostrils clean, but it wasn't moving or breathing. It was limp. The delay, the strain, and the stress seemed to have crushed the life out of the lamb.

Dad cleaned the nostrils again and blew into the nose, but nothing happened. He pressed on the lamb's chest and rubbed the stomach to get the blood flowing, but the lamb was still.

The first lamb kicked and started to flail. Dad checked its umbilical cord and dabbed it with iodine. The lamb let out a loud *baaah*, so Dad nudged it closer to its mother. She tried to smell her baby but was too weak to hold her head up. I rubbed her neck and encouraged her, "It's OK. It's OK. You're fine. You're doing fine." Dad positioned the living lamb so its face was close to its mother's stomach, the promise of milk. He checked the mother for bleeding, removed the placenta, and applied an antiseptic ointment.

I continued to stroke her head. Dad pulled a burlap sack from the feed bin. He picked up the dead lamb and wrapped it in the burlap. I noticed the other lamb had started nursing. Dad went to the corner and kneeled down, staring at the lamb swaddled in the burlap. My father was quiet. I couldn't tell whether he was sad or angry or disappointed. He closed his eyes. I wasn't sure, but it looked like he was praying. Dad placed the bundle in the corner of the feed bin. He would bury it when the sun came up.

Dad slipped his coat on and flicked off the light. He poured the water out of the buckets and set them by the side of the barn. He latched the door, and we started walking back to the house. The wind had blown away the clouds. Pinpoints of light, thousands and thousands of stars pulsated in the darkness. I remember thinking they looked like candle flames floating in ink. Dad walked ahead of me, scooting his boots and clearing the snow. I followed the path my father made; the world felt bigger, and I sensed that I was a part of everything.

I stopped typing and opened the file with my research. The day before, I had saved an article from the Smithsonian that stated: "The total amount of energy and matter in the universe remains constant, merely changing from one form

86

to another." As I sat in my robe staring at the computer screen, I envisioned that all life is connected to the birth of the universe, and someday my father would die, and I would die, and stars would explode and die, and our energy would merge with filaments of light floating among the hundred million galaxies in the Milky Way and the two trillion galaxies spiraling in dark matter and the billion trillion stars in an expanding universe, where father and son, sheep and snow, stardust and spiders are all connected by a cosmic web inside the mind of God.

9

NO SCARVES

God beneath you, God in front of you,
God behind you, God above you, God within you.
—SAINT PATRICK'S BLESSING

When I moved to New York City in the late 1970s, I discovered I was an AAWYD. I knew no one, had no contacts in the entertainment industry, and had no union affiliations. I was young, ambitious, and eager to carve out a career in the theater. But no one would hire me, interview me, or even look at my picture and résumé. I was struggling, desperate, the proverbial starving artist. But then things changed.

I managed to worm my way into an audition with David Cohen, the casting director at Ogilvy & Mather, one of the largest advertising agencies in the world at the time. I had done a few local commercials in the Midwest so I knew how to hold up the product and not bob my head when speaking to the camera. David had me read some copy. I believe it was

89

for Folgers coffee. Then he had me read copy for a new soap product. David grinned, took off his glasses, and said, "You will make a lot of money." I thought, *Hell, I would be thrilled if I could just pay my rent and eat occasionally.*

David explained, "You will constantly work because you are an AAWYD, an All-American WASP young daddy." And David was right. I started acting in commercials, a lot of them. I was the pipe-smoking husband in a Lysol spray commercial. I filled it to the rim with Brim. I changed diapers while explaining to the camera how Pampers keep your baby super dry. I played football with a bunch of sweating guys, but my armpits were dry because of Mennen Speed Stick deodorant. It wasn't high art, but I was surviving.

One afternoon, I had an audition for a new breakfast cereal. There was no dialogue or sales pitch. They were looking for a type. I went to a Midtown office building and stepped into the waiting area filled with other AAWYDs. Television had little diversity in the late seventies and early eighties, especially in commercials. But there were hordes of AAWYDs. I scribbled my name on the sign-in sheet and looked around. It was like standing in a house of mirrors. All the men in the room were the same size, shape, and age; eye and hair color were the only variables. We were all anxious. There was the usual nervous chatter, the studied insouciance, the offhand bragging about landing a part in a Sam Shepard one-act at La MaMa or booking an under-five on a soap opera. We were all fidgety and tense; we knew booking this commercial could mean the difference between paying or not paying our rent. My name was called. I went into the adjoining room for my audition.

The room was small, stuffy, with no windows. There was a camera on a tripod and three individuals. A brunette in her late twenties, wearing a stretchy orange sweater, leopard-print leggings, and Capezio flats, sat with a clipboard in her lap. She smiled a tight smile, her right leg crossed over her left, and she kept smacking her Capezio flat against her heel— plap, plap, plap. The second assistant was a swan. She was wearing some kind of white flowing thing that looked like someone had cut up a parachute or bedsheets and draped them over her body, the folds falling off her pale shoulders. Her hair was piled on top of her head, exposing her neck, the longest neck I had ever seen. Between these two creatures sat the director. He was wedged into a director's chair, rolls of butt fat splaying over the sides of the canvas. A scraggly beard sprouted out of his puffy face. He kept twisting his fingers in his beard as he silently eyeballed me. In my mind, I nick-named him Fuzzy. Fuzzy was dressed in all black except for his aborigine scarf.

I fought back nerves, nodded, and grinned. "Hi. How are you?" Leopard Lady snapped her Capezios—plap, plap, plap. The Swan smiled, a genuine smile, as she adjusted the buttons on the camera. The director stared, twisting tight clumps of beard around his finger. Fuzzy explained the narrative of the commercial. His accent was faux British, Mid-Atlantic, East Coast, with a touch of Harvard Yard. I thought, *Where the hell is this guy from?* Obviously, he came from a place with an abundance of food and a scarcity of razors.

Fuzzy untangled his finger and pointed at a table. There was an empty foam bowl and a pile of plastic spoons. He explained the action. I was to take the empty bowl, scoop up a spoonful of imaginary cereal, take a bite, and react. Simple.

I grabbed the empty bowl and what I hoped was a clean spoon, looked into the camera, and stated my name. Before the director nodded action, I interrupted and said I had a few questions. I thought, *Why not?* I was a trained professional. I had spent four years getting a BFA in theater and three years earning an MFA. That's seven years of voice lessons, dance lessons, Alexander technique, sense memory, scene work, and improvisation. Fuzzy raised an eyebrow and nodded. I stepped forward and asked, "Is this the first time I have tasted this cereal, and I'm surprised by the crunchy, delicious taste? Or is this a cereal I eat every morning and look forward to savoring that first bite? Am I alone in the kitchen eating this cereal? Or am I sitting at a dining room table with my beautiful wife and kids enjoying the honey, nutty, oat flakes?" Fuzzy leaned back in the chair, flicked his aborigine scarf, and said, "Show me your range."

I held up the bowl, scooped a big spoonful of invisible cereal, and stuck the spoon in my right ear. I smiled, chewed, and nodded my appreciation with the spoon lodged in my ear cavity. Swamp sounds. Nothing. Zilch. Total silence. The Swan stared. Leopard Lady's foot stopped flapping. Fuzzy squinted, shooting darts of disdain in my general direction. I knew this was the moment, the moment to decide. I could laugh and say, "I'm sorry. I was just joking. Let me do it again." Or I could scream, "You pretentious poser! I will not share my cereal-eating talents with the likes of you." Or I could do what I did. Say thank you and walk out of the room.

In the waiting area, nine AAWYD heads turned toward me, all anxious, all silently asking, "How is it in there?" I shrugged and said, "Guys, relax. I set the bar pretty low. You're all going to do just fine." And I left the building.

Years later, I stopped acting and started writing plays, then television series, and producing and directing feature films. I have auditioned thousands of actors. And before every audition, I thought about Fuzzy. I reminded myself: Don't grow a scraggly beard. Don't speak with a faux-British, Mid-Atlantic, East Coast, Harvard Yard accent. Don't flick my scarf. In fact, do not ever wear a scarf. And remember, the talent stepping into the room is a solitary soul, a child of God, and has trained for years to prepare for this moment. Every time an actor walked into the room, I imagined a warm, white light surrounding them. I answered any questions they had about the script. And then I blessed them with a silent blessing. And I never said, "Show me your range."

10

THE STORM

The gladiators battled, a fierce fight to the death. The imaginary crowd cheered us on. Randy used a garbage-can lid as a shield and wielded a wooden sword made from an old lettuce crate. I was armed with a volleyball net and a pitchfork. We circled each other, feinting and stabbing. I twirled the net just the way I had seen gladiators do in *Spartacus*. The film starring Kirk Douglas inflamed our warrior spirits, so we enacted all the battle scenes. "I'm Spartacus!"

Like most childhood tussles, this one started out benign, more posturing than pain, until Randy smacked my arm with the wooden sword. That pissed me off. So I tried to stab his bare feet with the pitchfork. He hit me again with the sword and banged the garbage-can lid into my shoulder. I whipped the volleyball net. Randy dropped his shield and grabbed the netting. Big mistake. I raced around my younger brother a couple of times, entangling him in the net like a trapped fish. Then I walked over and punched him in the face. A flash. In my peripheral vision, I saw a blur of flesh racing across the field, knees pumping, arms swinging, a body streaking toward me. It was my father, in cutoff denim shorts, slip-on cloth sneakers, and no shirt. He grabbed me, yanked the pitchfork away, and slammed it to the ground. He picked me up with one hand, splayed me over his knee, and spanked my ass. I was twelve years old and big for my age, but my father was strong. He swung from ropes tied to the oak tree, jumped out of the hayloft, rode horses bareback, and taught us how to shoot a bow and arrow. My father was the real Spartacus. As I was bent over his knee, my hair brushing the dirt, Dad whacked my behind three times, then plopped me on the ground.

"Don't ever hit your brother in the face," Dad said, pointing a finger. "You can wrestle him, sit on him, throw him in the dirt, but you do not punch your brother in the face. Do you understand?"

I nodded.

"Do you understand?"

"Yes," I whispered.

I sat there, more humiliated than hurt. I considered myself a grown man, but my father had treated me like a little child. Randy gathered up the weapons, smiled at me over his shoulder, and followed Dad back to the barn.

For the rest of the afternoon, I avoided going to the house. I didn't want to see my father. I was ashamed. I hung out in the field with our two horses, Gypsy and Stormy, and Cindy, our ancient donkey. I found comfort in their smell. That scent, the dusty sweetness of a horse's hide, is one of

God's gifts to humanity. I am not sure how long I was out there, but I noticed the temperature dropped. Leaves fluttered. I smelled rain. I waved my arms, driving the two horses into the barn. Cindy hobbled along behind them. I slammed the barn door shut and jogged toward the house.

My father stood at the top of the driveway, hands on his hips, studying the storm. He was still shirtless. I tried to avoid him by going behind the garage, but he waved me over. I stood beside him, and we watched flashes of light explode inside the gray-green clouds tumbling in from the northwest.

"It's going to be big but won't last long," he said. The rumble of thunder washed over us. Dad patted my back, "Come on, let's go." He trotted away, but instead of going to the house, he veered toward the sycamore that loomed over our driveway. It was massive, with thick branches and peeling bark. Dad grabbed the lowest limb, threw his leg up, and started climbing. I wasn't sure what to do, so I followed him. The first raindrops pelted us. The tree swayed as we climbed higher and higher, until the branches became thin and would no longer support our weight.

"Hold on," Dad grinned. "Hold on tight."

I planted my feet in the crook where a limb grew out of the trunk. I grabbed two branches above my head just as the tree bent sideways. Leaves ripped off and blew away. Cold rain slashed us. A ribbon of lightning shot down and struck our neighbor's yard, a flashbulb of white.

"Here we go!" Dad yelled. The tree whipped back and

forth. A streak of lightning, the air crackled, and an electric charge enveloped us. There was a metallic taste on my tongue. My scalp tingled. I yelled, "Wow! Oh, my God, wow!" We were inside the storm. Another crash of thunder. I threw back my head and howled. I no longer thought of us as humans. My father and I were elements, molecules of water, particles of ice, positive and negative ions colliding and exploding into thunder carried on the wind.

The storm didn't last long, fewer than five minutes. The earth was soaked, the field was puddled with rain. Rivulets of water slinked down our driveway, pushing pebbles into the grass. Out of breath, hair plastered to our scalps, my father and I looked at each other and laughed. Dad said, "That was fun." We started back down. The descent was precarious because the sycamore bark was slick, so we moved cautiously. Dad swung out of the tree, landing with a splash. I hung on the limb for a moment and then dropped back down to earth.

11
SNAKES

Randy and I were at the bottom of the driveway building a go-kart out of old lettuce crates and the discarded wheels from a Radio Flyer when we heard the scream. The scream was long and shrill and definitely our mother's. And it was coming from inside the house. We raced up the driveway, but the pebbles hurt our feet, so we veered into the grass. We slammed into the house to find our mother standing in the corner, hand to her mouth, pointing at the phone mounted on the wall. She kept jabbing her finger, pointing and mumbling something into her left hand.

"What? What is it?" I asked.

She removed her hand and said, "Snake."

"What?"

"In the phone. There is a snake in the phone."

The black phone was mounted on a patch of wall between our tiny kitchen and the living room. The receiver dangled on its cord, and, sure enough, a little green garter snake was coming out of the telephone. When Mom dropped the receiver, the metal cradle flipped up and more or less trapped the snake, strangling him. His round eyes bulged. His mouth was open, his tongue flicking madly. Randy reached up and pulled the cradle down. The snake retracted back inside the phone. I grabbed the receiver and hung it up. I jiggled the thin wire running down the wall into the baseboard. I looked inside the small opening where the wire entered the phone. No snake. Randy turned to me and said, "I think that was Baby."

"What should we do?" I asked my mother.

"Wait for your father to get home from work," Mom said, raking her fingers through her hair.

There were no cell phones in those days, so we had to wait for Dad to get off the first shift on the assembly line at Whirlpool. When he arrived home, our father checked the phone, fiddled with the cord, then decided to call the phone company. I remember the conversation vividly. Dad had the receiver in his left hand, phone to his ear, his right hand supporting him as he leaned on the door frame.

"Yes, we have uh . . . a problem with our phone. No, it works. I'm calling you from it. But there is a problem . . . inside the phone."

My eleven-year-old brain took note that he never said the word *snake*.

"OK, thank you. See you soon." Dad hung up. "They're sending someone out." He turned to Randy and me. "I don't want you making a big deal out of this. In fact, you two should go outside. Go on. And don't say anything to the neighbors."

SNAKES

Randy and I shot out of the house and immediately ran through the neighborhood, telling every kid we saw that we had a snake trapped in our telephone. Before long, we had a gang of twelve sweaty kids following us home. Randy and I raced into the yard just as the AT&T truck pulled into the driveway. Randy and the neighbor kids banged open the screen door and rushed into the kitchen. I hung back in the driveway to see how Dad would handle the technician. The telephone repairman, a beefy guy with strawberry-blond hair and freckles across his nose, crawled out of the truck. He grabbed his tool kit and asked my father, "What seems to be the problem?"

My dad told him the truth. "We have a snake in our phone."

The man stopped dead in his tracks. He looked at my dad, then at me, then back at my dad. "Have you been drinking?"

"No. I don't drink. There is a snake, a small one, trapped inside our telephone."

What Dad didn't explain was that the snake was our pet. Randy had caught the little green garter that spring and kept it in an aquarium in the living room with a screen on top, weighed down with two rocks. Randy had named the snake Baby. Every day after school, Randy took Baby out of the aquarium to play with him (we assumed it was *him*). Randy would spread out on the floor in front of the television, watching afternoon cartoons, as Baby wriggled around his fingers. One afternoon, while watching TV with Baby, Randy fell asleep. When he woke up, the snake was gone. Vanished. We checked under furniture, in the closets, and even down in the basement. We tore the house apart looking for Baby. No snake. My mother would use a broomstick to pry the dirty clothes out of the hamper when doing the laundry, anticipating a green flash. Every time she opened a kitchen cabinet, Mom flung the door open and stepped back, expecting Baby to plop out onto the counter. But the snake was gone, and after two weeks we assumed that he had escaped and returned to the wild. That was until Mom went to call my aunt Phyllis, yanked the phone receiver out of the cradle, and strangled Baby.

"Right this way," my father said, opening the kitchen door for the repair guy. He stepped into our kitchen and found a pack of grimy kids crammed along the walls, standing on chairs, smiling. Mom was hiding in the bedroom with my sister and baby brother. The technician studied the phone, tapped it a few times, then asked my father, "Are you sure it was a snake?"

"Oh, yeah, but he's a little one. I hope you are not Irish, because Irishmen are supposed to be terrified of snakes."

"I am one hundred percent Irish. On both sides." He set his toolbox down and grabbed a screwdriver. My brother offered to help. Dad shot Randy a look and whispered, "Be normal, act normal." Randy shrugged, confused. He had no idea what *normal* meant.

The technician unscrewed the bottom screw, removed the top screw, and lifted the black plastic case off the frame. Baby's head popped up. The poor man leaped across the room, over the kitchen table, and pinned himself against the wall. The neighborhood kids cheered. Randy approached the innards of the exposed phone, and there was the snake, curled in a perfect figure eight around the two bells. Baby's head darted back and forth, confused. I assumed his eyes were adjusting to the light. Randy lifted Baby out of the phone. The snake wrapped itself around his wrist, hugging him for security. "There's my Baby," Randy said, "my sweet Baby." I thought I heard the phone guy gasp.

Randy took the snake and went out to the yard, the gang clapping and following him outside. The technician was pinned to the wall, silent, shaking his head back and forth, still clutching the screwdriver. Dad pointed to the dismantled phone. "Uh, could you . . .?"

The man replaced the plastic cover, tightened the two screws, and stared at the phone. Dad thanked him and carried the technician's toolbox out to the truck. "Is there a bill or anything? What do we owe you?"

The man just shook his head one last time, got into the truck, and drove away.

I found Randy and the others out in the vegetable garden. All the kids were petting Baby. Everyone wanted to hold him. But Randy said the poor thing had suffered enough. Two weeks in a telephone without food or water. And the phone ringing, scaring him every time it rang. Randy decided it was time to set Baby free. He walked farther into the garden, bent over, and released the snake. Baby hesitated.

He lay perfectly still for several seconds and then shot away, wiggling across the dirt and disappearing behind the Bibb lettuce. We all stood there, silent as supplicants.

That would be the last summer of my innocence. Castro would aim missiles at the United States, threatening to blow us up. A year or so later, a sniper's bullet would shatter JFK's skull. A year later, boys with bangs would sing "I Want to Hold Your Hand." The television would show freedom marchers attacked by dogs and body bags loaded into helicopters. MLK would die on the balcony of a hotel in Memphis. There would be riots. My mother would take a job as a waitress. She would meet a man who told her she was beautiful. Eventually, she would run away with him. My parents would divorce. We would lose the house. The court would award the four of us kids to my father. He would move us in with his lover, Wayne. I would detach from the family and bury myself in school and sports, determined to be perfect, beyond reproach. I would push myself to get an education, move away, and build a career in the entertainment industry. I would create a television program called *Home Improvement.* In the first season, I would write an episode about a snake getting loose in the Taylor house. The episode would culminate with the snake crawling out of a hole in the wall and slithering down Tim Taylor's shirt. It would produce one of the longest laughs in the show's history. And at that moment, I would realize that I had recreated the family I had lost.

12
FLAMING COUCH

The heart that breaks open can contain the whole universe.
—JOANNA MACY

When I was in the eighth grade, I combed my hair like Elvis and slouched like James Dean. I was cool. Or at least I tried to be. It was the year of my confirmation in the Lutheran church. For memorizing passages from Luther's catechism and reaffirming Jesus as my Savior, my grandmother Schmitt, Momo, awarded me a Bible. She had saved her pennies and bought me a black leather-bound Holy Bible, the Revised Standard Version. It is the Bible that I still use today. The black leather binding is held together with duct tape, and a few strips of Scotch tape patch the torn pages. My full legal name, Mark Allen Williams, is still embossed in gold on the cover as well as the date 1965: the year I became a man, or at least accepted responsibilities for my actions, the year I listened to Motown and James Brown and had a mad crush on Joan Baez, the year I discovered the joy of kissing Cindy Wolf in our hayloft and tracing the curved mysteries of her body with my fingertips. It was the year of the flaming couch.

This happened immediately following the confirmation service: I hold the freshly embossed Bible in my lap and look out the window of our Rambler station wagon as my mother steers up the driveway. My father lounges in the passenger seat as we approach the one-car garage connected to our house by a breezeway. Behind and to the left of the garage, I see the white barn on the hill that houses all the guinea pig cages. The hayloft door is cracked open, and tendrils of gray smoke roll out of it. The smoke ascends. The breeze catches the curls and blows them toward the sycamore tree, where the branches shred the smoke, sending gray ghosts out over the field where they hover and then disappear in the wind. I am captivated by the poetry of it all until Randy says, "Oh, shit! Fire!"

The station wagon slams to a stop, pitching the family forward. Heads bang, and arms fly. The passenger door flies open, and my father runs up the drive to the barn before I can reach the car door's silver handle. He slams the sliding doors open and charges inside the barn as I tumble out of the car. I scramble up, still holding the Bible, and run toward the smoke. My two younger brothers and sister waddle behind me like drunken ducks, just as the hayloft doors bang open and a smoldering brown couch flies out and sails through the air, then bursts into flames with a loud whoosh. The fireball seems suspended for a brief moment before it plummets to earth, lands in the yard, and blows apart, sending heat and fragments of burning wool heavenward. A chorus of young voices exclaims, "Holy shit! Wow! Cool!" My mother saunters up and joins the congregation gathered around the funeral pyre. She shoots Randy and then me a sardonic look, reaches into her purse, and pulls out a Salem. She lights the cigarette and blows a lungful of smoke toward the flames. She knows what caused this conflagration.

Let me back up a bit. Each spring, as school let out for the summer, Randy and I would move out of the house and sleep in the hayloft. The heat in the attic that served as our bedroom was stifling during the summer months, but the hayloft had doors and a back window for ventilation, so we would arrange bales of hay into beds, spread out sleeping bags and old blankets, and more or less bed down for the summer. Neighbor kids often joined us. Every night was a campout where we discussed the unfathomable allure of girls, especially the Reed sisters, and told ghost stories or listened to a crackly transistor radio play Top Forty hits. One day we decided to make the hayloft a little homier by adding furniture. First was a couple of lettuce crates that we used as end tables. We found a frayed sisal rug that we laid out to define our living area among the hay bales. Two chipped and wobbly kitchen chairs were pulled out of a neighbor's dumpster and dragged up to the loft. Then we found the pièce de résistance: a chocolate-brown couch, a three-seater stuffed with foam rubber and covered with coarse wool. It had been orphaned on the side of the road near Jim Beverly's house, so Randy,

Doug Wilson, Jim Beverly, and I decided to rescue it. It took us almost an hour to bang it up the wooden stairs of the hayloft, but at last our hangout was complete.

The couch was perfect, except for the fact that if you slept on it with a bare back, the wool itched and raised red patches on your skin. Now, none of us was burdened with the weight of intelligence, so we decided it would be a good idea to smoke cigarettes while lying on cotton sheets on a wool couch on top of bales of hay. We'd lounge and light up the Salems I snuck from my mother's purse. I'd strike a kitchen match, light a cigarette, then cavalierly toss the smoking match into the hay dust. I taught myself to inhale, pulling the smoke deep into my lungs, hacking and coughing, never mind the shards of searing pain or beads of sweat popping out on my forehead. It was worth it because I looked cool, like James Dean.

It is said that God works in mysterious ways, and the greatest mystery that spring was why the couch didn't immediately go up in flames. Somehow, the embers of a less-than-dead cigarette ended up in the sofa's crevices and kept burning. The only thing that saved the couch from spontaneous combustion was that the window was closed and the hayloft doors were only slightly cracked, allowing very little ventilation. The smoldering cigarette must have stayed between the cushions overnight into the following morning until we returned from church and saw the smoke, and Dad flung the couch out of the barn, where the blast of oxygen caused the embers to burst into flames. I still marvel how my father, fueled by adrenaline and fear, could single-handedly send an ugly piece of furniture airborne. There was another mystery. None of us kids got spanked, grounded, or punished. There were no raised voices or threats, only tension. Something was going on between my parents that I didn't understand but felt in my gut, a deep gnawing.

The next day, Randy and I raked the ashes out of the singed grass, scooped the burnt remnants into a bucket, and buried them in a hole behind the barn. As I cleaned up the mess, I thought about my confirmation. I had worn a navy-blue suit purchased at Robert Hall and a clip-on bowtie. During the confirmation service, I felt grown up and realized I was not afraid to speak in front of the congregation. I was comfortable with a crowd. It felt good to stand before the altar, recite memorized verses, and tell stories from the Bible. The sound of a car engine pulled me back to reality, and I saw my grandmother's gray Plymouth glide up the driveway. Momo often drove out to the country to help our mother with the laundry, cooking, and wrangling four free-range children.

Momo closed the car door and smoothed the wrinkles of her housedress. Randy gave her a quick hug, then ran inside to get a drink of water, an excuse to stop working. I thanked her again for the Bible. My grandmother tussled my Elvis pompadour, opened her arms, and invited me into her embrace. Momo always smelled like her home: cinnamon, melted butter, Ivory soap, and hints of lavender. She released me and said, "Let's talk."

Momo led me to the army cot my mother used for sunbathing. We sat on the sagging canvas, the sun warm on our backs. I assumed Momo would lecture me about the sins of smoking or kissing girls in the hayloft. Instead, she took my hand, ran her fingers over my knuckles, and said, "I listened to you speak in church yesterday, and I believe you have a pastor's heart." She must have felt me involuntarily pull away because she tightened her grip. "I prayed about it. I think you should become a Lutheran minister." I tried to imagine Elvis Presley or James Dean wearing black robes and white surplices, handing out Communion wafers, but I couldn't bring the incongruity into focus. "If you make good grades in high school," Momo said, "somehow, someway, I will find the money and pay for you to go to college. Valparaiso, Concordia in Saint Louis, or anywhere you want to go."

Me? A preacher? That was the last thing on earth I wanted to be. But I loved this woman and didn't want to disappoint her, so I only nodded and mumbled a false promise that I would think about it. Before going into the house, she touched my cheek and said again, "You have a pastor's heart."

I went back to raking the ashes. A preacher? Why would she think that? All I wanted was to lean on a Porsche 550 Spyder and smoke cigarettes or sing in a nightclub in Acapulco or hopefully see Cindy Wolf naked someday. Those weren't very pastor-like. Then I looked at the mess I had made with the burning couch. I ran the rake's tines through the ashes, claw marks in the dust, and that deep gnawing came back. I didn't think about metaphors back then, but I knew this flaming couch symbolized something. The end of summer? The end of innocence? I didn't realize it was the end of our family.

My parents divorced when I was in high school. It was a bitter fight and an even more acrimonious custody battle. After a year of marital warfare, my mother was awarded the house and the Rambler station wagon. In exchange, my father got custody of the four children, a Studebaker pickup truck, and a few hundred dollars in a savings account. Mom sold the house and ran off with her lover and future husband, Gene. We had nowhere to live, so my father moved us in with his "friend" Wayne. Dad attempted to hold us together as a family, but it was a shitstorm from day one. Wayne, my father's lover, had never lived with a houseful of hormonal teenagers and rambunctious children. There were fights and screaming matches. Chaos reigned. Randy left home at fifteen, never to return, my sister got pregnant as a teenager and moved out, and Bradley, my youngest brother, was numbed out with drugs.

I went into survival mode, withdrew from everyone, and buried myself in school and sports. I saw less and less of my grandmother. Momo tried to help, but there wasn't much she could do to mend our broken family. She occasionally called to see how I was doing in school and inquire if my grades were good enough to get me into Valparaiso or Concordia. Momo was saving money and eager to keep her promise and pay for my education as a pastor. I graduated from high school with honors, but my grandmother didn't pay for my college education. I earned scholarships and studied theater instead, where I learned to tell stories on a stage, not from a pulpit. As I grew up, I only saw my grandmother for an hour or two on holidays or when I cut her grass. She paid me twenty dollars to mow her tiny patch of yard. I think it was her attempt to keep me in her life, even for an hour or two.

The summer before I moved to New Orleans for graduate school, I cut her grass for the last time. She stood on the back porch steps of her house, holding a tin cup filled with raspberries she had picked from the bushes in her backyard. Momo offered to wash the berries and put them in a bowl with a scoop of vanilla ice cream. I told her I was busy and had to go. She smiled and nodded, and for the briefest moment, I glimpsed her radiance, the glow of her soul. Then I noticed how drawn and wrinkled her face was from the chemo. Her skin had a soft brown hue from sitting in the sun. The oncologist told her there was a vitamin in the sunshine that was good for women with breast cancer.

I had no idea it would be the last time I would see her. But she must have sensed this was a permanent parting because she gazed at me with such tenderness I had to turn away. She pulled a crumpled twenty-dollar bill from her dress pocket and handed it to me, squeezing my hand. I hugged her awkwardly, knocking a few berries from her cup, and left without looking back.

Momo died a few months later while I was in New

Orleans. My mother called to see if I was coming to the funeral. I used the excuse of being a starving student and couldn't afford a plane flight or a train ride. Besides, I had my graduate studies, rehearsals, and a scholarship to maintain. I simply didn't have the time. I was too busy to take a few hours from my life and say goodbye to the woman who had rubbed Jergens lotion on my back and sang me to sleep with German lullabies, the woman who had propped up a glow-in-the-dark plastic cross on the nightstand so I wouldn't be afraid of the dark, the woman who had run her fingers through my hair as I stretched out on the church pew with my head on her lap, listening to the soft rustle of her slip, smelling lavender in her Sunday dress. This was the woman who'd molded and shaped my childhood with her tenderness, the woman whose funeral I didn't attend.

Several weeks after the burial, my mother and her sisters were at my grandmother's house going through her things. My mother opened the top drawer of Momo's bedroom dresser and found a little yellow-and-green checked sports coat with matching short pants. It was the outfit I wore to church on Easter Sunday when I was three years old. My grandmother had kept the outfit all those years, neatly folded in her top drawer, wedged between her slips and a lavender sachet. I realized that every morning when Momo opened the drawer, the first thing she saw was this fabric from my childhood. I imagined her running her hands over it and remembering when I was innocent, sweet, and adoring. Before I became ambitious, distracted, and selfish. I didn't take the time to attend the funeral of this precious woman whose fingerprints are all over my heart. The woman who thought I possessed a pastor's heart, who saw goodness in me that I knew did not exist.

I am seventy years old, and there is still a tiny tear in my soul that may never heal. I pray there is a heaven and that I will see Momo again so I can kneel before her, kiss her hand, and ask her to forgive my selfishness.

13

GLADYS

I am convinced we all have angels in our lives. They may
be photon-filled beings, traveling through space and time,
delivering spiritual telegrams, whispering in our ears, or
poking us in the ribs with a divine nudge. Some of us may
call that intuition, inspiration, or imagination, but I believe it
is angels doing their thing. Angels protect us, watch over us,
and deliver messages from the Almighty. They usually have
wings or halos or diaphanous gowns. Some carry swords.
They all glow in the dark. But some angels come in human
form, wearing work boots, aprons, or battered Crocs. They
drive buses and wait tables, heal the sick and teach toddlers
not to hit one another with toys. These fleshy angels may be
flawed, but they are here on earth to do God's work.

Gladys Welker was a terrestrial angel.

She was a short woman with a helmet of lacquered hair
who wore sweaters buttoned up to her chin and sensible shoes
that squeaked when she walked the linoleum floors of my
high school. Mrs. Welker was my sophomore English teacher.

She was nicknamed "The Witch" because of her perpetual scowl and stern demeanor. Gladys Welker patrolled the halls of Reitz High School with a vengeance, squeaking with every quick step, as she corrected rude behavior, jabbed her finger in the face of a loud or rowdy boy, and scolded girls who wore their skirts too short. It was rumored that she was a widow, but it didn't matter. Every student made fun of her.

One afternoon at the beginning of my sophomore year, Mrs. Welker stopped class because she spotted something that offended her. It was my ankles. I was not wearing socks. Between my penny loafers and the cuffs of my khaki slacks was a patch of bare skin. Keep in mind that this was 1967; there was a dress code, and I defied that code by not wearing socks. Mrs. Welker marched me down to the principal's office and demanded that he give me a demerit for not following the dress code. I got busted by The Witch!

But I quickly learned this woman was not a witch; she was a sorceress. She seduced the mind, awakened curiosity, and created new worlds with her words. After only three days in her class, Mrs. Welker's words penetrated my brain, expanded my thoughts, and opened my heart. She introduced me to metaphors and similes, alliteration and onomatopoeia. Shakespeare went from being an old dead British guy to a majestic storyteller. Years later, I would find this description of him in a Carl Sandburg poem: "the inkfish, Shakespeare." The inkfish swam in poetry, dove into characters, navigated tributaries of themes and cascading waterfalls of metaphors.

Who knew reading could be exciting? I asked and was granted permission to move to the front of the classroom so I wouldn't be distracted by my classmates passing notes or making faces behind Mrs. Welker's back. This little humped-over scowling woman gave me the gift of words. She explained the primary function of storytelling: to sensitize the tribe. She insisted that stories awaken something inside of us and remind us of our connectedness to humanity, nature, and God.

Years later, I found myself in New York City trying to eke out a living in the theater. I acted in a William Inge play in a church basement and directed one-acts in dust-filled, decaying nooks called off-off-Broadway. And occasionally, I would go to the hinterlands to direct plays in small regional or community theaters. I was driving back from Madison, Wisconsin, having directed a production of "The Runner Stumbles." It was winter. The trees were bare, ice on the ground, snow flurries slashing at the windshield.

When I traveled, I always had a yellow pad beside me to write down notes or directions given by a gas station attendant. This was years before cell phones and GPS. As I drove through the hills of Pennsylvania, I saw a small cluster of trailer houses parked in a semicircle on a bare patch of earth. They were decaying hulks of aluminum, with sagging stoops and dilapidated siding. A rusted truck sat on concrete blocks near a battered swing set with a broken slide. I asked myself, *Who lives there? How do these people exist in this makeshift community?* As I drove, I realized these trailers were the homes of coal miners' families. I knew that the men worked in the mines, but what did the women and children do all day? What did they talk about, worry about?

I imagined the families, the children, the pets. Faces appeared, and I heard snippets of dialogue. Without thinking, I picked up the ink pen with my right hand and started writing the dialogue down while I steered the car with my left hand. I drove for hours, eyes darting from the highway to the yellow pad, scribbling away without much conscious thought. By the time I crossed the George Washington Bridge, the pad was full of words. I read them over in my tiny apartment later that night and thought to myself, *Well, that was interesting.* Then I shoved the yellow pad into a drawer and went about my business trying to survive as an actor and director. But the faces of the women and the children I saw in my imagination kept floating up in my consciousness. I batted those images away because I needed to make money to pay the rent.

Then one morning, as I sipped coffee out of a paper cup with Greek lettering on the side, I opened the *New York Times,* and on the front page was a photograph of women, bone-tired, weary women, clutching children and waiting, waiting to see if their husbands and sons, nephews and uncles had survived the explosion in the mine. I studied the faces of those women, saw their pain, and imagined their fear. Maybe it was a divine nudge or an angel's whisper, but I went to the drawer, pulled out the yellow pad, reread all the scribbling, and realized this might be a play.

The words poured out over the following weeks. I wrote on yellow pads, scrap paper, and napkins in diners. I wrote and rewrote. I had informal readings and got feedback from friends, and continued writing. I didn't know what I was doing, but I knew I had to finish the play, one way or the other. It took me three years and many drafts to complete *Between Daylight and Boonville* before it was produced off-Broadway at Wonderhorse Theater. My former college professor John David Lutz directed the New York production. He decided to do a presentation at the University of Evansville and enter the play in the American College Theater Festival. During this time, I supported myself by acting in commercials and on a soap opera. I kept writing, but I never thought of myself as a writer.

I flew back to my hometown for the premiere of *Boonville* and was standing in the back of Shanklin Theatre when Mrs. Welker walked into the lobby. I almost didn't recognize her. The helmet on her head was softer, still dyed brown but wavy. The top two buttons of her sweater were unbuttoned, and a colorful scarf was tucked into the V crevice. Her shoes didn't squeak. They had heels. And she wore lipstick, soft and rose colored.

I knew she had retired from teaching several years ago, but I still imagined her scowling, sending students to the principal's office. My stomach tightened. Here she was, The Witch, to see my play, which dealt with infidelity and death and was laced with curse words. If she saw me, she certainly didn't acknowledge it. I watched her check her ticket and take a seat several rows in front of me. I thought this was ridiculous; I am a grown man with sweaty palms and a fluttery heart because a retired English teacher was sitting there, flipping through a program. The lights dimmed, and the play began. I didn't watch the stage; I watched Mrs. Welker's back. It was straight and still, and nothing moved as the drama unfolded on the stage. During the intermission, I found myself in the men's room. It wasn't because I didn't want to see her; I just needed to wash my hands excessively until she took her seat and the second act began.

Applause. The play ended, the house lights came up, and the crowd shuffled and bumped their way up the aisles. I stood there, back against the wall, and waited. And here she came. I knew she wouldn't scold me, because I was wearing socks. But still, I worried: Was she offended by the language? Was the writing dreadful and amateurish? Was the theme coherent? She adjusted the scarf, tucked one edge into her sweater, and looked up. When her eyes met mine, I held my breath. She looked at me with a half smile, raised both hands, held up two thumbs, and punched the air. She walked right past me without a word. She didn't have to say anything. Those two thumbs were a benediction, a blessing, and the divine nudge I needed to keep writing.

14

UNCLE LOUIE

He always rubbed his left hand to keep the blood flowing, the nerves alive. As he growled out instructions on where to park the dump truck or unload the bags of mortar, Louie Heuer massaged the scarred palm of his left hand. Years before, while cutting a sheet of plywood with a skill saw, the blade hit a knothole and torqued. The saw kicked back, and the blade tore between his forefinger and middle finger, severing the palm and crushing bones. Louie was alone on the jobsite at the time. He didn't panic because he had already faced formidable challenges.

During World War II, Louie Heuer had been a marine grunt on the island of Tarawa. As his platoon advanced over the ravaged terrain, a bullet slammed into his right side and exited just above his left hip. The impact spun him around, knocking the rifle out of his hand. He fell into a foxhole. My great-uncle explained how everything slowed down. His thoughts crystallized. He knew what to do. First, he rolled on to his back so he could see the edge of the foxhole, pulled out his pistol, and placed it on his chest. Then he tore two strips off his shirt, wadded them up, and plugged each hole to stop the bleeding. He sensed no organs had been damaged, no intestines punctured. But he wasn't sure. He tore a long strip off his shirt and wrapped it around the two self-made bandages. And he waited. Night was coming. Soon the sun would set, and his world would plunge into darkness. As he lay there in the mud, he heard other wounded marines call out for help. Their plea would often be met with the crack of a sniper's rifle, so Uncle Louie cocked the pistol and held it with both hands, waiting.

Throughout the night, he heard footsteps, the enemy patrolling the battlefield, bayonetting wounded Americans. Without any drama or hyperbole, Uncle Louie told me he listened to the screams of dying men as they called out "Medic!" Louie didn't call out for help because he didn't want to draw the attention of the creeping shadows with the deadly blades. He waited all night, pistol in hand, watching the clumps of dirt and rocks that edged the foxhole. As the sun rose, the marines mounted an offensive and pushed the Japanese back into the hills. Medics arrived and found my great-uncle, conscious, gun in hand, rust-stained bandages seeping blood. He was carried back behind the lines on a stretcher, awarded a Purple Heart, and sent home. He married my great-aunt Alma and started a family and a construction company. He worked as an independent contractor.

Louie saw the spray of blood before he felt the pain. He looked down and realized the skill saw had split his left hand in half. He whipped out his handkerchief, wrapped it tightly around the bleeding hand, and drove three miles to the nearest hospital. After hours of surgery, the doctor explained that the damage was severe: nerves severed, bones broken, and Uncle Louie would probably never use his left hand again. My uncle basically told the doctor that he was full of shit. He intended to have a full recovery and return to work—as soon as possible. The hand took weeks to heal and months to rehabilitate, but Uncle Louie willed the muscles and tendons to rejuvenate, the nerves to reattach, and the bones to mend. He carried a tennis ball around, squeezing life back into his fingers. And he returned to work laying bricks, hammering studs into walls, and pouring concrete driveways. As a teenager working a summer job, I marveled how this older man could work all day without stopping. He was a machine. We on the crew got one fifteen-minute break and a half hour for lunch during an eight-hour workday.

One afternoon, Uncle Louie asked me to take a truckload of broken cement down to the end of the cul-de-sac and dump it in the ravine. I had never driven a car, much less a twelve-ton dump truck. Eager to please and not look like a fool, I hopped into the cab and turned the key. The truck rumbled to life. I looked down at the gear shift. It was a manual. I hadn't thought about that. Years of sweat, grime, and grease had faded the numbers and the *R* on the black knob, so I had to guess what gear was where. I knew enough to put my foot on the brake and push in the clutch before shifting into gear. I grabbed the knob and jammed it into what I thought was first gear, grinding. As I released the clutch, the truck shuddered and died. I heard laughter. All the men on the site had stopped working, leaning on shovels or hanging from scaffolds, to watch the fifteen-year-old kid wrestle the massive truck. I knew that I was being tested, and I was determined to meet the challenge. Three more grinding attempts, and I finally got the truck in gear.

I weaved my way down the street through the subdivision, bumping a trash can but managing to stay between the curbs. When I got to the end of the cul-de-sac, I had to turn the truck around and back up between two cinderblock retaining walls. More grinding as I backed up to the ravine we used as a landfill. Then I realized I had no idea how to dump this thing. I studied the red knobs and a couple of levers and guessed. I was right on the first try. I watched the truck's bed elevate in halting movements in the rearview mirrors and slam to a stop. I heard the crunch and scrape of broken concrete slide down the metal truck bed and land with a dull thud in the ravine, kicking up plumes of powdery dust. The truck now emptied of the load, I pulled another lever and the bed descended with a slam that bounced the truck and rattled my teeth.

During the drive back up the cul-de-sac, I saw that the crew had gone back to work. The fun was over. I parked and climbed out of the cab and looked at Uncle Louie, expecting a "Good job" or "Attaboy" or some affirmation, but he was on the scaffold, sliding mortar off his trowel onto a row of bricks. He grabbed a brick in his left hand, looked over his shoulder, and said, "Mix some more mud, and move that scaffolding around to the south side of the house." He turned back to his work, but I caught a glimpse of a smile. My uncle tested me, and I passed the test.

I believe God tests us to see if we are up to the challenge. God doesn't jump down off the scaffolding and drive the truck for us. He watches and waits. Can we make it to the end of the cul-de-sac and back? Can we carry the weight we've been given and steer between the curbs? Can we return to the end of the street, ready to face more challenges? And if we do all of that, meet those challenges without compromise or complaint, does God go back to work with a smile on his face?

I worked that summer as a hod carrier. As the sun rose, my mother or father dropped me off at the job site each morning. I was always the first to arrive to mix the mortar and have it ready when Uncle Louie drove up at precisely 7:00 a.m. every day. He'd turn off the truck's engine, stride across the lot, climb the scaffolding, and lay the first brick by 7:05. I never missed a morning. He had me unload pallets of twelve-inch concrete blocks and dig a foundation in swampy gray mud, the sump pump gurgling up and spitting out the dirty water from the basement we were building. He showed me how to set a plumb line, how to use a level, and how to tuck-point. By the end of August, I was standing on top of the scaffolding laying bricks.

As we worked, I questioned my uncle about Tarawa. He was reticent to talk about it, but after hours together on the scaffolding, the stories emerged. The landing was rough. A shallow reef surrounds the island. The LTVs carrying the marines got caught on the reef, forcing the men to wade to shore under heavy sniper fire. The waves pounded the marines and repelled them as they struggled to get to dry land. Some marines, weighed down by heavy belts loaded with ammunition, drowned in the surging seas. My uncle explained that the real enemy, in many ways, was the waves.

That image has always stuck with me because I realize challenges are like waves. They keep coming, pounding against you, trying to knock you down. But if you stand firm and lean into the waves, you don't drown, you get stronger. Challenges strengthen character, build confidence, and encourage independence. Challenges keep us alert and alive and on point. Challenges force us to grow. That summer, Uncle Louie wasn't teaching me how to build a wall; he was teaching me how to build a life.

15
PUZZLES

My memory is a little hazy. I can't remember if it was someone from the theater department, the fraternity, or one of my college roommates. I do remember the empty beer cans and the thousand-piece puzzle spread out on the kitchen table. Between sips of beer, whoever he was would snap a colored puzzle piece into place. Or not. Frustration built. He would crush a Budweiser can, toss it onto the floor, and keep punching jagged pieces into the puzzle. He got so angry that he jumped up, disappeared into the bathroom, and returned with an emery board. He took the stubborn puzzle piece and rasped away the edges, shaping the cardboard to his liking. He'd then force the mutilated puzzle part into place with his thumb until it stuck. With a fresh can of beer and the emery board beside the puzzle, he kept filing and fitting, shaving and shoving. The image that emerged looked like something Picasso would have painted if he had eaten a bad burrito and puked on a strip of cardboard.

Why am I telling you this? Because that is exactly how

I prayed when I was in my twenties. I presented God my to-do list. The prayer went something like this: "Dear Lord, hi. I need your help. Please take care of this and this and that. Sorry, I don't have time for a longer prayer. I've got to run. Amen. Oh, and thank you." I would toss my prayer requests at God, turning the Supreme Creator of the universe into my personal assistant.

I imagine that is how many of us pray. We have a preconceived notion of what we want the picture to be, and we expect God to grant it to us. We don't wait for God to show us the pieces and help us snap them into place. We grab an emery board and start rasping away, pathetically attempting to get the Creator to conform to our perfect little picture puzzle. *Fit in there! This is what I want!*

I eventually realized that it is so much easier if I give over and let Spirit guide me. But prayer has taken discipline and hard work to become something approaching effortless. If I acknowledge God's greatness, embrace solitude and silence, put aside my to-do list and suffocate my ego with a pillow, then the puzzle evolves, and the pieces eventually fall into place, revealing God's plan. I don't need beer and an emery board. I just need patience and faith.

16

TOILET DANCING

Dance is the language of the soul.
—Martha Graham

If you and I were to have a contest about who had worked the worst job, I bet I would win. We've all had survival jobs, but working the graveyard shift and sweeping floors in a toilet factory would probably be at the top of most people's list of crappy employment. While an undergraduate, I worked at Peerless Pottery in Evansville, Indiana, during my Christmas break.

If I remember correctly, my hours were from 10:00 p.m. to 6:00 a.m. My duties on the night shift consisted of two parts. During the first half of my shift, I scooped up damp clay. A machine pours melted clay into different shapes and design molds when toilets are made. These molded clay shapes travel on conveyor belts to a furnace where the kiln bakes the clay, and then, on the other side of the kiln, the baked clay is sealed and sprayed with paint. I worked at the beginning of that process. As the molds traveled on the conveyor belt toward the furnace, the belt vibrated, shaking out air bubbles and settling the clay into the molds. The excess clay splashed out onto the cement floor. My job was to take a large snow shovel, scoop up the spilled clay before it cooled, and dump it into a wheelbarrow.

When the wheelbarrow was full, I pushed it down three floors on a series of wooden ramps, out the back door, and across the parking lot, where I dumped the clay into the dump pit. Now, here's the thing. It was December. So I would scoop clay by the roaring furnace, where temperatures hovered around 120 degrees, and wheel my way outside, where temperatures were usually in the low teens. I took off my shirt and heavy coat the first night, hung them on a peg by the door, and worked bare chested. Then wheeling my way outside, I stopped, put my shirt and coat back on, raced across the parking lot to the dump pit, came back inside, and removed and hung up my shirt and coat.

By the second night on the job, I realized the strip show was slowing me down, so I worked shirtless. I scooped clay by the furnace, my skin glistening with sweat, then ran down the ramps out to the parking lot and hit the frigid night air, where my sweat turned to steam as I wobbled the wheelbarrow across the parking lot. I was a vaporous cloud pushing two hundred pounds of moist clay through the cold night. By the time I got back inside, the sweat had turned to hard crystals, and I was covered in goose bumps and shivering. That was the first four hours of my night.

During the second half of my shift, the factory shut down,

and production was stopped. Everyone left the building except the security guard and me. I was given a large push broom and instructed to sweep the floors in the storage warehouse. The warehouse was almost a football field long, lined with rows and rows of toilets stacked about six high on metal shelves. It was just me, the toilets, and the broom. I don't have to tell you what I felt like. I thought about getting a T-shirt and printing TURD on its front, but I didn't think management would appreciate that.

I swept floors from 2:00 a.m. until 6:00 a.m., in the still of the night. This was before cell phones and I didn't own a Walkman, so I would sing and dance to break the monotony. I sang "My Girl" or "Ain't Too Proud to Beg," my voice echoing through the warehouse as I recreated the smooth moves of the Temptations. Step, step, turn and sweep. I'd toss the broom from hand to hand, occasionally dipping the handle dramatically, then sweep puffs of dust along the gray concrete floor. I had found a way to beat the boredom. Until one night, when I heard a tap-tap-tap. I looked up, and the security guard was standing at the end of the long row of toilets. His beer belly pushed against his black belt. His Fu Manchu mustache hid his upper lip. He didn't wear a tin badge. His badge was stitched into the fabric of his navy-blue shirt: SECURITY.

He tapped the metal rack again; I stopped singing and dancing. He raised his billy club, waved it back and forth like a wagging finger, and mouthed, "No. No. No." I shrugged *OK* and raised the broom in surrender. He yelled, "No singing. No dancing." Satisfied, the security guard tapped the metal rack one last time, pulled up his belt, and strolled away.

When I was a child, my idea of God was a punitive father figure, a police officer, or a fascist security guard. God was about power and control. God set the rules, and I had to follow those rules, or else I would be struck down, thrown into the fiery furnace of hell where demons would torture me and toss my battered body into a dump pit for eternity. My strict Lutheran upbringing, Sunday School every Sunday, and eight years of parochial grade school had taught me not to piss off Big Daddy. It wasn't enough that I loved the Lord; I had to fear Him. Fear and trembling. No dancing.

Long before Jesus of Nazareth walked across the Sea of Galilee, people perceived dancing as a spiritual expression. The dance of the Hindu god Shiva represents the creative cycles of creation and destruction, the source of all movement in the cosmos. Miriam, the sister of Moses, supposedly grabbed a tambourine and got the women of Israel on their feet and dancing after the parting of the Red Sea. King David joyfully danced before the ark of the covenant. So joyful was he that he took off his clothes and danced naked. When my children were little, they danced in puddles of rain. My wife and I dance in the kitchen while we prepare dinner. When the wind blows, the trees dance. Even stars and galaxies dance in the infinite darkness of an expanding universe. What would happen if we all stopped thinking of God as the great punisher and imagined God as our ultimate dance partner? I like the idea of swing dancing for eternity with the Lord.

17

DR. BEN

The baby was sick. Laurie had fallen into a deep depression. The medical clinic struggled to stay open, and Dr. Ben had lost hope. Satan attacked everything he loved—his family, work, and faith. These were desperate times in Kingsley.

I played the character Dr. Ben Martin for three years on the soap opera *Another Life*. The program was Pat Robertson's brainchild, produced by the Christian Broadcasting Network, CBN. The show was shot at the media complex Pat Robertson had built in Virginia Beach, the same studios where he recorded *The 700 Club*. The writers for *Another Life* were undergraduate students attending Pat Robertson's university, so you can imagine the quality of the writing. The producers quickly learned the scripts could be amateurish, but the actors on-screen had to be professionals. So the producers flew to New York City and held casting sessions.

I was a mediocre actor at best, but somehow I got cast as the clean-cut, heroic Dr. Ben Martin. On my first flight to Virginia Beach, I waited by the gate at LaGuardia, ready to board the plane. A stranger strolled up to me and sat down. He asked, "You flying down to Virginia Beach for the show?"

"Uh, yes, I am," I said.

"You're an actor," the stranger said.

"How did you know?"

"Come on," he gestured toward me. "You look like an actor."

The stranger had been cast in a recurring role and was flying down on the same flight. And he was right; I looked like an actor who played a doctor on a Christian soap opera. Christian soap opera? That was an oxymoron. Soap operas are about gorgeous people doing despicable things—stealing, lying, cheating, and murdering. They're about sleaze and sin! *Another Life* was supposed to be a tawdry soap opera in which the characters prayed, and Jesus played the lead role. I wasn't quite sure how that would work.

On the plane ride to Virginia, I tried to imagine what CBN employees would be like. Were they cultish? Did they have *Dawn of the Dead* eyes? Did they carry a Bible and a shotgun, insisting I claim Jesus as my personal Lord and Savior? I was leaving New York City to dwell in the land of Pat Robertson.

When I arrived, I was pleasantly surprised. For the most part, everyone at CBN was congenial and good natured; they were genuinely nice folks. They patted me on the back and said, "Praise the Lord!" Or waved as I pulled out of the parking lot and shouted, "God bless you!" I enjoyed working there, despite Pat Robertson's fundamentalist views and conservative politics. I disagreed with everything the man represented except the part about loving God and being kind to neighbors. But the most challenging aspect of the job was asking viewers for money.

The actors in the series were required to work the phones during pledge drives. That meant we had to talk to people around the country and take donations for *The 700 Club*. I envisioned the wrinkled octogenarian on the other end of the phone emptying her savings accounts to buy her way into heaven. I imagined a retired farmer cashing his Social Security check and tithing so Pat Robertson could expand his empire. I kept my mouth shut, answered the phones, and collected my paycheck. But spiritually, I was in a constant tug-of-war. I was *in* Pat Robertson's world, but not *of* his world. I was a practicing Christian, but not that kind of Christian. Yet deep inside I sensed I was at CBN for a reason.

Before each show's taping, the cast and crew members gathered in the studio to sing hymns and pray. Occasionally, a cameraman or the hairstylist prayed in tongues. They raised hands and uttered a strange guttural language, which scared the hell out of the secular/humanist/heathen/atheist New York actors. I prayed daily, so all the God stuff never bothered me. I was comfortable around prayer. If a camera malfunctioned, production stopped and the crew would lay hands on the camera and pray. The New York actors snickered or covered grins with their hands and left the studio, shaking their heads in disbelief. But I was fascinated. I knew faith could move mountains. I wanted to see if faith could resurrect a television camera.

I was never a great actor because I was distracted by every aspect of production—the cameras, lights, and scene design. I was curious. Linwood Boomer, the show's executive producer, was a kind and generous man. He sensed my curiosity and invited me into the booth to watch the director. *Another Life* was a multicam show, which meant three cameras ran simultaneously. The director sat in a booth in front of a bank of monitors and snapped his finger to cut from camera to camera, editing the program as we shot it. When I wasn't acting in a scene, I stood in the back of the booth and observed while Linwood explained the coverage and the camera angles for a multicam program. Eventually, Linwood asked if I was interested in the editing process. I jumped at the chance to sit in the editing bay and learn how the editors cut and sound mixed the episodes. Is that why I was in Virginia Beach—to learn production? Is that why Spirit had placed me in this environment? I didn't know. But I knew I had to stay busy or fall into a crippling depression.

This was around the time my marriage to Peggy was disintegrating. I was heartbroken, so I buried myself in work. I rented a condo on the Chesapeake Bay and stayed busy. I would wake up at 6:00 a.m. to review the scenes we were shooting that day, drive to the studio, and shoot until two or three in the afternoon. Then I drove back to the condo, went for a long run, and prayed while jogging on the beach. I showered and wrote for about three hours. I was teaching myself how to write plays, studying every book I could find on dramaturgy, and was determined to hone my craft.

After a light dinner, I sat down to memorize the next day's scenes. The memorization came easily to me. I had attended grade school at Trinity Lutheran School in Darmstadt, Indiana, and we had memory work every night. Every night of the school year, the students had to memorize Bible verses, hymns, or large chunks of Martin Luther's catechism. As a child, I hated poring over words and searing them into my memory so I could recite the Nicene Creed or the Apostles' Creed in front of the class. But God works in mysterious ways; I developed an almost photographic memory because of all the practice. I could look at a page, mentally take a snapshot, and see every word on the page in my mind, recreating every line of dialogue and all the stage directions. So after dinner, I'd resist calling my soon-to-be ex-wife and memorize the pages we were shooting the next day. I'd go to bed around ten thirty or eleven and then repeat the routine until I finished that week's shooting and flew back to NYC. But I kept asking myself, *Why am I down here?* I sensed it was for something more than acting.

And boy, did I act, with a capital *A*. I could chew scenery with the best of them. I learned to cry on cue and how to hold a distant, troubled stare as the camera fades to black. I learned all the tricks, like not blinking during a close-up, not bopping my head around or waving my arms too much when portraying anger. Hold all that rage inside and let the audience do the work. Dreadful. Embarrassing. I promised myself (and God) that I would stop acting if I started earning a living as a writer. I mean, you can subject the audience to only so much ham.

I started rewriting my scenes because the scripts for *Another Life* were so poorly written. As I studied the lines, I would restructure the dialogue, clarify the intention, build an arc, and identify the defining moment of the scene. Eventually, the rewrites became part of the process. When the director saw me walk into the rehearsal hall, he asked if I had any changes. I usually did, so a production assistant would xerox those pages, which is what we rehearsed and shot. Without realizing it, I learned to write for television, and Linwood Boomer had taught me every aspect of multicam production.

My marriage ended about the time *Another Life* stopped production. I had been on the program for three years and two weeks. One week to the day after I shot my last episode, I got an unexpected call from the executive producers of *The Cosby Show*. They had read some of the plays I had written in Virginia Beach and wanted to interview me as a possible writer for the show. On the phone call, they asked if I had any experience working on a multicam show. I smiled and told them I did. I went to the interview. I got the writing job. I kept my promise and stopped acting. Audiences around the country cheered and exclaimed, "Thank God!"

18

SHARING

I met an angel while working as an actor on *Another Life*. She didn't have a halo or wings; she wore dark pleated slacks dotted with lint, baggy sweaters with the sleeves pushed up over her elbows, and glasses that dangled on a faux-silver chain around her neck. She was a wardrobe assistant. I can't remember her name; I remember only her sweet spirit. Her job was to gather the dirty costumes, wash and iron them, and ensure each actor's wardrobe was camera ready again the next morning. In the dressing room, actors threw clothes on the floor or slung them over chairs. As the angel gathered the soiled garments, she never spoke or looked at the actors. She worked quietly with great dignity, humbly serving others. That touched my heart. After several attempts to engage her, she finally gave me a shy nod. I thanked her for taking such good care of the costumes. She said, "You're welcome," and walked out the door with an armful of shirts.

As the months passed, the angel occasionally stopped

working long enough to have a conversation with me. I started putting together the puzzle pieces of her life. She was divorced. Her ex-husband was a truck driver who had abandoned her without any support. Through the studio gossip in the hair and makeup department, I learned the angel had an ailing mother she cared for and a rebellious teenage daughter she was trying to get through high school. I also discovered this woman worked a second job. How was that possible? After completing her tasks at the studio, she worked part-time in the evenings cleaning a local motel. She never complained. She never said an unkind word. I wanted to hug this woman, give her money, do something, anything, so the angel could get some rest. But I did nothing other than offer her kind words and the occasional prayer.

One afternoon, I was leaving the CBN studios for the day. I had shot my scenes in the morning and headed home for lunch. As I passed the wardrobe department, I saw the angel sitting on a stool wedged between a sewing machine and a clothes rack. She had a white napkin across her dark slacks as she pulled a sandwich out of a crumpled paper bag. I gave a quick wave and said, "Bye, I will see you tomorrow."

"Would you like some?" she said, unwrapping the plastic around the sandwich.

"No, thank you."

"It's good. Here." And before I could protest, she tore the sandwich in half and offered me the bigger half. "It's turkey with lettuce and tomato."

SHARING

There was no way I could refuse her. I took the half she offered. "Thank you."

"You're welcome," she said.

We both took a bite of the sandwich. I mumbled, "Delicious."

She chewed and smiled and started to glow.

19

MIKE

Frankly, there isn't anyone you couldn't learn to love
once you've heard their story.
—MR. ROGERS

Mike Forche has been my closest friend for more than fifty years. He was the best man at my wedding to Angelina, as I was at his. He is godfather to my daughter, Matisse, and I am godfather to his daughter, Ellie. Mike is lean, fit, and cowboy handsome, like the actor Sam Elliott. He has a thick mustache like Sam's, except Mike's mustache is still black.

Let me give you a glimpse of the kind of person Mike is. During our bachelor days in the early 1980s, Mike and I flew to Aspen, Colorado, for what we hoped would be a weekend of mild debauchery. I didn't ski. Never have. Never will. Freezing my ass off, tumbling down a hill, and breaking bones is not my idea of fun. We were headed to Aspen to drink and meet women.

We boarded a small commuter jet, squeezed down the narrow aisle to our assigned seats in the front row of the plane. As I stuffed my bag into the overhead bin, I glanced across the aisle and saw an older couple in their late sixties. The husband had silver hair and wore a gold Rolex the size of a Volkswagen. Next to him, in the aisle seat, was his wife, the grande dame. She had puffy lacquered hair and sparkly rocks on both hands, and wore a massive fur coat that looked as if a hairy animal had swallowed her body, leaving her glossy head exposed for the world to admire. I rolled my eyes, and words like *rich bitch*, *pretentious*, and *entitled* popped into my head. I took my seat by the window. Mike settled into the aisle seat.

Before the plane took off, Mike turned to the woman, pointed at her fur, and said, "Did you shoot that thing this morning?" The woman laughed a warm growl and replied, "No. I bagged it last night." Her husband hung his silver head, shaking it from side to side, and chuckled. Mike and the couple talked the entire flight to Aspen. By the time we landed, they had traded contact information and business cards. The grande dame invited Mike to visit their Texas ranch anytime he wanted.

I was judgmental; Mike was gracious. I made a snap judgment; Mike started a conversation. I saw the label on the jar; Mike looked inside and saw the contents. Mike is very successful, and I believe what accounts for that success is his ability to talk to anyone without judgment. He has lived and worked in Las Vegas for thirty-eight years, working at a title insurance company and building apartment complexes, shopping centers, and high-end subdivisions. Mike's gregarious nature and midwestern work ethic catapulted him to success during the boom years in Vegas and carried him through some desperate years.

On September 15, 2008, Lehman Brothers filed for bankruptcy. Deregulations, negative amortization, and derivatives triggered the meltdown, the crash. Armageddon. Fannie Mae and Freddie Mac fueled the conflagration. Mike explained, "If you could fog a mirror, these guys would lend you money." Corporate greed had once again crashed a global economy. The Vegas bubble burst and billion-dollar projects were abandoned. New construction halted, development died, and Mike found himself out of work.

A local judge approached Mike to work as a receiver for the court. Receivership is like being a referee. The court appoints an objective third party to help settle bad real estate deals to prevent financial loss, control accounts, assess the property, and make proposals to the judge. Judges depend on receiverships, and the judge in Las Vegas respected Mike because he was honest and had an impeccable reputation. Mike accepted the offer and was appointed the receiver of a run-down, fleabag hotel off the strip on Paradise Road, not far from the airport. There were 340 units. The ceilings were stuffed with asbestos; mold and mildew streaked the bathroom walls. The swimming pools were drained. Rooms were rented for about seven dollars a day. Mike put up a chain-link fence surrounding the entire building to discourage squatters, keep out trespassers, and prevent the owner from burning down the place to collect insurance money. Mike's job was to protect and refurbish the decaying hotel and bring it back to life. He hired two sets of security guards to patrol the property 24-7. All the employees at this particular company were either ex-cops or ex-cons. The ex-cops had arrested many of the ex-cons, but now they worked side by side. Ironic, to say the least.

A thick concrete wall divided the hotel property from a nearby car-rental lot. One morning, Mike went to inspect the site, and while walking the perimeter of the property, he noticed a hole dug under the retaining wall. As he approached the wall, he heard grunts and moans. A creature covered in dirt crawled out of the hole. Mike stepped back, spilling his coffee. The beast was a man, a bundle of rags, with a matted beard and grime streaking his weathered face. Mike didn't yell at the man, reprimand him for trespassing, or report him to the police. He struck up a conversation. The man's name was Gary. He was homeless and had been living under the retaining wall for several months. He had dug a hole next to the fence and created a makeshift cave crammed with plastic bags, a sleeping bag, cardboard boxes, and a butane gas stove. Mike learned Gary was a former drug addict, an alcoholic, and a veteran of the Gulf War.

Mike saw Gary most mornings. He brought him coffee and sometimes breakfast sandwiches from 7-Eleven. They would eat and sip coffee as the sun rose, burning the chill off the desert floor. Breakfast became a ritual. Mike noticed Gary had a cell phone. Gary explained that he kept it active to contact distant family members and use it for emergencies. He showed Mike how he charged the phone by furtively running an electric cord from the car-rental place to his cave. Gary made Mike an offer. Gary volunteered to keep an eye on the property since he had a direct view of the chain-link fence and crumbling hotel. Mike tried to pay him, but Gary said the coffee was enough. Mike punched his cell number into Gary's phone.

About a week later, Mike was awakened at 2:00 a.m. by his cell phone's buzzing. It was Gary. He said that men dressed in black and wearing ski masks had cut through the chain-link fence. They were carrying gas cans.

As I was writing this, my gut went off. I stopped typing to check this story's veracity. I wasn't sure if I remembered it correctly. So I called Mike in Vegas. We hadn't seen each other for almost a year because of the pandemic, but as soon as Mike answered the phone, it was as if we were continuing our previous conversation. I told Mike what I was writing and explained that I wanted to confirm the story, make sure the narrative was rooted in facts, and ensure I wasn't fabricating fiction. As my gut had told me, I had veered off into fiction.

Mike confirmed that everything I had written was accurate, except for the gas cans. That night, the security guards had cut a large hole in the fence, and men wearing black clothes and ski masks had slipped through the opening, but they weren't arsonists. They were stealing three hundred air conditioners, window units still in their shipping crates. The men carried the crates to an idling truck, loaded them up, and disappeared into the night. Hearing the commotion, Gary crawled out of his hole to check. That was when he called Mike. Mike called the police, hopped into his truck, and drove to the hotel. He never got the air conditioners back. And he had a dilemma: Which security guards were the crooks—the ex-cops or the ex-cons? It didn't matter. Mike fired them all. He hired a new security firm and continued the renovation. Mike thanked Gary and gave him a little money, a show of gratitude. Gary reluctantly accepted the cash.

Mike and Gary didn't become lifelong friends. They never shared an actual sit-down meal together. In fact, shortly after the air-conditioning incident, Gary vanished. The hole was empty. Gary was gone. But a bond had been formed, a connection made. On the phone call, I asked Mike, "What was it about this man that made you trust him?" Mike thought a moment and said, "When you talked to the guy, you could see a spark of intelligence in his eyes. You could tell he was a good guy." I realized I needed to be more like Mike. More open, less judgmental. He didn't see a filthy animal crawling out of a hole, a drug addict, or a drunk. Mike looked for and found the man's humanity and caught a glimpse of God.

20
PART OF THE FAMILY

During my morning meditation the other day, I was doodling on a yellow pad, daydreaming and reminiscing. As I sat at my desk, sipping coffee, faded images floated into my consciousness—memories of a moment, a glimpse from almost forty years ago, a glimpse that changed the course of my career.

As I recalled earlier, my first job writing for television was *The Cosby Show*. Jay Sandrich, the director of such popular programs as *The Mary Tyler Moore Show, Rhoda, Phyllis,* and *The Cosby Show*, plucked me from the obscurity of off-off-Broadway. He had read a collection of one-act plays that I had written and managed to get produced in tiny theaters behind fish stores or musty church basements. Jay, without informing me, passed the plays to Tom Werner and Marcy Carsey, the executive producers of *The Cosby Show*. They responded to my writing. I was called in for an interview. This was September 18, 1984, two days before *The Cosby Show*

149

premiered on NBC. The show had been in production for weeks. Still, no episodes had aired, the audience had not met the Huxtable family, no one had seen the sitcom destined to become one of the most popular shows in television history. I showered and shaved, dashed out of my studio apartment, hopped on the subway, and headed to Avenue M in Brooklyn for the interview.

Tom Werner greeted me in front of a redbrick, pre-war apartment building. He escorted me inside, up a flight of stairs, and down a long hallway. Muffled voices and television noise seeped through the walls. The smell of chicken soup and cooked cabbage lingered in the hallway. A frail older man wearing a bathrobe, house slippers, and a yarmulke shuffled past, smiled, and nodded hello. Tom opened a door and we stepped into the production office, an eclectic jumble of chairs and tables crammed into a two-bedroom apartment. I settled into a folding chair that pinched the backs of my thighs. Tom sat across from me. I shifted, trying to get comfortable. Tom seemed anxious. I thought, *Why is this guy nervous? I'm the one being interviewed.* Tom explained they shot *The Cosby Show* in front of a live audience just around the corner, the same studio where they filmed the soap opera *Another World.* Tom complimented my one-act plays. I thanked him. Then he grew serious and asked, "Do you think you can write for television?"

"I have no idea," I said.

My honesty must have stumped him because Tom sat silent, eyes blinking. Finally, he nodded and mumbled, "OK,

OK." He shuffled the pages of my plays.

"Are you funny?" he asked.

"Not necessarily," I said.

More nodding. More blinking. Things got quiet. So I filled the silence. I explained that I write characters, not jokes, and sometimes the writing is funny if the characters are funny. Tom blinked and nodded, so I continued. "I don't know how to write jokes," I said. "I couldn't write a joke to save my life. But I know basic dramaturgy, and I have worked very hard to hone my craft. I'm organized. And I show up on time." More nodding. More blinking. I walked out of the interview, convinced I had blown it big time.

I was hired. (Later, I discovered that almost every writer on the *Cosby* staff had been fired. The producers were desperate and would have hired any warm-blooded creature with opposable thumbs who could hold a pencil.) I worked there as a writer/producer for three and a half seasons.

It was my third or fourth week on the show, and the writers and producers were gathered in the studio to watch a rehearsal. Jay Sandrich was "the general" on the floor, blocking scenes, giving notes, and encouraging the actors to have fun and delight in the material. I stood with the other writers, along with Tom and Marcy, watching the rehearsal. I was like a cub reporter with my pen in hand, scribbling away on a notepad, eager to make a suggestion that might help the scene or perhaps tweak a line of dialogue to make it funnier when we did a final polish pass of the script that evening.

The scene being rehearsed was between Theo (Malcom-Jamal Warner) and Rudy (Keisha Knight Pulliam). As child actors, these two had natural comedic instincts. Keisha was so genuinely funny it was as if she had toured the comedy circuit for years. Jay finished giving notes and had Theo and Rudy run the scene. It was charming because their behavior and their relationship felt authentic. Nothing was forced, neither of them straining to be funny, only honest human behavior.

As they finished the scene, I heard someone say in passing, "If you were sitting at home right now watching, wouldn't you want to be a part of this family?" I thought, *YES! Yes, I would!* That moment was more than a glimpse. It was like getting smacked on the head with an angel's wing. An epiphany. I thought about that phrase for weeks, ". . . wouldn't you want to be a part of this family?"

The more I thought about it, the more I realized that all of my favorite sitcoms did just that—invited the audience to be a part of a family, whether it was a biological or surrogate family. *The Mary Tyler Moore Show*, *Cheers*, and later *Seinfeld* and *Friends* invited the audience to hang around the newsroom with Mary and the gang, pull up a stool at the Cheers bar, or have a cup of coffee with clever friends and neighbors. That was the key: instead of blasting comedy through the screen and machine-gunning the audience with jokes, invite the audience to become a part of a family.

I consciously incorporated this idea when conceiving

the opening credits of *Roseanne*. I wanted the camera to do what they call in the business a 360, a complete circle around the table as the Conners gathered, plopped into chairs, grabbed food, teased, joked, and told stories. The opening credits were designed to subliminally invite the audience to pull up a chair and become part of the family. Dan Foliart and Howard Pearl composed a brilliant bluesy theme song that captured the rough and rugged fun of a working-class family.

This gathering at the table was also inspired by my Midwestern upbringing. When family and friends gathered at our house, they always sat around the kitchen table, usually with a coffee pot placed in the middle of it. Everyone told stories. As a small child, I would sit under the table with all the dirty work boots, tennis shoes, and bare feet and listen to story after story. The stories were usually our family's history—reminiscing about a hilarious mishap or disparaging a marginally sane relative who ruined every Christmas holiday. Occasionally, the stories turned dark and melancholy, retelling tales of tornadoes tearing through small towns or sudden death by accident or bemoaning the alienation of a loved one. I would ride an emotional roller-coaster with each story as family members tried to out-talk and top the others with an even funnier or sadder story. I didn't realize it at the time, but our kitchen table was the campfire, the sacred circle where the oral histories were shared, and ancestors lived on in my imagination.

While writing and rewriting the pilot episode of *Home Improvement*, I kept in mind that phrase I overheard during the Cosby rehearsal, ". . . wouldn't you want to be a part of this family?" When David, Carmen, and I created *Home Improvement*, we had a clear intention: we wanted the program to be a celebration of an American family. We consciously decided the show should be aspirational, creating a family the audience would want to be a part of. We designed the sets and shot the program in order to invite the audience into the Taylor home, stand in the backyard and listen to Wilson, or be an audience member in the bleachers at *Tool Time*.

When you think about it, the television is like our ancestors' campfires. We gather around its flickering light to hear stories, share moments of joy and heartbreak, and learn about the world and one another. I used to criticize people for spending hours sitting in front of a television, thinking it was a total waste of time. I know this sounds hypocritical since I spent most of my career creating content for television. Yes, people watch television to numb out after a stressful day at work. Sometimes the television is background noise, moving wallpaper as people scroll on their phones or flip the pages of a magazine. But really, the television is our electronic campfire where we gather to share stories and connect with others. And that is so important because it seems there is an atavistic need to belong to something bigger than ourselves.

PART OF THE FAMILY

Ultimately, we are herd animals, and we seek out the comfort of the community. We all want to belong, to be part of a family, even if that family is made up of fictional characters on a television screen with a laugh track.

21

ISN'T IT ROMANTIC?

We are made for love.
—Julian of Norwich

In romantic comedies, there is a concept known as the "meet-cute." The two future lovers crash bicycles in the park or fight over a taxi, or the cocky lawyer doesn't realize the spitfire attorney striding into the courtroom is his future wife. The audience knows, but the lovers haven't a clue. The first time I met Angelina, she was scrubbing a toilet. The woman was on her knees, wearing yellow plastic gloves, Lysol in one hand and a scrub brush in the other, polishing the porcelain throne. Angelina swears it was not the toilet; it was the bathtub, and the gloves were not yellow, they were blue. It doesn't matter. She was spring cleaning.

Her best friend, Susann Brinkley, was directing a collection of one-act plays that I had written. Susann shared an apartment with Angelina Fiordellisi in Hell's Kitchen and offered to bring me there to select interstitial music for the production. When we stepped into the first-floor apartment, I heard singing, a smoky female voice growling out Motown, Martha Reeves and the Vandellas. Susann walked over and rapped on the door frame. I peeked into the bathroom, and there was Angelina Fiordellisi in a torn *Flash Dance*–type sweatshirt and baggy sweatpants, her hair twisted into a bird's nest on top of her head. Beads of sweat dotted her forehead. Angelina stopped singing and blew a fallen curl out of her face. And at that moment, the spirit voice inside me said, *This is the mother of your children. What?* It was as if a cherub had karate chopped me in the heart. And I heard my spirit voice, the true voice that never lies, say, *You will marry this woman and have children.*

We exchanged hellos. I managed to mumble something; I don't remember what. Angelina seemed more concerned with removing stubborn stains than talking to a neurotic play-wright. I walked into the next room, turned to Susann, and said, "I am going to marry Angelina Fiordellisi, move to New Jersey, and have six kids." Susann crinkled her eyebrows and shook her head. *WTF?* But I had glimpsed my future. I repeated what my spirit knew. I said, "I am going to marry Angelina Fiordellisi, move to New Jersey, and have six children." Susann dismissed my temporary insanity with a wave of her hand and insisted we sit down and choose music for the plays.

I saw a lot of Angelina. She was between acting gigs so she came down to the Westbeth Theatre to support Susann. Angelina rolled up her sleeves and did everything from moving set pieces to collecting tickets. I would watch her pass through the theater during rehearsals, and I'd whisper to Susann, "I am going to marry Angelina Fiordellisi, move to New Jersey, and have six children." My mantra became a running joke until Susann snapped at me one day, "Don't joke! Angelina takes this shit seriously!" But I wasn't joking. My spirit was at peace because it knew this woman was my future wife.

But my brain was screaming in terror. I had just survived a painful divorce and was a jumbled bag of broken parts. I married for the first time in college when I was twenty years old and was divorced at twenty-one. My first wife, Marilyn, was a beautiful, bright spirit, but I was too young and insane and self-absorbed. I cheated and lied and destroyed our marriage in less than twelve months. I married Peggy right after graduation. We remained married for more than ten years, but it was a cold marriage between two friends, not lovers. I always wanted children, but Peggy insisted she would never get pregnant. So I talked myself out of wanting a child. But the longing lingered; the desire for a family was always there. Once Peggy moved out, I threw myself into my work. I spent every waking moment working as a writer on *The Cosby Show* or writing plays. I convinced myself that if I stayed busy, I wouldn't hurt. Seeing Angelina in a sweatshirt, scrubbing a toilet, had thrown me. The last thing I wanted was a relationship. A long-term commitment? No way. But my spirit knew.

Opening night of the play, I found myself sitting beside Angelina. There were two broken seats in the back row of the theater, so we took them. The one-acts I had written were comedies, and much of the humor depended on timing and pacing. But the actors loved to "act" by slowing down, making every moment meaningful, killing the comedy. I squirmed in my seat, going insane. I kept snapping my fingers, whispering, "Faster. Faster. Move it. Pick up the pace." I felt this iron claw grip my thigh and fingers squeeze so hard the blood stopped flowing. Angelina leaned over and whispered, "Shut the fuck up!" Shocked, I turned to her. She silently mouthed the words, *Stop it.* I sat quietly with my hands in my lap for the rest of the play.

As the audience exited the theater, Angelina pulled me aside and told me I was a major asshole. "You were a distraction," she said, insisting the audience and actors onstage probably heard me snapping my fingers and grumbling in the dark. She shook my arm and said, "Cut it out." I realized my spirit voice had been very wrong. There was no way I wanted to move to New Jersey and have babies with this woman. Angelina was from Detroit, an angry street dog. She barks. And bites.

But God works in mysterious ways, because I found myself walking down a sun-filled street in Manhattan with Angelina a few days later. We were discussing the rewrites of the play, and I looked over and saw her seven months pregnant in my mind's eye. She was beautiful, aglow, her body holding

160

new life. This wasn't a hallucination. It wasn't some misogynistic barefoot-and-pregnant fantasy. My spirit showed me this was my life partner, my twin flame, my future. I didn't say anything to her, but inside, I did one of those frantic cartoon head shakes, attempting to rattle the vision out of my head. Angelina and I had not kissed or held hands, and I was already making babies with her.

On that walk, Angelina told me that we had met before the day of spring cleaning. She was with Susann at one of the early auditions for the one-acts. Really? I didn't remember. Because of long hours on *The Cosby Show* and longer hours rewriting the plays, I was sleep deprived, distracted, and wrapped up in my narcissism. And I was depressed and angry from the divorce. Angelina confessed that when she first saw me, I was standing in the back of the theater, leaning against the wall. My fedora was pulled down, covering my eyes, and my arms were crossed tightly across my chest. She took one look at me and thought, *Damaged goods. This guy is a wreck. Stay away from him.* I stopped walking and said, "Well, I'm glad I made an excellent first impression." It was the first time I heard her genuinely laugh. The sun suddenly felt warmer as we turned the corner.

We continued to work together, but the play finished its run at the Westbeth Theatre, and I didn't know if I would see her again. But Spirit, and Susann Brinkley, had other plans. The Double Image Theater was throwing a gala, and Susann invited me to the party. The night of the event, I worked my way through the crowded lobby to pick up my ticket, and there was Angelina. She was stunning, radiant, with a head full of cascading curls. It was the eighties, the era of Big Hair. Angelina wore an off-the-shoulder white dress, and she had taken (I later learned) a pair of fishnet hose and cut out long Madonna-like gloves that caressed her forearms. She had transformed from a toilet scrubber into an Italian goddess. Angelina handed me a ticket, and I reminded myself to close my mouth.

It just so happened Susann sat me next to Angelina that night. I don't remember the evening. I remember the intoxicating scent of Angelina's Big Hair shampoo. Maybe my spirit voice had been right after all. Angelina was the goddess of my idolatry, my future wife, and the mother of our children.

After the gala, I walked Angelina home. She and Susann had moved out of Hell's Kitchen to a sublet on the Upper West Side. We strolled the night streets and sat on a bench in Riverside Park until three in the morning, talking about our careers, spiritual beliefs, God, and higher purpose. I took her hand and explained that I was flying to Europe later that morning to visit my best friend, Mike, who was living and working in Monte Carlo. I told Angelina I would be away for two weeks and would call her as soon as I returned to New York. She pulled her hand away. I don't think she believed me. I walked her to her apartment building, and we stopped by a wrought iron fence. I kissed her good night. If this had been a romantic comedy, the camera would rack to soft focus, buildings would disappear, and, above us, the stars would explode and turn into fireflies. As I walked back to my apartment, the camera would track with me, then pull back to reveal that I was floating six inches off the sidewalk as fireflies made of stardust drifted down to earth and landed in the trees.

When I was in Monte Carlo, I thought about that kiss. I thought about Angelina and her perfect lips while jogging along the Côte d'Azur with Mike, driving down to Èze for lunch, or watching sunsets dapple the Mediterranean. I flew back from Europe and called Angelina before I unpacked my bags. We started dating. Angelina got cast as the Widow in a production of the musical *Zorba* with Anthony Quinn. She toured the country while I wrote on *The Cosby Show*. Every break from the show, I hopped on a plane and flew to various cities—Buffalo, Chicago, San Francisco—to be with Angelina. And no matter where she was in the country, Angelina could transform a sterile hotel room into a lovely home. She draped scarves over tables, placed cut flowers around the room, and lit candles. And always set out a bowl of fresh fruit.

One day, Angelina was in a slip, leaning on the kitchenette counter. She grabbed a ripe peach and took a bite. The juice ran down her chin. She licked her lips and said, "You have to try this. It's perfect." And she offered me the fruit. I took a bite. The juice exploded up my nose. We laughed and kissed. I didn't think her kisses could ever be sweeter, but they were. This was the person I had longed for; she was everything I desired: a talented, intelligent, passionate woman with a fierce spirit and tender heart.

So what did I do? I did everything in my power to drive her away. The more I longed for her, the more I withdrew. When she was sweet and cuddly, I said something hurtful or started an argument. My spirit voice had told me, "You will marry this woman and have children." My spirit knew. But my brain held up clenched fists, ready to beat the crap out of Spirit. While in California, Spirit lost the fight.

In Los Angeles, *Zorba* played the Pantages Theatre, and Angelina lived in the Oakwood Apartments in Marina del Rey. I waited weeks to see her again, counting the minutes until I finally had a break from *The Cosby Show*. I flew out to California for the week. On my first day there, Angelina placed a purple scarf on a coffee table and set out a bowl of fresh fruit. She lit a scented candle. And I started a fight. It was one of those hissing hurtful arguments. I slammed out of the apartment, dragged my bag to the airport, and flew to Las Vegas.

Mike had returned from Monte Carlo and started a successful career in Las Vegas in the title insurance and real estate business. When Mike went to his office, I moped around his condo on Flamingo Drive with the curtains drawn. I sat in the dark and argued with myself: *That was so stupid. Why did I leave? Because she set out a bowl of fruit. That was a trap. I am not a monkey. She can't trap me with a piece of fruit. She is trying to control me. But I want her, need her. But I am not going to let her manipulate me.*

Mike came home from work one afternoon and found me talking to myself in the dark. He threw open the curtains and said, "Hey, man, you're starting to look like a mushroom. You need to get outside." He took me to dinners and lunches and introduced me to his friends. And we ran. Every morning, we ran countless miles. As we jogged through the desert, I talked about Angelina and how she was beautiful, intelligent, and intuitive. She was volatile, passionate, and a little insane at times, but in a good way. She was perfect. Mike stopped running. He wiped the sweat from his eyes and, between breaths, asked, "Then what the hell are you doing in Vegas?" I didn't have a clue.

The next day, a mutual friend from our hometown, Charlie Hobgood, arrived with his new wife, Toni. They stayed with Mike for a few days. Charlie was a midwestern mongrel, like me. Toni was full-blooded Italian. I watched Charlie and his Italian wife dote on each other, splash in the pool, kiss, and cuddle with a fruit-and-cheese platter on a lounge chair. They fed each other grapes. I wanted to eat grapes with my Italian woman. I got very drunk that night and decided to call Angelina. Mike stopped me and said, "That's not a good idea. Wait until morning."

"You are a bachelor," I said.

"Yes, I am," Mike agreed.

"I know what I am doing. I have been married twice before."

"Yes, and three strikes, you're out."

I stumbled past Mike into the guest room. This was before cell phones, so I locked the door and called Angelina.

I declared my love. I pleaded with her to move in with me once the tour was finished and she returned to New York. Angelina's answer was simple: "No." She would not move in with me. In fact, she didn't know if she ever wanted to see me again. I swore that I loved her and wanted to be with her. She said, "The only time you want to be with me is when you are not with me. And when you are with me, we fight. Don't you find that strange?"

And there it was. Angelina was right: I was damaged goods. I was irrational and erratic and did everything I could to destroy our relationship. That's when I decided I needed professional help, a psychotherapist to help me untangle this knot of confusion in my brain. When Angelina returned to New York, I took her for coffee and told her I was starting therapy. She was thrilled. But I warned her, "This may bring us closer. Or it could very well end our relationship." She said with a sigh, "Just what every woman wants to hear."

Dr. Philip Luloff helped me untangle all the knots: my parents' tumultuous divorce, my father's failure as a husband, and my mother's multiple marriages. My mother had abandoned the family when I was a teenager. I pulled that thread and realized I expected women to leave and hurt me. I unknotted my two failed marriages and examined the threads of fear, doubt, and insecurity. I pulled a thread I didn't know was part of the knot: my desire to seduce and win a woman, but not commit to her. If I didn't fully commit, I wouldn't get hurt. And with the final thread, I learned that vulnerability was not a weakness but a gift. Vulnerability is where you find the good stuff—the delicate parts of your soul, gentleness, and sweetness. I acknowledged my past mistakes and vowed not to repeat them. Instead of therapy ending the relationship, it brought Angelina and me closer. She became my lover and most intimate friend.

One night in Little Italy, we were in a candlelit restaurant on Mulberry Street. The tiny table was wedged in the corner with two chairs and a red-and-white checkered tablecloth. We had been dating for almost two years. The therapy was working. I felt good about us. As we sat there, I recalled the lyrics from an old love song: "What a lovely way to spend an evening." But then Angelina folded both hands on the table, looked me dead in the eye, and said, "Where is this going?"

"Huh?"

"Who are we? What are we? Are we exclusive? Is this something long term?" It was like sitting in the back row of that theater again; she had metaphorically reached under the table, grabbed my leg, and stopped the blood flow. She repeated, "I want to know where we are in this relationship."

I didn't have time to think, so I spoke from my heart. "I think we should get married. What do you think?"

Angelina didn't move. She didn't say a word. She blinked once. Then she bent over, grabbed her purse, and pulled out a day planner. She flipped to the calendar and said, "When?"

"W-w-what?" I stammered.

And she repeated, "When? What date?"

"Well, I thought that maybe we could get married this spring. When *The Cosby Show* goes on hiatus."

"What date?"

I was scrambling. "I don't know. Maybe we could, you know, plan a wedding sometime in May."

She flipped pages in her day planner to the month of May, turned the book toward me, and said, "What date?"

My mind reeled. I saw a weekend on the calendar and said, "May ninth."

She circled the date and wrote something on her calendar.

Angelina never agreed to marry me. She never said, "Yes, Matt, I would love to be your wife." Or even "Sure, OK." But on May 9, 1987, in Rochester, Michigan, Angelina said "I do." Susann Brinkley was Angelina's maid of honor, and Mike Forche was my best man. On our honeymoon, I asked Angelina why she never said yes to my bumbling proposal. Why only ask for a date? She said, "Because I knew when I called my mother with the news, the first question she would ask was, 'What date?'"

Angelina and I didn't have six kids. We had two. And we didn't move to New Jersey. We moved to Los Angeles. So you see, Spirit doesn't know everything.

22

FRISSON

Awe is what moves us forward.
—Joseph Campbell

The baby was stressed, so the doctor decided to insert wires through the birth canal and attach them to our unborn daughter's head to monitor her heartbeat. This being our first child, we were anxious and scared. We had rushed to the hospital twice before thinking Angelina was in labor, but it turned out to be Braxton-Hicks contractions, or false labor. On the third trip, Dr. John Williams (no relation) decided to induce. Angelina was in full labor, but she received the epidural too late. When it came time to push, she was numb and unable to bear down. The lights in the birthing room were dim; soothing music wafted through the sound system. It was after midnight. The halls of Cedars-Sinai were quiet. I watched the monitor beep, each flutter of our daughter's heart as she strained to come into the world. I folded my hands, but I wasn't praying. Part of me was calm, knowing everything

169

would be fine, while another part was terrified, fearing that this baby, a being I already loved more than myself, would die before she took her first breath.

A door slammed open. The squat, redheaded nurse who had checked on us constantly for the past twelve and a half hours finally lost patience, flipped on all the lights, turned off the music, and climbed on top of my wife. She placed her hands on Angelina's stomach and more or less attempted to push the baby out. Dr. Williams calmed the nurse down and patiently coaxed, cooed, and encouraged our baby to come out and join us.

The head emerged, then the body, and Matisse entered the world. Our daughter rolled her face from side to side and opened her eyes, blinking at the lights in the ceiling. Then she turned her head toward me and stuck out her tongue. Angelina and I laughed. And we wept. We couldn't speak. Dr. Williams asked if I wanted to cut the cord. As the scissors chewed through the umbilical cord, I mumbled something like "This feels like cutting calamari." The nurse smiled, wrapped Matisse in a blanket, and placed her on Angelina's chest. At 12:55 a.m. on April 3, 1988, Easter Sunday, Matisse Elizabeth Williams was born.

Fathers who are present at the birth of their child talk about the miracle, the joy, and the love they feel when the baby is born. But words are inadequate, a feeble attempt to express something that cannot be described. Words reduce a moment of vast importance and meaning to a cliché. Dr. Jay

Lombard, in his book *The Mind of God*, explains this feeling: "We cannot communicate our wonder. All we can do is gasp. Or, still in the delivery room, we marvel at the newborn babe in our arms. We are grateful. We are staggered. But no words can come. We can only weep. Surely we are tapping into the intangible then. We have come to the limits of our language and have experienced something beyond language. In doing so, our minds have brushed against God. We have encountered, however limited, the echoes of another world."[1]

Standing in the labor room, I felt "the echoes of another world," as if a veil had been pierced and God energy had poured into the room. *Awe* is the only word to describe this feeling, a combination of fear and wonder, joy and dread and elation, something sublime, something sacred. I felt tiny yet vast, a part of something greater than myself, like a single grain of sand on an endless beach. Eight years would pass before I experienced this feeling again.

Angelina and I had moved back east and were living in New York City when I got the call. My paternal grandmother, Vonda Grace Brown, was dying. The doctors were unsure how long she had. It could be days or minutes. I shoved a shaving kit and a few clothes into a bag and caught the first flight back

---

[1] Jay Lombard, *The Mind of God: Neuroscience, Faith, and a Search for the Soul* (New York: Harmony, 2017), 79–80.

to Evansville, Indiana. I don't remember the flight or driving the rental car to the assisted-living facility. I do remember the smell of the corridors as I entered the nursing home, a scent of soap and disinfectant, wilted flowers, and mothballs. I had no idea what I would find or what I would say or do.

I stopped at the nurses' station and was directed to a room on the first floor. I opened the door; heads turned. There was my father and his partner, Wayne, my uncle Cyril, and Betty, a family friend. They were seated in a tight cluster by the window.

Before any of them spoke, I simply asked, "How is she?"

Uncle Cyril, who was always the loudest person in the room, got even louder when nervous or excited. He blurted out, "Hey, buddy! She's on the ropes, but she's not down. She's hanging in there. She's a fighter."

He pointed to the bed in the corner, where my ninety-three-year-old grandmother lay. She was on her back, eyes wide, staring at the ceiling. Cyril laughed a nervous laugh and shook his head. "She's tough. She won't go down without a fight. She's still swinging." I held up my hand to stop Cyril's blather and noticed my father. He was quiet, looking at the floor. I rubbed Dad's back and then walked over to the bed. Grandma Brown rolled her head from side to side and squinted, as if trying to bring the room into focus. Her hands were raised, and she kept grabbing at something, her fingers clutching air.

I kneeled beside the bed and held her hands. They were cold, bird bones under the skin. I rubbed her fingers, warming them, and recalled how these hands could grab a hot skillet off the stove, fry a chicken, cast a fishing line, gut a catfish, and shoot a shotgun. They were the hands of a country-woman who lived out her last years in the city.

Her house on Richardt Avenue was a box of four small rooms, a bathroom, and a basement. If you were to stop by Grandma Brown's house anytime, day or night, you would find three strips of fried bacon on a paper napkin resting on top of the stove next to the coffee pot. Just in case someone wanted a bacon sandwich and a hot cup of coffee. The kitchen was her domain. She ruled. Grandma always sat in *her chair* at the Formica-topped table with the chrome legs. She would fold and unfold a napkin as she listened, gave advice, or scolded. "Put your mind in gear before you run your mouth." To anyone who tried to dodge the truth, she would urge, "Say what you mean, mean what you say." She laughed often, a wheezy, warm laugh that made her eyes squint. She called everyone *suggie*, her slang for sugar. "Hey, suggie, you want a bacon sandwich?" And she always demanded, "You are not leaving here until you give me some sugar." Sugar was a kiss on her cheek. You didn't leave the house without giving her some sugar, a blessing.

In her youth, my grandmother looked like Judy Garland. I have a faded photograph of her in my study, and the resemblance to the star is staggering. Vonda Grace was a petite woman, just over five feet tall, and weighed about 110 pounds, but she was loaded with grit and gumption, as if someone had yanked a 250-pound, six-foot-tall cowboy off the range and stuffed him inside this little package. Grandma shot quail better than any man, bass fished with the best of them, drank highballs, and smoked unfiltered cigarettes. She was married a couple of times, supposedly wild in her younger days, and gave birth to three children during the Great Depression. She worked as a bacon inspector at the Swift packinghouse for a while. I am not sure about her education. It stopped somewhere around the seventh grade, but she was wise. She had heart wisdom.

Her kitchen was a therapist's office and confessional, where people came to confess their sins, work out their problems, or simply vent. If someone was going through a divorce, got hurt on the job, or was simply overwhelmed by life, they came to Grandma Brown's house for healing. She put them down in the basement, a makeshift den with a jerry-rigged shower and slop sink in the corner, a foldout couch, and a Philco phonograph that played 78s and had a radio that still worked. She would love on these folks, cook their meals, wash their clothes, and wipe their asses if necessary, until broken hearts were mended, wounds healed, or they died. Many a soul transitioned under her care: her mother, two brothers, her youngest child, and only daughter. I don't remember my grandmother going to church. I don't remember her ever saying a prayer. She loved with her heart and her hands.

I ran my thumb over the blue veins under the tissue-paper flesh. Her pulse was rapid and weak. I had no idea what to say, so I said a silent prayer, asking God to give me words. Grandma turned and looked at me. There was fear in her eyes. I brushed back her hair, leaned close to her ear, and said, "Grandma, it's OK. You don't have to be afraid. Perfect love casts out fear. And you are loved perfectly, so there is nothing to fear." Her eyebrows crinkled, and her mouth tightened. I whispered, "If you let go, peace and love and light will surround you. You will be enveloped in that light and become eternal." She looked into my eyes. I don't think she saw me. I don't know if she heard me. I stroked her hand. "It's OK, Grandma. It's time."

"Excuse me," the nurse said, lightly rapping on the door. "I need to check her vitals." She walked into the room. Cyril and Betty said they had to run an errand but would return later. I checked on Dad. He was silent, still staring at the floor. His hands were folded. The knuckles were white. The nurse removed her stethoscope and informed us it was only a matter of time. "She's near the end," the nurse said, nodding her condolences and closing the door. Cyril and Betty offered Dad and Wayne a ride home, but I said I would drive them. Betty gathered her things, and, before they left, Uncle Cyril turned back to me and said, "Hey, bub. Thank you for coming." He winked and left. The room grew quiet.

"Dad?" I asked.

"Yes?"

"Do you want to stay here? Do you want to stay?"

"No, I don't think so."

"OK."

"I don't know if . . . I don't think I can be here."

175

"All right. I understand."

Wayne interrupted. "We should probably go home."

Wayne squeezed Grandma's hand goodbye. Dad leaned over and kissed his mother on the cheek. He didn't leave without giving her some sugar. I drove Dad and Wayne to the house. The drive was only five miles round trip. I got them settled and then went straight back to the facility. The nurse was at her station when I returned. She looked up. I saw her eyes, and I knew. "You were gone only five, maybe ten minutes when she passed," the nurse said. "It happens that way sometimes." I nodded without speaking. The nurse tilted her chin in the direction of the room. "You can go in if you want, you know, before we transport the body. I'll give you all the time you need."

I stepped inside the room. My grandmother was on the bed, eyes closed, head back, and mouth open. Her hands were still, resting on her chest. Suddenly, I felt something immense, overwhelming, warm, and vibrating, like brushing against God. *Frisson* is the French word for the shivering thrill we sometimes feel on our skin. The body feels something extraordinary before the mind can conceive it. But I knew what I felt. It was her spirit filling the space. I burst into tears and started laughing and said, "I love you, Grandma. I love you so much, so very much. And I am so happy for you." At that moment, I felt something bigger, the echoes of another world. And I realized that I knew this feeling. It was the same feeling I had when my daughter was born.

23

QUIRKY

Angelina tells everyone that I cursed our son the moment he was born. When Fredrick Emerson Stefan Williams decided to come into this world on March 22, 1990, he came fast. I was at the Disney Studios in Burbank, watching a rehearsal of *Home Improvement*, when I felt a tap on my shoulder. One of the interns whispered, "You have a phone call. It's urgent."

When I arrived at Cedars-Sinai, Angelina was already in labor. Matisse had been born two years earlier in the same hospital, so we knew the drill and had taken all the Lamaze classes. My job during labor was simple: be supportive, offer encouragement, and remind my wife to breathe. "Breathe. Push, push, push, push. Breathe." I watched the monitor, charting every contraction, following the beeping line as it ascended and descended. I could see a contraction starting before Angelina felt the pain, so I could warn her. Things were smooth and right on course, but then . . . Angelina began ranting about every time she had auditioned for a part and didn't get the role. In English and broken Italian, she cussed out every writer, producer, and casting director that had ever rejected her. "*Figlio di puttana. Va'all inferno!* How can you make the casting director cry and not get the part?!" I was smart enough not to answer that question.

Standing at the bedside, reminding Angelina to breathe, I realized my toes hurt. I was wearing brand-new cowboy boots, designer boots with pointy toes and narrow heels. (Why did idiots like me think wearing cowboy boots with pleated dress slacks was the epitome of elegance in the early nineties?) Anyway, the boots were pinching my toes, so between Angelina's contractions, I happened to mention, "Honey, these new boots are really hurting my feet. I need to sit down." The monitor started beeping. Faster. Louder. Angelina's blood pressure shot up. She dilated another two centimeters. Growling. Teeth grinding. Veins throbbing. I thanked God repeatedly that my wife was on her back with her feet in metal stirrups, or she would have ripped my heart out and swallowed it without chewing. But all of that rage helped move things along, because Fred popped out right into my hands shortly after that. And with the umbilical cord still attached, I looked into my son's face and said the first thing that came to mind: "He is so *quirky*."

Angelina sat up (I think I saw flames shooting out of her eyeballs) and growled, "I don't want to hear *quirky*!" But he was. Our son was wrinkled, slightly jaundiced, and quirky.

Back at the house, we introduced Matisse to her new baby brother. She took one look and screamed, "Take him back!"

I said, "Oh, honey, you will come to love him because he is your brother. And he is so—" I stopped because I saw Angelina glaring at me, flames flickering in her pupils. "He is so sweet," I said to Matisse. "Now you'll have someone to play with."

Matisse stomped away, went into her room, and tore all the hair out of her favorite doll's head. Fred started crying. Angelina clutched our son, staring at me like one of those emaciated, Depression-era women in a Dorothea Lange photograph. She was very quiet. Which always terrifies me.

"What?" I asked.

She shook her head from side to side, slowly, without taking her eyes off me.

"I didn't curse him," I said.

"No. It wasn't the *malocchio*," she said. "You didn't put the evil eye on him. But you labeled him."

"Labeled? I just said—"

"You labeled him, you christened him with that word." She shook her head some more and went into our bedroom to nurse the baby. I checked on Matisse. She was in her room punching a teddy bear. So I left her alone. After a while, I peeked into our bedroom. Angelina and Fred were both sound asleep. While they slept, I hid the cowboy boots in the back of the closet.

With both of our babies, I developed a technique for getting them to sleep. Angelina would wrap them in a swaddling blanket, and I would hold them to my chest, walk around the room, and hum. I hummed old hymns and Sinatra songs, but the most effective tune was "House of the Rising Sun." After a verse or two about a whorehouse in New Orleans, the baby's eyelids would flutter and the tiny head would sag. While I hummed Fred to sleep that night, I watched his fontanel pulsate softly. When I was little, my grandmother told me that the soft spot on a newborn's head was where an angel kissed the baby before it left heaven and came down to earth. Is that what happened? Had a quirky angel kissed my son? I pressed Fred to my chest and thought, *Why did I use the word* quirky? *Why did I call him that?* I could have said he is so *zany, wacky, kooky, unusual, unconventional, exuberant, joyful,* but I used the word *quirky*. I guess I meant that Fred seemed different; he possessed a unique, ineffable soul. I couldn't articulate what it was. But then I saw his essence a few years later and understood.

It was early morning and there had been a light sprinkle of rain. The sun had come out. Fred and I were walking down the sidewalk in Santa Monica. He was three and a half, maybe four years old. And on the street, near the curb, was a puddle of oil. A car engine had leaked and left an oil slick. My cell rang. I answered it. And as I talked, Fred went to the curb, ran his hands through the sticky oil, and smeared it all over his body— his face and hair, all over his clothes, up and down his arms.

I yelled, "Fred! What the hell are you doing?"

He looked up and grinned and said, "I'm painting myself with rainbows." And he pointed at the dark smudge. When the sunlight hit the puddle of oil just right, shimmering rainbows rippled off the stain. I saw oil. My son saw rainbows.

24
THE KEY

I am convinced that if you look up the word *chaos* in the dictionary, in any language, you will find an asterisk: *see *Italian*. I am not disparaging Italians. The most fabulous food, fashion, art, architecture, ice cream, and operas have come out of Italy. But have you ever tried to get six Italians out of the house at the same time? Impossible.

I say this because my wife's family is 100 percent Italian on both sides. I have witnessed the chaos of an Italian family eating a meal. They yell, laugh, cry, slap the table, and occasionally throw a bowl of spaghetti against the wall. Then they kiss and hug, eat biscotti, and drink coffee. I grew up in the Midwest and come from an Irish-German lineage. If family members raised voices, it meant someone was getting a divorce.

The morning I asked for Angelina's hand in marriage is a perfect example of what I am talking about. We had flown to Detroit to announce our engagement. I had been warned that Angelina's father, Stefano Fiordellisi, was old-school, so

I wanted to do it right. It was early morning, and we were drinking our first cups of espresso for the day.

I waited until Stefano had a few sips of coffee, then I said, "Mr. Fiordellisi, I love your daughter very much, and we have decided to get married. I would like your blessing."

He stared at me for about twenty seconds without blinking. Then he smacked the table, rattling the espresso cups, stood up, and screamed, "You can't just decide to get married!" The veins in his neck throbbed, his eyeballs bulged, and his face turned scarlet. "You have to talk to a priest. It takes time! You can't just decide to get married!"

He downed the last of his espresso, went to the sink, and started washing the cup. Angelina's mother, Caterina, stood in the corner crossing herself and mumbling the rosary. Stefano washed and washed and washed that one little cup with a sponge until Angelina walked up behind him, put her arms around his waist, and said, "Daddy, we're getting married. Be happy for us." Stefano burst into tears, hugged his daughter, kissed her cheeks, then hugged me, kissed my cheeks, and then he made us more espresso. Angelina's mother wasn't sure what to do, so she started cooking sauce.

Stefano Fiordellisi and Caterina Sgambati were married for fifty-three years. They became Nonno and Nonna when grandchildren came along, the quintessential Italian grand-parents. For the remainder of their lives, everyone called them Nonno and Nonna. They were childhood sweethearts, grew up in the same village in Italy, on the same street, and would sneak away to hold hands and kiss in the shadows of stone archways. They were forced to hide because Nonna's father, Mr. Francesco Saverio Sgambati, threatened to blow a hole in the Fiordellisi boy with his shotgun and on one occasion took a potshot at his daughter. That is the truth.

So they hid from an irate father and German soldiers. When Nonno and Nonna were teenagers, Nazis occupied the town. Nonno told us stories of how the Nazis marched down the streets, and how families hid food from the soldiers in the hills, among the chestnut trees, and how you couldn't trust anyone—Brownshirts, Blackshirts, neighbors—and how they cheered when the American army liberated the town and handed out chewing gum and chocolates.

After the war, Stefano finally got up enough courage to approach Mr. Francesco Saverio Sgambati. He went to his house, sat across the table from the man, kissed the back of his hand, and formally asked permission to marry his daughter Caterina. Mr. Francesco Saverio Sgambati didn't reach for his shotgun; instead, he reached across the table, hugged and kissed Stefano, and made them both a cup of espresso.

Nonno and Nonna were married in a small church in their hometown, Baiano, Italy. Baiano is a village in the province of Avellino in the Campania region, about twenty miles inland from Naples. If you get on a train in Naples and ride it until you run out of track, you are in Baiano.

Nonno and Nonna's third daughter, Caterina "Cat" Fiordellisi, and her fiancé, Victor Nelli, married in the same church where Nonno and Nonna were married. This was May of 1992. Family, friends, and relatives from around the world packed up kids and suitcases and headed for Baiano. Like the Nazis, the wedding guests invaded and took over the town.

When we drove into Baiano, my first thought was that we had entered a time warp. The entire village looked like a Fellini film from 1957. Couples on Vespas zipped down cobblestone streets; every male over the age of twelve had a cigarette dangling from his mouth; older men sat in the piazza sipping amaro, playing cards; grandmothers knitted and gossiped about the neighbors, while hormonal teenagers flirted and squealing children played tag around the water fountain.

The week we arrived in Baiano, a very odd thing happened. The Italian government discovered they had run out of cells in the local prison in Naples. The jail was overcrowded, so the government rented apartments, put a gang of "minimum risk" prisoners on a train, and sent them to Baiano to serve the remainder of their sentences. God's truth, they actually did this. I had an image of hardened criminals standing before a magistrate, locking fingers and pinkie-swearing they wouldn't kill anyone, steal anything, or leave town.

The rental car we picked up at the airport was the size of a shoebox. To this day, I don't know how we got four suitcases, a baby stroller, a duffel bag of toys and coloring books, our four-year-old daughter, Matisse, our two-year-old son, Fred, Angelina, me, my sister, Beth, and her husband, Rick, into that car. There were few hotels in Baiano, so we stayed in a cousin's home on the edge of town. Word must have gotten out that the Americans were coming because, on our first day in the apartment, the cousins arrived before we unpacked a single bag. Armies of cousins invaded, armed with an arsenal of food—cheese, olives, bread, pastries, sauce, and an entire cow. OK, it wasn't an entire cow, but it was enough meatballs to make a cow. I was jet-lagged and grumpy and trying to take a nap, but every time my head hit the pillow, someone knocked on the door. More cousins. They came in waves, arthritic aunts, knobby-kneed teenagers, chain-smoking uncles, crying babies, everyone talking at once, pinching and kissing cheeks. Total chaos.

At one point, I turned to Angelina and said, "How many friggin' cousins do you have?"

She smiled and replied, "Oh, this is just my mother's side."

Angelina's two sisters, Cat and Mary, her brother, Stevie, and the other wedding guests were spread out all over Baiano, crammed into more cousins' apartments, sleeping on couches, floors, and roofs. Nonno, the patriarch, stayed in the Fiordellisi family home, the house where he was born and raised, the house that had been damaged in the 1980 earthquake, the house that was condemned, deemed unsafe for habitation. The Italian government had promised to build new homes for all the families with condemned houses. But it had only been twelve years since the earthquake, so the government was still organizing the paperwork. In the meantime, Nonno, Nonna, and other family members ate meals and slept between cracked and crumbling walls, crooked stairs, and buckled floors. The Fiordellisi house was a two-story stone structure on the corner of a cobblestone street. The street was so old and narrow that a deep notch had been carved into the side of the house from the axles of Roman chariots. That is the truth.

The one crucial feature, the one iconic object for the Fiordellisi house, was the key. The house had a massive wooden door so thick it could withstand flames and arrows and Italian temper tantrums. The key looked like something from a monster movie. It was iron, about eight inches long, and it weighed about the same as a clawhammer. I imagined a hump-backed Igor scurrying into a dungeon carrying the key to his master. One key. One key for ten people. Anytime anyone left the house, they had to lock the door to keep out aging Nazis or invading cousins—one key, which meant that someone was locked out of the house every minute of every day. Keep in mind this was 1992, no cell phones, and the key was so ancient there was no way to make a duplicate. So people ran around Baiano looking for the key: "Who's got the key?"

Three days before the wedding, the entire Fiordellisi family scrambled from house to house, apartment to apartment, to the piazza, trying to track down the key. Mary asked my wife, "Who's got the key?"

"Cat has the key."

"No, she gave it to Stevie."

"I don't have the key. I gave it to Victor."

"Victor doesn't have the key."

"Who's got it?"

"I don't know."

"Well, we're locked out!"

This daily argument started early in the morning and continued late into the night. People fell asleep mumbling, "Who's got the key?" I'm not good with chaos, so when things got crazy, I would go into the bedroom, roll my belts, line up my shoes, and color-coordinate the few things hanging in the closet. I craved control, needed organization, and insisted on punctuality. I've always gotten a little jittery when things spin out of control.

One afternoon, the chaos reached a crescendo when Angelina and her siblings gathered in the apartment where we were staying. Everyone was yelling, accusing, trying to figure out *who has the key?* Tempers flared. I went into the kitchen, hid the knives, and organized the pantry. I noticed Nonna sitting in a corner, her hands raised to the heavens, pleading with God to help us find the key.

Then Nonno charged into the apartment, veins throbbing, eyeballs bulging, scarlet streaks running up his neck. "I have had enough of this shit! Enough!" He smacked the table and demanded, "Who's got the key?" No one answered. In frustration, he slapped his chest. Then he stopped, reached into his jacket pocket, and pulled out the key. He shrugged. "Oh, I've got the key."

After a few days in the apartment, the kids got bored and

started chewing the furniture, so my brother-in-law Rick and I decided to take Matisse and Fred to the piazza to get gelato. The streets of Baiano were bustling—shoppers with carts, mothers with strollers, Vespas, cars, and bicycles, weaving this way and that. I got jittery. There was no order to anything; no one followed traffic patterns. I assumed the traffic lights and street signs were only for decoration. As we weaved our way down the narrow streets, I studied every face trying to discern who was a prisoner and who was a local resident. As far as I could tell, the prisoners had blended in reasonably well unless they all got on a train and went back to Naples. Rick and I walked with the kids hand in hand. I noticed doors slamming, people peeking out from behind curtains, middle-aged women hovering in doorways clutching rosaries, eyeing us suspiciously. Was it because we were Americans or because two grown men were wearing short pants? Did they think we were a couple of prisoners from Naples stealing children? Two withered old crones dressed in black glared at us from under a crumbling Roman archway. I smiled and waved. They gave us the devil-horn sign, the *malocchio*, and spat on the ground in Rick's direction. Ah, then I realized—Rick is six feet, two inches tall, 220 pounds of ripped muscle, with blond hair and Ayran features. They thought he was a Nazi.

We bought Fred and Matisse the gelato and wandered around the piazza when I heard a commotion. There was some kind of procession coming up the street. The scene was right out of *The Godfather Part II*, with the big drum, the sad trumpet, and a ragtag caravan of mourners walking the stone streets, crying into handkerchiefs. I recognized one of the cousins who had dropped off food that first day and asked him what was going on. In broken English, he explained that one of the uncles had died suddenly of a heart attack. The cousin wiped away tears and mumbled, "He was a good man. The best. And God took him."

Pedestrians stopped, removed caps, and bowed heads as the procession passed. About twenty minutes later, Rick and I were dragging two sticky kids back to the apartment for a nap when I heard a horn honking and saw a car driving slowly down the street. The radio was blasting an Italian rock song. A handsome man with three days of stubble, a man I recognized as one of the chain-smoking uncles, hung out of the car window waving a jug of wine. He and another man handed out paper cups of vino to everyone they passed as the chain-smoking uncle proclaimed, "He's dead. The son of a bitch is dead. We are celebrating because today he burns in hell!" He smiled and handed me a cup of wine.

Two days before the wedding, all the family members went to the church to meet the priest and discuss the rehearsal. Stevie showed up with his right arm in a cast. He'd gotten pissed off about something and punched a brick wall, breaking several bones in his hand. He probably got angry because he was locked out of the house.

Anyway, while we were waiting for the priest to arrive, everyone started arguing about the seating arrangements for the wedding. Could you put cousins in mourning next to cousins who passed out wine? More yelling, no one could agree.

Then a car pulled up and honked. It was Marcel, my wife's best friend from high school back in Detroit. She had driven down from northern Italy in a rental car with no GPS or map and was randomly driving the streets of Baiano looking for Angelina and her family. That's when she pulled right up to the church and waved. Angelina shouted, "Oh, my God, Marcel! How did you find us?" Marcel explained that she drove the streets of Baiano until she heard arguing.

The priest finally arrived. And he flatly refused to have a rehearsal. I guess he thought it was a ridiculous American custom to have structure, order, and some semblance of sanity during a wedding. With Angelina translating, I learned he essentially said, "No rehearsal. You show up, say the Mass, and get married." He scowled at all of us, pointed his finger, and warned us that the wedding would start at 2:00 p.m. sharp. Not a minute later. With or without the bride and groom. No one would be allowed into the church if they came late. No exceptions.

So, you've probably already guessed—the day of the wedding, no priest; 2:00 p.m., no priest; 2:25 p.m., no priest; 2:40 p.m., not a cleric in sight. All the family members, cousins, and friends were gathered in front of the church, sweating, cursing, and smoking cigarette after cigarette. Matisse was the flower girl, and this four-year-old child took her job seriously. She had actually practiced and mimed reaching into the basket and tossing flower petals from side to side. But Matisse was crying, holding an empty basket. Someone forgot the flowers.

Another argument broke out. "Who's got the flowers?" Somebody, I believe it may have been my sister, Beth, snuck off and picked flowers out of a garden behind a house. They tore up the stolen petals and dropped them into Matisse's basket.

Then Mary looked around and asked, "Where is Ma?" Angelina's mother was missing. Everyone scanned the crowd. No Nonna. Where was she? Another argument. "Ma was supposed to come with you."

"You were supposed to bring her!"

"No, you said you were bringing her."

"Cat was supposed to bring her!"

"Cat is the bride!"

"Stevie had the keys to the car!"

"Stevie has a broken hand. He can't shift gears!"

Nonno lit another cigarette and blew smoke out of his nostrils like a cartoon bull. Everyone started yelling, "Where's Nonna?" Cousins wandered the churchyard looking behind bushes for an Italian grandmother. Then Marcel drove up. She found Nonna waiting at a cousin's house, holding the flowers for Matisse's basket.

Fred, our adorable two-year-old, was the ring bearer. He was dressed in a brand-new suit and tie, very spiffy. But standing around waiting for the priest to arrive, Fred got bored and jumped headfirst into a pile of dirt beside the church steps. The soil, I swear, was left over from a bomb crater from World War II. Bridesmaids were melting, hairdos wilting. Nonno and the uncles smoked so many cigarettes that it looked like we were standing in the middle of a forest fire. I was scraping dirt and grime off Fred when the priest finally arrived. He clapped his hands and said, without a hint of irony, "What are you waiting for? Let's begin the ceremony."

Of course, the wedding was beautiful. Sunlight shimmered through the stained-glass windows; stolen flower petals adorned the marble floors. Two young people deeply in love knelt in front of the same altar where Nonno and Nonna had said their vows. Fred, his face streaked with dirt from World War II, sat quietly on my lap, and I was wedged between my beautiful wife and lovely daughter, who had sprinkled her petals perfectly. I glanced over at Nonna and Nonno; they were regal. I listened to the words of the priest, words I didn't understand but somehow felt, and I sensed the Holy Spirit hovering above the kneeling couple, blessing all those gathered in the sight of God.

As Cat and Vic said their vows, I thought about my parents' wedding. They had married relatively young, but it ended in a bitter divorce. No one ever yelled or argued or smacked a table. Our family quietly imploded and then splintered apart. So I created order. I rolled my belts, color-coordinated my closet, and alphabetized the cans in the pantry. I got organized and focused on my studies, going from a C-plus student to an honor-roll student. I decided that I would be perfect, beyond reproach, and successful. My life became ordered, regimented, and unwavering. I was productive and efficient, winning awards, earning college scholarships, and launching a successful career.

But years of that kind of regimentation can squeeze the life out of life; it doesn't leave room for spontaneity and joy. After the past week in Baiano, with the cousins and the fights and the arguments and the lost key, I found myself sitting in a church pew smiling, smiling because I had given over to the joyful chaos of life.

"Amen," the congregation murmured. The couple kissed. The crowd applauded. A hymn was sung. The church was filled with music, incense, love, light, and crazy Italians. *Va tutto bene.*

25

BALLOONS

I can't remember whose birthday it was, Matisse's or Fred's, but there was a wave of preschoolers heading to our house for a birthday party. This was the calm before the tsunami of slobbering and sticky, sugar-buzzed kids would tear through our house, terrorizing the dog and destroying furniture. Matisse and Fred jumped up and down on the couch anticipating the joyful chaos.

So to keep my children occupied, I recruited them to help me blow up balloons. I grabbed a purple balloon out of the bag, gave it a good stretch, and started huffing and puffing.

With each breath, the balloon got bigger and bigger and more beautiful. It was as big as my head. Then I turned to the kids and said, "Hey, watch." I released it, and the balloon sputtered and jetted around the room, wiggled up to the ceiling.

Matisse and Fred squealed and clapped. Then the balloon fluttered down and flopped onto the floor, wrinkled, lifeless, and kind of ugly. I thought, *Humans are like balloons: we are useless, empty, and kind of ugly until God's breath is blown into us, and then we become something bigger and beautiful.*

26

POKÉMON

I called my mother on her sixtieth birthday. She was between husbands at the time, so I didn't know how or with whom she was celebrating it. Probably with my sister, Beth. On the phone call, I asked Mom if she had any regrets from the past sixty years. She said her only regret was not going to college. My mother had done what most women of the post–World War II generation did: she graduated from high school, married, and started having babies. When I pressed her about regrets, my mother explained that she was always bright and had graduated from high school with top honors. She loved learning. She didn't regret abandoning her kids, marrying multiple men, or wrecking her life with drinking. My mother regretted not going to college. I was at the peak of my success in Hollywood, so I told her, "Mom, you can choose any college you want, and I will pay for it."

"Really?"

"I will pay for everything—tuition, books, room and board. Everything."

"OK, praise the Lord!"

She got very excited and started researching colleges. A few weeks later, she called me back. "I made a decision."

"Good," I said.

"I want to go to Oral Roberts University."

"Oral Roberts?"

"Yes, it's in Tulsa, Oklahoma."

"Oral Roberts, the televangelist guy?"

"Yes, he's got a school, a university. That's where I want to go."

She enrolled at Oral Roberts University, packed up, and moved to Tulsa. In the spring of 1992, she started her undergraduate studies. Every semester my mother mailed me her report card, proving my money wasn't being wasted. At the end of one semester, she had made the dean's list, so I called her. A male voice answered the phone. "Hello?" The voice had a smoker's growl, with a little bit of hill-country twang.

"Uh, is Lillian there?" I asked.

"Lil?"

"Yes."

"Hold on." Without covering the phone, the man yelled, "Lil, you got a phone call."

I heard the receiver clunk on the desk. There was a pause. I listened to the patter of feet and then Mom's voice. "Hello?"

"Mom, it's Mark."

"Oh, hi. How are you?"

"Uh, Mom. Who answered the phone? Who was that man?"

She laughed. "That's my husband."

"Husband? You got married again?"

"Yeah, I did."

"When?"

"Oh, I don't know, about three or four weeks ago."

"Why didn't you tell us?"

"I didn't think about it."

"You didn't think to let your kids know you were getting married?"

"Well, sweetie, I was busy with school."

"Mom, wait. Hold on. Who is this man? What's his name?"

"Hansel. Hansel Bull. He's nice. He watches the dog while I study."

As we talked, I calculated—was this number four, five? I had lost track. One time I went to call my mother, and I couldn't remember her last name. I turned to my assistant at the time, Helen, and asked her if she knew my mother's last name. She flipped through a Rolodex (it was that long ago), and Helen mumbled, "I think it is Crowe or maybe Wilkie. I know it's not Schmitt or Hinton."

"Sweetie, are you there?"

"Yes."

"Did you want something?"

"I just wanted to say that I am very proud of you. The dean's list is kind of a big deal. You made all As and Bs."

"I used flash cards. Hansel held them up and tested me. I did OK."

"Well, that's wonderful. I'm very proud of—"

"Oh, and I learned how to lay on hands and speak in tongues."

"You're speaking in tongues? Did they teach that in a class?"

"No, I learned it at my church, the church where I met Hansel."

I heard Wim, the little shih tzu she inherited from me, barking in the background. "Sweetie, Hansel has to walk the dog. I'll call you later. Love you." And she hung up.

I hung up the phone and thought: *My mother has another husband.* And she has married a man named *Hansel Bull?* It sounded like the name of a German wrestler. I had no idea where he was from, where they got married. Was Hansel gentle with her? Was he fierce? Did he have a temper? My only impression of the man was a gravelly voice with a country twang. My mother had always been eccentric. But now she was a full-time college student who spoke in tongues.

At the end of one semester, my mother took a short break from Oral Roberts University and visited us in Santa Monica. I don't remember why Hansel didn't come with her. I had not met the man yet. It was as if my mother kept him a secret, hiding him from me. If I recall correctly, he was visiting family in Arkansas. Anyway, my mother spent a long weekend with Angelina, the kids, and me. One afternoon, Mom sat on the porch swing watching Fred play in the dirt with his Pokémon collection. Fred went through obsessive phases. There was the Thomas the Tank Engine phase, the dinosaur phase, and later a Power Rangers phase. But as a three-year-old, he was obsessed with Pokémon.

He played with his toys and sipped grape juice from a cardboard box with a plastic straw. The sticky goo stained his mouth and attracted a fly. This big-ass horsefly dive-bombed Fred's face, bounced off his chin, buzzed around his head. Fred swatted it away, but the fly would circle back to irritate him some more. Mom watched this from the swing, until finally she had enough. My mother stood up, pointed at the fly, and said, "In the name of Jesus, *die*!" The fly obviously didn't hear her or chose to ignore her because it dive-bombed Fred again. Mom stomped her foot and yelled, "I command you in the name of Jesus Christ to die!" Fred stopped playing with Pikachu and looked up at me with bugged eyes to see how I would react to the angry woman condemning flies to their death. I nodded at Fred and mouthed, *It's OK.* He watched his grandmother sit back down on the porch swing, convinced her rebuke had solved the problem. The fly wasn't buzzing around Fred anymore. If it was dead, it died from a heart attack.

And there was the incident with Matisse. She was playing kickball, fell on the tiles by the front door, and scraped her knee. The scrape wasn't bad, but she was crying. So my mother took her by the hand and led her inside the house to the kitchen. "Oil. I need oil," she told me.

"Why? What kind of oil?" I asked.

"Any kind. I am going to anoint her with oil and heal her."

I went to the pantry and grabbed a bottle of safflower oil. Mom sprinkled a few drops into her palm, then laid her hand on Matisse's knee. My mother closed her eyes and prayed silently over the scrape. She rocked back and forth and began speaking in tongues. It sounded like this: "Garish ne, nosh alla mah kareem." Matisse never looked at me. Her five-year-old mind was fully engaged as she watched her grand-mother sway and spew a strange guttural language over her wound. After a few minutes, my mother stopped praying. She lifted her hand from Matisse's knee. The scrape was still there but now had safflower oil smeared on it. I didn't want to be a smart-ass, but I said something like "The scrape looks pretty much the same." Mom studied the injury. "Yeah, but now it won't get infected." She looked up at me and smiled.

I glimpsed her radiance. For the briefest moment, I saw a holy spark inside this woman, the glow of Spirit. I may have questioned some of her Pentecostal views, but I respected her beliefs. After all, this was the woman who insisted that I go to Sunday School and church every week and attend eight years of parochial grade school. This was the woman who made sure her children folded their hands in prayer before every meal and kneeled in prayer before crawling into bed. While my father stayed home on Sunday mornings tending to his guinea pigs or grooming the horses, my mother wrestled four squirming, raucous children into our good clothes and carted us to Sunday School. Then she drove back home, showered, dressed, and arrived back at church. She gathered all four of us after Sunday School, led us into the church, and planted us in a pew, where we were required to sit still and listen. Despite being exhausted from her endless household chores and feeding a family of six on a minuscule budget, my mother was determined that her children have a relationship with the almighty God.

Before she left to go back to Tulsa, my mother gathered all of Fred's Pokémon toys, every single figurine, and put them in a basket. She told me to destroy them. *What?* Fred loved his Pokémon. He was obsessed with them. She insisted they needed to be destroyed because they were possessed. She said the people in Japan who manufactured the toys had infused the Pokémon figures with evil spirits. Mom wasn't drinking. This was during her sober years. She was emphatic and absolutely convinced that Japan was shipping millions of demon-possessed toys to the United States to create chaos and destroy the souls of American children. I didn't argue with her. I put the basket of Pokémon toys on the top shelf of a hallway closet. After I dropped off my mother at the airport, I went straight home, pulled the basket down, and gave the toys back to Fred. He looked concerned because he had heard my mother's accusations. I think Fred expected the toys to growl or burst into flames. So I knelt down and assured him the toys were not demon-possessed—unless he used them to hit his sister.

27

ONE MORE YEAR

As soon as he saw the Big Boots,
Pooh knew that an Adventure was going to happen.
—WINNIE-THE-POOH

Angelina and I got married in May 1987 and got pregnant that July. I had codeveloped *A Different World* with John Markus and Carmen Finestra and was working part-time on *The Cosby Show* while writing the *Roseanne* pilot. Angelina and I bought a little house outside New York City and set up the baby's room. We furnished it with a cradle, crib, and changing table, anticipating the baby's arrival that coming April. Life was good.

Then, right before Christmas, I got a call from Tom Werner and Marcy Carsey, the executive producers.

"Matt, we have good news. The *Roseanne* pilot is a go."

"Really? That's great!"

"ABC is excited and wants to get started right away."

"OK. When?"

"We'll need you in Los Angeles in February to start production."

February? *This* February? I thought I had six or seven months. Oh, crap. I had to break the news to Angelina. In my writer's imagination, this is the scene I envisioned: Angelina hangs a colorful mobile of bouncing birds on the crib's railing. I kiss her on the cheek and say, "Hey, honey. Great news. The pilot is a go. We're moving to Los Angeles in February." She throws her arms around me and says, "Oh, my darling! How wonderful! I am so proud of you."

A writer's brain doesn't always make sense. The reality was when I told Angelina, she cried.

We had just bought the house. We were expecting a child. Angelina found a wonderful ob-gyn to deliver our baby. And although she was pregnant, Angelina continued working as an actress. She did a guest spot on *The Cosby Show* and was still auditioning for other parts.

"Do you realize I will be seven months pregnant when we move?"

"Yes."

"Do you have any idea how that makes me feel?"

"No, I don't."

"We have to find a place to live, a hospital, and a doctor to deliver the baby."

"I know."

I phoned Mike Forche and told him about our dilemma. Mike being Mike, he said, "Hey, man, don't stress. I got you covered." Mike flew from Las Vegas to Los Angeles, rented us a furnished home in Westwood, completed all the paperwork, and found a hospital and an excellent doctor, Dr. John Williams (no relation), to deliver our child. There's a reason Mike was my best man.

Angelina and I packed up and flew out to California. My wife was leaving her new home, career, and all her friends behind so I could create a television program for ABC. But this was an opportunity of a lifetime, everything I had been working for. When the plane's wheels touched the tarmac, Angelina said, "I want to go back to New York." I promised her we would be in Los Angeles for only one year. *One year.*

I plopped my pregnant wife in the rented house and went to work fifteen hours a day, seven days a week. After several setbacks, the *Roseanne* pilot was made, and ABC picked up the show. Matisse was born on April 3, 1988. The writing staff was gearing up for production, so I would have no time with our new baby.

But God works in mysterious ways: the Writers Guild of America went on strike. Writers had to put down their pencils and walk the picket line. I had a month at home with our newborn, a month to love on our angel and give my wife some much-needed nap time.

The strike ended, and I plunged into the production of *Roseanne*, working insane hours. Angelina brought the baby and a change of clothes for me out to the studio so I could kiss Matisse, shower, change, and continue writing. After my well-publicized battle with the lovely and talented Roseanne Barr, I left the show after the first thirteen episodes. I signed a deal with Walt Disney Studios and co-created the series *Carol & Company*, starring Carol Burnett. Our second child, Fred, was born on March 22, 1990. That same year, three programs I had worked on or created were in the top ten: *Roseanne*, *The Cosby Show*, and *A Different World*. Then David McFadzean, Carmen Finestra, and I created *Home Improvement*, starring Tim Allen. My family was growing. My production company, Wind Dancer, was expanding. The company went from three people to more than thirty employees.

One more year.

David, Carmen, and I created other television programs and started developing feature films. I was riding the crest of the wave, surfing the success of Hollywood. Everything at work was excellent. But at home, Angelina and I fought every day.

She had given up her career as a Broadway actress to be a hausfrau in Hollywood. Angelina was a fantastic mother, but she was stuck at home with two toddlers in diapers, and I was never there. When I had a day off, I cooked animal-shaped pancakes for the kids, took them to the park so Angelina could rest, gave Matisse and Fred baths, and watched kiddie videos with them. But that was only a few hours while Angelina hauled the heavy load the rest of the week.

I was torn. When I was working at the studio, all I wanted was to be home with my wife and children, and when I was at home, I worried about the unwritten scripts, the writers we were firing and hiring, and the films in development. The membrane of our marriage was about to tear.

Every argument Angelina and I had was like Ali and Frazier throwing punches in the ring. Our punches weren't physical, they were verbal. We threw word punches until one of us hit the mat. The verbal barrage went something like this.

"You are never home."

"I am working."

"That is all you do!"

"I am providing for my family."

I caught her with a quick jab. She retreated.

"Yes, and I am glad. I appreciate it."

"Do you know how many hours I work during a given week?"

"And do you know many hours I work? Alone!"

"Hire an assistant. Get help!"

"Like you. You have an entire company of assistants."

She landed a sweeping roundhouse to my jaw. I shook it off.

"You make me not want to come home. Because all you do is bitch and complain."

"I'm not bitching. I am fighting for my life."

"Is it going to be something every damn day?"

"Would you like me to keep my mouth shut for ten years and walk out on you like your last wife?"

Oh! She rattled me with an uppercut to the chin. I saw stars and staggered backward.

"I'm under constant pressure from the studio, the network. Pressure to produce a top-ten show!"

"How about producing a top-ten family? Why don't you try that!"

A solid blow to my rib cage knocked the air out of my lungs. I had to go to my corner.

But she was right. I practically lived on the Disney lot in Burbank. To see my family, Angelina would schlep the kids out on Friday afternoons, fighting rush-hour traffic, to come to the studio for the taping of *Home Improvement*. We squeezed in our family time while on a soundstage, surrounded by cast members, the crew, and three hundred strangers in the audience.

One more year.

One afternoon, Angelina surprised me and brought the kids to the studio for a visit. Fred was stuffing his three-year-old face with jelly beans from craft services. Matisse was on the set of *Home Improvement*, cuddled up on the couch between Jonathan Taylor Thomas and Zachery Ty Bryan. Our five-year-old was a terrible flirt, batting her eyelashes at the boys and laughing at their jokes. She was completely comfortable on the *Home Improvement* set. Angelina watched our daughter and said, "This is not real. This is not reality. I don't want our children to grow up in a make-believe world. We have to get them out of Hollywood."

I knew she was right.

One more year.

Then God stepped in, in a massive way, with the Northridge earthquake. The earthquake struck at 4:30 a.m. (PST) on January 17, 1994. It was one of the largest quakes in California's history, measuring 6.7 in magnitude, rattling the valley and all of Los Angeles. The quake lasted only about twenty seconds, but it did billions of dollars of damage.

Thunder Alley, a new series we had created starring Ed Asner, was in production. Monday, January 17, we were scheduled to have a table reading for the first episode. I went to bed early the night before. The earthquake hit. It felt like a giant had picked up our house in Santa Monica and shaken it. There was a loud boom. Our bed bounced. The headboard banged against the wall. Objects flew off shelves. Without saying a word, Angelina and I ran out of our bedroom, criss-crossed in the hallway, and went into the children's rooms. The large mirror in our bedroom shot across the room and crashed onto our bed. All the doors banged wildly. The house swayed.

We stumbled in pitch darkness. I snatched Fred from his bed. Angelina grabbed Matisse. We carried them down the stairs toward the front door. I heard screaming. I had forgotten about Angelina's parents, who were visiting us. Angelina's mother pulled on a robe and stumbled out of the guest room. As we ran outside, Angelina's father, Stefano, grabbed his wife's arm and steadied her. The sun hadn't come up yet. It was cold. We huddled in the front yard shivering with our children in our arms. And then I realized I was naked.

I went back into the house to get clothes and blankets. As I searched through the closet, an aftershock hit, slamming me against the wall and knocking me to the floor. I pulled on jeans and a sweatshirt, grabbed an armful of jackets and a few blankets, and ran outside. We all huddled in my father-in-law's car parked at the curb. And waited. Sirens screamed in the distance. We weren't sure if gas lines had broken or electrical wires were down. One Good Samaritan, an older man from the neighborhood, ran up and down the alley with a wrench, turning off gas lines to people's houses. We later learned that more than fifty people died and thousands were injured. But the following day I had to go back to work. Angelina's parents packed up the children and flew to Detroit.

We were fortunate because our home received minimal structural damage, while other homes in our neighborhood had lost chimneys or entire walls, or had cracked foundations. It took us weeks to clean up. Dishes had flown out of every cupboard and crashed onto the floor. Every object in the pantry had bounced off the shelves and cracked open. There were more than forty aftershocks, some measuring 5.0.

You could never completely relax. In the middle of a rewrite, the buildings at the studio would tremble and shake. The writers would freeze and ride it out, then continue writing. When not at the studio, I was home cleaning up.

One afternoon, while Angelina and I were putting our house back together, I looked out the window at the children's swing set in the backyard. The swings began to sway back and forth. I grabbed Angelina and said, "Get ready. Here comes another one." Boom! An aftershock jolted the house like a hard punch. Angelina turned to me and said, "We are out of here." I had the good sense to say, "Yes, dear."

One more year had come to an end.

The family moved back to New York, and I commuted to LA for years. I would spend a few days in New York, a week in Los Angeles, then hurry back and spend the weekend in New York. I racked up over a million air miles. Angelina was setting up our home in New York while refurbishing the Cherry Lane Theatre, creating new programs for writers, producing plays, and raising our children. I was running myself to death in the hamster wheel of Hollywood.

The notion of being bicoastal, a jet-setter, fed my insatiable ego. And having multiple shows in the top ten was intoxicating. But, still, it felt like someone had pulled a plug and my soul was seeping out. I stopped hearing my spirit voice, and I stopped feeling divine nudges. I lost my connection to Spirit. Abstractly, I knew God was there, but I didn't feel God's presence the way I had in the past. During one flight to Los Angeles, I remembered something I had read years before in a devotional: "If you don't feel God in your life, guess who stepped away?"

During my bicoastal commute, I often saw birds in JFK or LAX. The birds were trapped inside the airport terminals, living out their lives swooping over commuters' heads, pecking at crumbs in a Chili's, or sailing past a Hudson bookstore. I stopped one morning and watched a sparrow glide through a shaft of sunlight. Was this some kind of message? Was it a metaphor? Was God trying to tell me something? If so, I didn't hear it. I had a plane to catch.

28
THE LUNCH

I had no interest in working with another stand-up comedian. But Jeffrey Katzenberg, the chairman of Walt Disney Studios, insisted I meet this up-and-coming comic. Wind Dancer, the company I formed with David McFadzean and Carmen Finestra, had set up production offices on the Disney lot in Burbank. Every other day, Jeffrey would call my office and ask me to meet this new guy with whom Disney had signed a deal, Tim Allen.

I didn't want to have lunch with Tim Allen. After my experiences with Roseanne Barr, the last thing I wanted was to work with another neurotic stand-up. Comedians may trigger laughter, but they tend to be psychological train wrecks. Every comedian I know has a tributary of rage running through their soul. But Jeffrey kept calling and insisting. And I kept refusing to meet Tim Allen. Finally, Jeffrey snapped, "Matt, I am not asking you to marry the guy. I just want you to have lunch. One lunch. Here on the Disney lot."

Gene Blythe, the casting director for Disney Television,

had "discovered" Tim at the Montreal Comedy Festival. Gene told me that when he first saw Tim perform, he thought this clean-cut comedian had a spark, something special. And at the festival, Tim had to follow a very tough act. The comedian before him had gone off on a crazy comedy riff and ended his set by sticking a lit Roman candle between his butt cheeks and shooting fireballs across the stage. A hard act to follow. But as they say in the biz, Tim killed his set and impressed Gene Blythe.

I reluctantly dragged myself to the lunch with Gene and Tim. I brought David, my partner at Wind Dancer, to more or less be an objective observer and keep me from saying something stupid. Tim was affable and charming. I refused to be swayed by charm. But five minutes into the lunch, Tim and I started trading stories about our midwestern upbringings, families, and wives. We laughed about how oblivious men can be at times and complained about how our wives drove us crazy. How obsessive they can be about loading a dishwasher or folding hand towels. Tim grew up in Detroit in a large, rambunctious family. I grew up in Evansville, Indiana, in a chaotic household where the kids ran free range. And Tim and I discussed going to church.

The discussion wasn't about spiritual matters; it was about the pranks we pulled while sitting in a church pew, bored out of our minds—teasing and taunting our brothers, whispering jokes, trying to get them to crack up during the sermon. I told Tim how my brother Randy would slip off his shoes during the service. I would wait until the right moment, then steal his shoe with my foot and flip the shoe out into the aisle or kick it three pews away. As we traded stories, it seemed as if Tim and I had grown up in the same household. Our experiences were similar, our sense of humor was the same, and we mirrored each other. As we finished lunch, I heard my spirit voice say, *Do this.* I listened to the conversation around the table with my ears, but I listened to my heart when the spirit repeated, *Partner with this man. Do this series.*

Walking back to the production offices, I turned to David and said, "If we do this series with Tim, it will be a top-ten show." David looked skeptical. He enjoyed meeting Tim, but jumping from one lunch to a hit television series seemed presumptuous. But there was no question in my mind. I had glimpsed the future. I repeated, "This will be a top-ten show."

I don't know about you, but when I'm making a decision and there is a debate between my head and heart, the heart usually wins. It's not that I don't think something through. I do. I analyze, prioritize, and plan. But at the end of the day, I trust Spirit. If you trust the true voice that lives inside you, there is peace that comes with that, a deep knowing. It is summed up fairly well in Paul's letter to the Philippians: "And the peace of God, which surpasses all understanding, will guard your hearts and your minds in Christ Jesus."[1] I trusted what I heard in my heart at that lunch, and I never wavered. *Home Improvement* premiered in the top ten and remained there all eight seasons. Spirit knew.

---

[1] Philippians 4:7.

29

THANK YOU

*If the only prayer you ever say in your life
is thank you, it will be enough.*
—Meister Eckhart

Angelina and I were arguing—again—fists clenched, whispered screams, hissing like snakes behind closed doors so our children wouldn't hear us. It was one of those arguments in which objects get thrown across the room. I was working at Disney Studios six, sometimes seven, days a week—twelve-, fourteen-, sixteen-hour days. Angelina was stuck at home with two toddlers in diapers, a full-time mother and, in essence, single parent. The tension built up over several weeks until we both snapped. Hateful words were hurled, cruel and cutting. I held up my hand to stop her. We squared off, both of us catching our breath.

"Does this mean we're getting a divorce?" I asked.

"What?"

"Are we getting a divorce?"

Angelina looked at me like I had just turned into a frog or a billy goat in a tutu. I had been divorced twice before. My parents divorced, my grandparents divorced, my mother married and divorced a multitude of men. In my family, divorce is how arguments were resolved.

Angelina shook her head, confused. "What are you talking about? My family doesn't get a divorce. We're just arguing. Don't you know that we will *never* get a divorce?"

At that moment, I glimpsed the intensity of her love and the depth of her commitment. Inside my head, I shouted: *Thank you! Thank you, universe! Thank you, God! Thank you, fierce, wonderful wife!* That assurance from Angelina concretized our union. I never questioned it after that day. We were bound together forever.

Talking to my therapist, he confirmed that Angelina was probably right. He said, "I believe the two of you are inseparable because the membrane of your marriage is very strong." I liked that: the membrane of our marriage.

Throughout the years, Angelina and I continued to fight and make up, argue and make love, like most married couples. What I eventually learned is that, for us, arguments were like road trips. When we were first married, those early arguments lasted for days, racing over bumpy ground and around dangerous curves, fighting to keep the marriage on track. But the longer we were married, the road trips got shorter. They would last a day, or maybe only a few hours. And after thirty-six years together, our arguments have sort of run out of gas. We steer the marriage and settle on the side of the road. We could get out and push the argument along, but why do that? So we just sit there and enjoy the view.

30

LAUGHING JESUS

I remember in college going to a friend's apartment to drink beer and hang out and seeing a poster of Jesus, laughing. The unframed print was taped on the wall. Now, I was used to seeing the face of Jesus in churches, but not between a lava lamp and a giant bong. The figure in the portrait looked like the traditional Jesus, with long hair, a beard, and a hint of a hippie vibe. But in this particular portrait, the Son of God had his head thrown back, mouth open, all of his teeth exposed, guffawing. It startled me because I always thought of Jesus as the emaciated figure with protruding ribs hanging from the cross. Until that moment, I never connected that the laughing Buddha and the laughing Jesus were perhaps cousins. Maybe they hung out together in the same celestial comedy club.

In the New Testament, the historical Jesus is described as a man of sorrow. That doesn't sound like the life of the party. He carried the heaviest of burdens, the sins of the world, and the salvation of humankind. I am not seeing the fun. He wandered in the desert for days and prayed so hard in Gethsemane that he sweat beads of blood. Not many laughs there. In Matthew 5 and Luke 6, Jesus mentioned joy and happiness in the Beatitudes, but I couldn't remember Jesus laughing. I did some research and discovered that I couldn't find a single scripture that described Jesus laughing in all four of the Gospels. Really? Was frivolity forbidden? Mirth outlawed? Wouldn't a belly laugh enhance the Lord's humanity? Or at least release some stress? So I tried to imagine Jesus having fun.

Did Jesus ever turn the wine back into water at a wedding, just for laughs? Between miracles, did Jesus and his disciples eat loaves and fishes and tell knock-knock jokes? We know Jesus enjoyed the company of children because he said to his disciples not to keep the children away but to have them "come to me."[1] Did Jesus kick off his sandals and play crack the whip with the kids in the neighborhood? When he told them stories, did he do funny impersonations of the Pharisees? Or did the children do comedic pratfalls or dance a wild wiggle-butt dance for Jesus to get him to unfurl his brow and chuckle a little? Jesus wept. We know that from John 11:35. He got angry, overthrew the money changers' tables and kicked them out of the temple. He healed the sick and raised the dead. He suffered, he died, he rose again and ascended into heaven. But did Jesus ever laugh? I like to think that he did, at least a couple of times, because laughter

[1] Mark 10:14.

heals. It releases endorphins, the "feel good" chemicals, and decreases stress hormones. Laughter increases immune cells and triggers healthy antibodies. Laughter may be the purest expression of God's love.

A couple of days after *Home Improvement* premiered on ABC on September 17, 1991, we received our first fan letter. It was a sheet of typing paper with a handwritten scrawl that read: "God! That was funny!!!" The woman signed her name at the bottom of the page. I taped that note on my office wall as a reminder that we were bringing joy into the world and serving God in some small way.

31

DATE NIGHT

It was a miracle. We were going home early on a Tuesday. *Home Improvement* was in production on the Disney lot in Burbank, California. I created the show with my two partners, David McFadzean and Carmen Finestra. As the showrunners, we were responsible for every aspect of production, including writing and supervising the scripts. The job was demanding and stressful. We worked incredibly long hours, usually six days a week, but it was worth it because *Home Improvement* was the number one show on television at the time.

We shot the show in front of a live audience, which meant the scripts had to be "locked" by midweek so the camera crew could rehearse and prepare for Friday's taping. Tuesdays were always exceptionally long days. We often worked past midnight and sometimes into the wee hours of the morning, reworking and refining that week's script. But this particular Tuesday was an exception. We had a great rehearsal, and the script needed only a few adjustments. The writers could go home early.

I called Angelina. "Hey, honey, great news. No rewrite tonight. I'm coming home."

"Oh, that's wonderful," she said.

"Depending on traffic, I can probably get home within an hour."

"That's perfect because the kids are with Nonna and Nonno. We'll have a night together. Just the two of us."

Even the LA traffic cooperated and was lighter than usual, so I drove home in record time. I was feeling good. I walked through the door, imitating a cheerful sitcom husband, and said, "Honey, I'm home!" I kissed Angelina on the cheek, popped a beer, put my feet up on the coffee table, and clicked on the evening news. Time to relax. Angelina was in the kitchen unloading the dishwasher, loudly and emphatically. I heard the clatter of silverware; forks slammed into drawers, knives stabbed back into the knife holder. There were heavy sighs and a few snorts, like a bull about to charge.

"Honey, are you OK?" I called out.

"Fine."

"Anything wrong?"

"What would be wrong?" Angelina asked, slamming the cabinet door and rattling all the glasses in the cupboard.

"Well, it's just that I sense a little tension." More slamming and snorting. I took my feet off the coffee table and said, "Come on, what is it?"

Angelina charged into the room, "Since you got off work early, I thought you and I would drive up the coast to

Moonshadows, watch the sun go down, and have a romantic dinner."

"A what?"

"A romantic sunset dinner."

"Did you tell me that's what you wanted to do?" I asked.

"No."

"Did you tell my assistant, Helen, that you wanted to go to Moonshadows tonight?"

"No."

"OK, I'm a little confused. Did you tell anyone about this plan?"

Then I noticed her hair was done up, and she was wearing lovely earrings. And lipstick. Angelina put her hands on her hips and lasered me with the stink eye. I didn't have the good sense to stop myself. I continued, "I mean, seriously, did you happen to mention to anyone—anyone on the entire planet—that you wanted to go to Moonshadows, watch the sunset, and have a romantic dinner tonight?"

"No."

"Then how was I supposed to know that's what you wanted to do?"

Angelina snapped the dish towel and growled, "If you were tuned in to me, you would know that's what I wanted." She stormed out of the room. Papers fluttered off the counter. The curtains billowed like a matador's cape. I sat on the couch with a half-empty bottle of Heineken, totally confused.

I hate to admit it, but my first thought was this: *Can*

this argument be written into a Home Improvement *episode?* Everything that happened in our marriage, the joyful moments, the frustration, the arguments, I brought into the writers' room. We kicked the ideas around and often incorporated those real-life moments into the show. But now was not the time to write future episodes. I came home to be with my wife, and she was upstairs planning ways to strangle me in my sleep.

I told myself not to overreact. To think about this. Was I that oblivious? Am I supposed to read her mind? I walked out to the backyard, went to the swing set, and wedged my butt into a kiddie swing. Swaying back and forth, I realized I hadn't tuned in to Angelina. I missed the subtle hint on the phone call, ". . . a night together, just the two of us." I hadn't noticed the lovely earrings and lipstick when I walked through the door. I hadn't tuned in to her because I was busy thinking about myself.

I think that is what God wants us to do: *tune in.* I doubt God slams silverware drawers or snaps dish towels, but I can imagine the Supreme Deity patiently waiting for us to pay attention, to check in, to stay connected. *Tune in to me.* Tune in through prayer, meditation, chanting, kneeling on a rug, fingering prayer beads or rosaries, dancing a sun dance, or simply sitting quietly and listening to that still, small voice, the true voice that lives inside us. Tune in. Angelina and I have been married for thirty-five years, and I have learned that the three most important words in our relationship are not "I love you." They are "I hear you."

DATE NIGHT

I wiggled my way out of the swing and went upstairs to Angelina. I didn't exactly apologize, but I did offer to cook a delicious meal. We had missed the sunset, but there were candles. And champagne. We had a date at home, dining by candlelight and talking about everything except my work and the kids. No phone calls from the studio. No baby banging a spoon on a high chair. No spilled milk. Just two people tuning in.

Angelina must have enjoyed the dinner. The following morning when I woke up, she was cuddled next to me in bed. I was happy and relieved and thanked God that my wife hadn't strangled me in my sleep.

32

THUNDER ALLEY

On the set of *Thunder Alley*, I met God. He wasn't anything like I expected. He was nice. I had been expecting the God of my childhood: an angry older man in a cloud of thunder wielding a lightning bolt. In the Old Testament, God seems pissed off a lot of the time. I have struggled with the wrath of God and how he occasionally strikes down the unrepentant and disobedient. I remember as a child hearing the story of poor Uzzah. It scared the crap out of me.

David and the Israelites had wrestled the Ark of the Covenant away from the Philistines and carried it back to Jerusalem. They had put it on a cart with Ahio and Uzzah leading the way. The ox pulling the cart stumbled, and the ark tilted. Uzzah put out his hand and grabbed the ark to keep it from falling. And God struck Uzzah down on the spot. He dropped dead. Harsh, to say the least. But God wasn't just angry because someone laid hands on the ark; God was mad because of how David and the gang were transporting the Ark of the Covenant. It should never have been plopped onto a cart drawn by an ox. It was to be carried by priests on poles that ran through rings mounted on the sides of the ark. Litters were for transporting royalty; carts were for transporting cargo. Uzzah's demise was an effective scare tactic because the Israelites carried the ark properly after he was smitten. (You can read the full story in the two books of Samuel.) And I am not even getting into the flood, the plagues of Egypt, and the fire and brimstone that rained down on Sodom and Gomorrah. Scary guy, this Lord of ours. But then I met Ed on the set of *Thunder Alley*.

Thunder Alley was a short-lived television series I created with David McFadzean and Carmen Finestra after we launched *Home Improvement*. It starred Ed Asner. This was in his later years, long after *The Mary Tyler Moore Show* and *Lou Grant*. Ed was a curmudgeon. He loved everyone, or at least tolerated them, and was grumpy most of the time, but tears welled up in his eyes if you gave him a birthday card. Ed was fun and impish and a flirt. When Angelina, who was in the cast of *Thunder Alley*, walked into the studio one day wearing a yellow sundress, Ed grabbed her by both arms, kissed her on the cheek, and said, "My dear, you look enchanting." My wife has had a crush on the man ever since. Ed would pepper his curmudgeonly rants with sprinkles of Yiddish: "*Bupkes, alte kaker, schmegegge.*" Ed Asner was a Jewish love muffin. No, he was a sweet babka.

I was the showrunner and executive producer, the person in charge. When I stepped into the studio, people listened. One day, I was giving notes to our director. I had my script in hand, going through it note by note. Ed walked up behind me and pinched my butt. I jumped back, and he winked at me, instantly deflating my bubble of self-importance. And the thing about Ed is that he was generous with his time and energy, and he was altruistic. Ed Asner was president of the Screen Actors Guild, a board member for the wildlife conservation organization Defenders of Wildlife, and the founder of the Ed Asner Family Center, which provides help to neurodivergent individuals and their families. Ed was, in the truest sense, a mensch. So I didn't actually meet God on the set of *Thunder Alley*. But I met a man who represented the kind of God I had longed for as a child—kind, generous, fun, with love in his heart, who would occasionally pinch your butt and wink.

33

RODEO DRIVE

"Here, let me help you with that," I said, reaching for the shopping bags.

"That's OK. I've got it," my mother insisted, settling into the wicker chair under a red umbrella. Instead of placing the Bergdorf Goodman bags next to her, my mother tucked the bags under her legs, holding them prisoner against the chair.

"Why are you sitting on your shopping bags?"

"I don't want anyone to steal the new shoes and the scarf you bought me."

"Mom, we are on Rodeo Drive. I don't think there are marauding packs of shoe thieves prowling the streets of Beverly Hills."

"You never know," she said, picking up the menu, fanning herself, and looking around the sidewalk café. "Do you think we will see anyone famous?"

"You never know," I said. A waiter approached. He had a dancer's posture, the cheekbones of a model, and a perfect head of ebony hair. Another theater major waiting tables. I was sure he had played Sky Masterson in a college production of *Guys and Dolls*.

"Good afternoon," he said in a rich baritone. Yep, definitely Sky Masterson. He pointed at my mother's face. "I love your sunglasses."

"Well, thank you," my mother said, removing her glasses and batting the lashes of her blue-green eyes. She did look glamorous. Her hair was cut in a sassy bob. The earrings matched her blouse and rose-colored lipstick. Flirting with a handsome waiter on Rodeo Drive, she was in hog heaven.

"Something to drink?" the waiter asked.

"I'll have iced tea, unsweetened," my mother said sweetly.

"I will have the same," I said. The waiter bowed slightly toward my mother and left.

As she perused the menu, I realized it was the first time in many years that I was alone with her. Just the two of us. She had graduated from Oral Roberts University with a master of divinity degree and planned to open a home for unwed mothers. But her fifth husband, Hansel Bull, had died of cancer, so my mother moved to Florida to be closer to my sister, Beth.

"I think I'll have the Cobb salad," she said.

"That's what every executive in Hollywood eats for lunch."

My mother opened her arms and gestured toward me. "Just look at you."

"Yeah? What about me?"

"My mother always said you had a pastor's heart. Your

grandmother wanted you to be a Lutheran minister."

"Yes, that was Momo's dream. You know she offered to pay for my college if I became a minister."

"And she would have too."

"Instead of a pulpit, I ended up out here in La-La Land."

"But just look at all you've done." Mother smiled. "I mean, when you moved to New York City, you didn't know a soul. And look what you accomplished. You have a new home, beautiful children, and are happily married. You're making television shows and movies. You buy your mother expensive shoes."

"I know how much you love shoes."

"Just stop and think about all that you have accomplished."

"Mom, everything I have ever done is so that you would love me."

The explosion was instantaneous. My mother burst into tears and sobbed uncontrollably. Patrons stopped eating their lunch and stared. The handsome waiter rushed over, spilling iced tea. "Is everything all right?"

"Yes, we're fine," I assured him. "We are good." He set the glasses of tea on the table and hurried away. Mom's face was buried in her hands, her body shaking. I reached out and touched her forearm. She gave my hand a quick pat, snatched up her purse, and searched for a nonexistent tissue. I gave her my handkerchief. She covered her mouth with it and continued to cry.

"I'm sorry. I didn't mean to upset you."

She nodded and took a shaky breath. Her hands quivered. I slid the glass of tea closer to her. "Here, take a sip of tea." She pulled the paper off the tip of the straw and sipped. Then she took another deep breath and settled a little.

I didn't mean to hurt her. I told her the truth. I longed for her approval and approbation. I always thought I had to earn her affection. There were years when our relationship was distant and undefined. There were times when I didn't know where she lived or to whom she was married. Months would go by without a phone call or a letter. My mother moved constantly, a leaf in the wind. Beth told me that Mom moved to three different apartments in one year. She moved so often that the cardboard boxes never got fully unpacked before she packed up and moved again. As she sat there with tears streaking her cheeks, I was stunned by the fragility of this fierce woman's soul. And Mom was, indeed, fierce.

When we lived on Read Street, I remember my mother screaming at the corner tavern next to our house. There was a narrow breezeway between the bar and our home. We could hear the laughter and raucous conversations throughout the night. My mother would throw open windows and yell at the patrons, "Quiet! Hold it down!" On Saturday nights, the bar brought in a live band that played until the wee hours of the morning. My mother couldn't sleep, and we had to get up early and go to church the following morning. Mom finally had enough of this shit. She charged next door wearing a bathrobe, hair in curlers, and threatened to shove the drum-sticks very far up the drummer's ass. The entire bar cheered. She gave them all the finger and told them to go to hell!

My brother Bradley lived with Mom and her second husband, Gene, for a while. Bradley told me that Gene and my mother used to have knock-down, drag-out fights. After one especially raucous fight, my mother waited for Gene to fall asleep on the couch, and she put out a lit cigarette on his bare chest. My mother chased Beth's Italian boyfriend down the street with a butcher knife. I had no idea this ferocious woman could break so easily. With only a few words, I had shattered her.

My mother blew her nose into my handkerchief and took another sip of tea. Her mascara was smudged. As I waited for her to stop crying, I recalled catching a butterfly. I was very young but had somehow trapped a butterfly inside a mason jar. I tilted the jar, grabbed each wing, and ran to show my mother. The powdery wings were burnt orange and peri-winkle blue, with wisps of red. My mother exclaimed that it was beautiful but I should probably let it go. When I released the butterfly, it dropped to the ground and lay there, trem-bling. The powdery colors had come off on my fingers. I had smeared its beauty and crippled its flight.

My mom finished crying, wiped her eyes.

"Well, that was a surprise. I didn't expect to do that," my mother whispered.

"I'm sorry, Mom. Really."

"I always loved you, Mark, always. I may not have shown

it. But there was never a moment that I didn't love you."

"I know that now. I do."

She twisted the handkerchief into a knot. I sensed the deep sadness in her soul, the guilt and self-loathing. All the past hurts. My mother had three nervous breakdowns. Back in the 1960s, working-class families didn't ship emotionally damaged members off to an institution. They went to Florida for a week, which my mother did three times. She'd come back rested, tanned, and smiling, but the grind of domestic chores and the constant chaos wore her down. She was isolated outside the city on five acres of land with horses, sheep, goats, guinea pigs, and four free-range children. We were restless and ran wild and never once thought about how the house got cleaned or how food ended up on the table. With little money and no help, Mom was trapped. She finally escaped when she took a job as a waitress and met a man who told her she was lovely.

"When we lived in the country on Park Road, I was busy all the time," Mom said. "I guess I was like Martha in the Bible. I was so busy feeding you kids, doing laundry, and cleaning the house I didn't pay attention. Your father was always at work or in the barn with his animals. But I should have left the house a mess and paid attention to you kids. I should have spent more time with all of you. Especially you. I was a piss-poor mother. I know that."

"No, you weren't. You were overwhelmed."

"I couldn't take it anymore."

"I understand, Mom. I do."

"When I left, after I ran off with Gene, you were playing football at Reitz High School. Gene and I would come to your games and watch you play."

"I didn't know that. I never saw you."

"We always sat in the back of the bleachers, but we were there. I kept your letters and the birthday cards you sent me. I lost them because I moved so damn many times. But what are you going to do?" She shrugged.

"I guess what I meant earlier is that I always wanted you to be proud of me."

"But, Mark, I was always—"

I raised my hand, cutting her off. "It wasn't you. It was me. I thought I had to be worthy of your love. I created that scenario. Not you. I knew you loved me, and I've had years of therapy. And yet, I still feel this compulsive need to impress you, to win you with my magnificence."

"That's silly."

"I bought you expensive shoes to impress you. I brought you to a café on Rodeo Drive to impress you. I secretly hope we see someone famous today, so you will be impressed. Are you impressed?"

"We are both so screwed up," she said, shaking her head.

"Yes, we are. Big-time."

My mother smiled, and I saw a flash of God's shimmering grace in her blue-green eyes, a flicker of ineffable love inside this beautiful, damaged creature. It took my breath away. My mother dabbed at her eyes and fluffed her hair. "I must look like a darn shitting mess."

"Why are you worried? You trying to impress me?"

"Oh, be quiet."

"Or do you want to look good for your new boyfriend?"

"Boyfriend?"

"The handsome waiter. Maybe he's attracted to an older woman who blows snot wads into her son's handkerchief."

Mom laughed. It was deep and warm and genuine. "Here, you want it back?" she teased, offering me the handkerchief.

"That's OK. You can keep it."

She shoved the handkerchief into her purse and grabbed the menu. She fanned her cheeks, looking up and down Rodeo Drive. "Seriously, do you think we will see anyone famous today?"

"Probably. If we wait long enough."

34

LOST AND FOUND

There is no way of telling people
that they are all walking around shining like the sun.
—THOMAS MERTON

"Are we lost?" Angelina asked.

"No, we're not lost," I assured.

"I think we should go back."

"I don't know which way is back," I said. My instinct told me to turn right, so we did. Angelina and I walked past rows of clapboard houses, the paint sun-bleached and peeling. Beside one crippled place, a vegetable garden had been scratched in the dirt. A dog charged across the yard and lunged at us.

"Oh, shit!" I yelled, jumping back. The chain snapped tight around the dog's neck, holding the animal up on his hind legs as he barked maniacally.

"Is this worth it?" Angelina frowned. "I mean, really!"

Angelina's friend Eduardo, who had arranged our trip,

assured us that if we wanted authentic Cuban cuisine, we must eat at a *paladar*, a clandestine restaurant that Cubans run out of their homes. Eduardo had written down the address and given us directions, but we had made a wrong turn. I held up the crumpled piece of paper. "We will find the place or find a way out of this neighborhood. We just have to keep walking."

We attended the Havana Film Festival and stayed at the Hotel Nacional de Cuba, a grand old beauty built in 1930. The majestic bones of the building were still intact, but the facade had cracks and fissures, like the face of an aging starlet. White tables and chairs dotted the sweeping lawn in front of the hotel. Every afternoon a uniformed bartender served mojitos under swaying palms to the gathered filmmakers. The festival was a chaotic jumble of movie premieres, interviews, panel discussions, and armies of interns running around with clipboards and dangling lanyards. A film I'd directed, *Where the Heart Is*, was to be screened at the festival, but the Spanish version of the movie had not yet arrived from Barcelona. So Angelina and I decided to leave the tourist area around the hotel and find the *paladar*.

I checked the address of each house, but none of them matched the address scribbled on the hotel stationery. A breeze kicked up little dirt devils in the street. An unseen rooster crowed. Angelina grabbed my hand. I looked up and saw three young men sauntering toward us. The youngest was a chubby kid, trailing behind two angular teenagers. All three wore faded jeans, threadbare T-shirts, and frowns. Angelina tightened her grip. We kept walking, not making eye contact, but the leader stepped in front of us, blocking our path. He raised his hand to shade the sun from his eyes and machine-gunned us with a burst of Spanish.

"I don't . . . I'm sorry. Don't speak Hispaniola," I said.

With a mix of Italian and Spanish, Angelina explained that we were lost. The two skinny teens exchanged a look and grinned. Then the leader said in perfect English, "Where are you from?"

"We live in New York City," I said.

"Ah, New York. We love New York. Are you a Mets or a Yankees fan?"

"I'm not really a baseball guy, but I would cheer the Yankees."

"Me too. I love the Yankees." His two companions nodded. The leader chanted, "Yankees, Yankees, Yankees . . ." Hearing the chant, the chubby kid made a thumbs-up sign. The leader shoved his hands into his back pockets and studied us. "Where are you going?"

Angelina explained that we were looking for a particular *paladar*. "We heard it was one of the best," she said.

"It's illegal, you know, these restaurants," the leader said. "The government doesn't like it."

"We know," I said, showing him the address.

"No." He shook his head. "I'll take you to get the best food in the neighborhood. Guaranteed. Follow me."

Angelina and I hesitated.

"Come on," he said, waving his hand for us to follow.

There was a split second when a decision had to be made. I could feel Angelina's grip, the energy running up my arm. I glanced at her. She glanced at me. And without a word being said, we followed the three young men deeper into the neighborhood, where damp clothes hung on stretched ropes and barefoot children squatted in the dirt, hitting something with a stick. Salsa music crackled from a battered transistor radio propped up on the roof of an ancient Ford Fairlane. Two gray-haired men studied the engine like surgeons, passing a wrench back and forth. All the while, the leader, facing us and walking backward, rambled on and on about the wonders of New York City. "Someday, I am going to visit New York," he said, "as soon as I have enough money. You have to have a lot of money to live in New York City, right?"

"Right," I agreed.

"My dream. My absolute dream is to go to Times Square, Central Park, the Empire State Building," he said, hitting a different finger as he rattled off his dream list. "And, of course, my dream, my absolute dream, is to eat a hot dog in Yankee Stadium."

After about five minutes, we arrived in front of a yellow house with spindled columns and a sagging porch. The leader threw open his arms and said, "This is it!" He yelled someone's name, and a middle-aged woman stepped out onto the porch, wiping her hands on a towel. The leader pointed at us and rattled off another burst of Spanish. The woman nodded and opened the door, inviting Angelina and me inside. "*Gracias. Mille grazia.* Thank you." Angelina said to the leader, "Thank you so much." I pulled a ten-dollar bill out of my pocket and offered it to the kid. He stepped back, waving his hands. "No, man. No. You're from New York. Enjoy the meal." He smiled. "God bless." And at that moment, I glimpsed his bright spirit, his vulnerable essence. The three of them turned and shuffled off. The leader threw his arm around the chubby kid's head and put him in a playful headlock. That's when I realized they were brothers.

The restaurant was two wooden tables and eight mismatched chairs crammed into the tiny living room. The windows were open, so the kitchen's aroma wafted through the house. There were no menus. Paper napkins. Glasses of water. Two bottles of Cerveza Cristal arrived, plunked down in front of us by the woman and her daughter, a serious child with unplucked eyebrows and a severe ponytail. The girl gestured for us to drink the beer and disappeared into the kitchen. Then plates of food started coming: *ropa vieja, plátanos maduros fritos, arroz con pollo*, and the best rice pudding on the planet. I ate until I hurt. After the meal, we paid the woman with American dollars. Then, in broken English and Spanish, she gave us clear instructions on how to get back to the hotel. We made it back easily. Angelina went to our room, and I went to see if the movie had arrived from Spain.

Somewhere between Barcelona and Havana, the canisters of the film were lost or stolen. The woman running the festival was married to the head of Castro's security force, so she had clout and pulled some strings. Security forces searched the airport, as well as the hotel. The film was never found. So instead of a screening, I spoke on a panel with a couple of Latin American filmmakers before attending that night's screening.

The movie theater was packed. Angelina was excited because the festival honored the legendary Cuban singer and dancer Omara Portuondo, who had gained international fame as a founding member of the Buena Vista Social Club. We squeezed our way through the crowd and discovered that we had been given premier seats, dead center, about twelve rows from the front of the stage. Just as the lights came down, there was a stir, a murmur of voices as two uniformed soldiers marched down the aisle, pistols strapped to their hips. Behind them was a frail-looking, bearded Cuban man, someone I recognized.

The soldiers stopped a couple of rows in front of us. Audience members stood up, and the two soldiers, one in front and the other behind the older man, walked to the center seats and sat down directly in front of us. The lights faded, and projected images of Omara Portuondo flickered on the screen. It was a montage of her films as she sang and danced with big bands from Cuba's glory days when movie stars partied through the night and gangsters ran the island. I kept glancing at the woman on the screen and the back of Fidel Castro's head. This is the man I had watched on the news as a child, the revolutionary and the Communist, who aimed missiles at the United States and threatened to blow us up. I was a terrified eleven-year-old, standing in the front yard of our house in Indiana, scanning the skies, waiting for missiles to rain down and blow up our neighborhood. Every night I had prayed for God to protect my family and me from this cigar-smoking, angry man who hated America. And there he was, sitting two rows in front of me, slump shouldered, his head tilted back, watching old black-and-white film clips.

On the screen, a young Omara Portuondo crooned in a swanky nightclub. Then another voice was heard. An amplified voice from backstage blended perfectly with the voice on the screen. The screen retracted into the ceiling, and behind it, standing in a spotlight: Omara Portuondo. The woman was in her seventies, but still lithe and elegant, her voice warm and sensual. She seduced the microphone as she strolled to center stage and gestured to the crowd, acknowledging the bearded man in the audience. Then she wooed the president of Cuba with a love song as the crowd watched, mesmerized. When Omara Portuondo finished, she blew a kiss and took a sweeping bow. Castro held his hands high above his head and applauded the icon as she left the stage. The screen descended, and the film began.

I vaguely remember the movie that premiered that night. It was a Spanish film with English subtitles about a young artist and his tyrannical father. I didn't pay attention. The story on the screen became a blur because a movie flickered to life in my imagination. In that film, the camera dollies with three young men as they walk in the afternoon heat, their shadows rippling in the dirt. The skinny teenager puts his brother in a headlock. The younger boy pretend punches his brother in the ribs. They all chant, "Yankees, Yankees, Yankees . . ." The camera cranes up and away as the boys recede, laughing and stumbling down the street, kicking up dust that hangs in the sunlight, then floats away and disappears like a dream.

35

NEW ZEALAND

We had just returned to the hotel room. I was removing Angelina's jacket when her cell phone rang. The caller ID displayed our son's name.

"Hi, Fred," Angelina answered. She stopped, one arm still in the sleeve of her jacket. "What are you talking about? What . . .?" Angelina stammered, freeing her arm from the sleeve. "It's Fred," she said, putting him on speakerphone.

"Mom?"

"Yes?"

"I want you to know that I'm OK."

"What?"

"I'm OK . . ."

"Hey, honey," I said.

"Hey, Dad. I don't know if you two have seen the news."

"No, we haven't."

"There was an accident."

Angelina and I were celebrating our twenty-fifth wedding anniversary in Paris. We stayed in a small hotel in the Saint-Germaine district, enjoying our time alone, away from kids, work, and responsibilities. We had just returned from the Musée d'Orsay when Fred called. It was May 12, 2012. Fred was calling from Auckland, New Zealand, where he had lived the past few months as part of Boston University's study-abroad program.

"There was a van," Fred said. "A bunch of students were on a road trip. They were visiting, you know, those mountains where they shot *The Lord of the Rings*. And there was a wreck . . . a van flipped over. Three people were killed. Maybe more."

"Oh, my God," Angelina whispered.

"One of them was Roch."

Roch was Fred's roommate. When Roch and Fred met in Auckland, there was an instant connection; they became fast friends and were inseparable. Angelina and I never met Roch, but Fred had sent us videos from his cell phone of the two of them on a beach, playing ukuleles, clowning around, dancing, and improvising songs.

Angelina set her cell phone on the coffee table and turned up the volume. We leaned over the phone as Fred explained what had happened.

"There're three dead, maybe four. They're still gathering the bodies. I was supposed to be on that trip, but I didn't go. I'd already hiked the Tongariro Crossing. But Roch . . ."

There was a pause; Angelina and I waited.

"He's gone. His stuff is all here. He wanted me to come. I told him we'd have dinner when he got back. But he's dead."

In the background, Angelina and I heard knocking, muffled voices, more knocking, Fred's footsteps, the door opening, the voices growing louder, and several people talking at once. "Listen, there are people here. I got to go. I'll call you." And he hung up.

Angelina turned on the television in our room and clicked through the news channels. Nothing. No news of the accident. Then on CNN International, we found the story. Watching several reports, we pieced together the facts.

Three study-abroad students died in New Zealand while visiting locations where *The Lord of the Rings* movies had been filmed. The students were headed for the Tongariro Crossing, a World Heritage site known for its mountains and volcano. A van driven by one of the students swerved off the road and rolled over at around 7:30 a.m. The vehicle had drifted into the gravel on the side of the road and the driver had lost control. According to police, the driver overcorrected and jerked the steering wheel too hard. The vehicle flipped more than three times with eight people inside, flinging two passengers out of the van to their deaths. Another student died inside the vehicle. Five other students, one in critical condition, were airlifted to local hospitals.

Angelina stared at the screen, her hands to her mouth, and whispered, "Dear God. Oh, God. I can't even imagine . . ." A helicopter shot showed the carnage: the van on its side, cameras, backpacks, and blanketed bodies strewn along the road. I said a silent prayer for the deceased students, Roch, and his family, and, very selfishly, I thanked God for saving our son, our youngest child. I thanked God that our boy was not in that van. He had been spared.

Angelina and I stayed fixated on the television, scanning channels and searching for more information. I lost all sense of time. When I looked out the window, I noticed shadows had crept across the buildings. Streetlights clicked on.

The cell phone rang. Angelina answered. "Hey, sweetie. You OK?" Fred explained there had been a flurry of emails and telephone calls from the administration at Boston University and students and distraught parents. He was in his dorm apartment on campus, so Fred had inadvertently become the liaison, the conduit for information. Fred had also spoken with Roch's parents. He confirmed their son was gone. The school in Auckland arranged for grief counselors to meet with students, many in shock and crying, wandering the campus. They didn't know what to do, so they gathered in Fred's room, the room he shared with Roch. There were too many students to fit into the dorm apartment, so Fred led the group to the communal kitchen.

"I hope it's OK, I used the credit card," Fred said. We had given him a credit card for emergencies while he was away. "I spent about a hundred dollars. I hope that's OK."

"Sure, of course . . ." Angelina said.

"I bought milk and eggs, pancake mix, and syrup."

"OK . . ." I said, glancing at Angelina.

"Dad, I didn't know what to do, so I bought a bunch of

groceries and fixed everyone breakfast. I scrambled eggs and made pancakes. Everyone ate and talked and just sat there for a long time."

I realized that I was crying. I hadn't cried all day, but now I cried for the dead, the grieving parents, the mangled young bodies in hospitals, and the bereaved students gathered around a table. I cried because our son had made breakfast. He turned pain into a blessing, nourishing and comforting souls with food. Fred and Angelina continued talking on the phone, but I didn't hear them. I was thinking about manna from heaven, milk and honey, bread and wine, barley loaves and fishes, and pancakes.

36

JOY

Joy is the serious business of heaven.
—C. S. Lewis

I drank wine, staring at my reflection in the hotel window, reinforced glass panels fourteen floors above the concrete parking lot. There was no moon, only black sky and twinkling dots of light in the distant desert, streetlights in subdivisions. It felt like I was adrift in darkness, looking down on the stars. I had been in Albuquerque, New Mexico, for four weeks producing a film, *As Cool As I Am*, and we still had two more weeks of shooting before I could return home to my wife. It happened to be Good Friday so we weren't shooting, no production meetings were scheduled, and the cast and crew were off for the weekend. The hotel was quiet. I was alone.

Nothing was wrong. The production was on schedule, with no significant tantrums and no actors locking themselves in trailers refusing to come to the set. We didn't have to fire any crewmembers, and we were on budget. But as I sat there gazing at the distant lights, I thought: *What the hell am I doing?* The week before, I had turned sixty years old and celebrated my birthday away from my family. I was tired, burned out, and empty. Thirty years of constant production had worn me down, stripped away the joy of creating. Two impulses had driven me my entire career: crippling insecurity and raging ambition. They were the two pistons pumping away, driving me, pushing me, and I was determined to stay in the game, to prove to the industry that I still had some juice and that I still mattered, but I didn't know if I had the strength to continue the fight.

I drank much wine that night and more or less passed out, a premeditated drunk. I wanted to numb myself so that I wouldn't feel so sad. And, of course, drinking copious amounts of alcohol, a major depressant, is the perfect way to pull out of a funk. I woke up to a gray, cloud-covered Saturday morning, went straight to the gym, and punished myself with exercise. I ran on the treadmill, jumped rope, pumped weights, sweated, and exhausted myself. After my shower, I got on the computer and started researching churches in Albuquerque holding Easter services. I didn't need a sunrise service or a hallelujah choir. I just needed to find comfort in a community, even a community of strangers. I found a church online that looked interesting, a small congregation on the eastern edge of town. The website welcomed anyone and everyone to join the Easter celebration the following day.

Sunshine streaked the sky and burned away the clouds,

warming the empty streets. I drove past shuttered tattoo parlors. I don't know for a fact, but I would guess that Albuquerque, New Mexico, has more tattoo parlors per capita than any city in America. Tattoo parlors and bars. I passed a bundle of clothes. It looked as if someone had dumped a hamper of dirty rags on the sidewalk, and then I realized it was someone sleeping off Saturday night. Two bearded men sat on backpacks outside a coffee shop, passing a joint. An older woman wearing Nike sneakers walked her prancing dog on a red leash past the church.

The church was a restored movie theater. Like most of the architecture in Albuquerque, it was the adobe style, all stucco and earth tones. As I approached the building, I parked my rental car in the lot behind the theater and heard the muffled sound of drums, a bass, and electric guitars. The front of the building still looked very much like a theater. It had a ticket booth, a row of stringed lights outlining the awning, and two glass panels that once displayed movie posters but now displayed children's drawings of Easter eggs and bunnies, flowers, and a gold cross with white rays of light shooting out in all directions.

I stepped inside the theater, almost expecting someone to ask for my ticket, and was handed a pamphlet outlining the service and the words to all the hymns. I took a seat in the back, under a balcony. The balcony was large and covered more than half the theater. I didn't know how many people could sit up there, but I imagined quite a few. The fold-down velvet seats had been refurbished, and almost every seat on the main floor was filled with families: Black, white, brown, old, and young. A few children ran up and down the aisle, clapping to the music. An arm would reach out, snag one of the kids, and plop the squirming child onto a lap, but the little one would manage to slip away and run up toward the stage, where the four-piece band rocked out, filling the theater with celebratory songs.

I don't remember the sermon. While writing this, I tried to recall if the pastor was male or female, and I couldn't remember. What I remember was the music and the energy of the crowd, clapping, swaying, and singing. The service ended, the congregation stood, and we sang the closing hymn. As the song reached its crescendo, balloons cascaded down from the balcony, brightly colored balloons—yellow, red, bubblegum pink, cobalt blue—of all sizes, pouring down into the congregation. Children squealed. The adults laughed and applauded. Everyone started tapping and swatting the balloons, sending them floating up toward the ceiling, floating down to someone else in the crowd, who would tap and send a balloon spiraling up again. The colored balls bounced and ricocheted off walls, off hands, off heads as the band played. I found myself smiling and swept a balloon toward a toddler cradled in his father's arms, and something inside me opened as if a stone had been rolled away and a blade of light pierced the darkness.

37

LIVE YOU

"Do you love Jesus?" the preacher roars, eyes bulging, veins throbbing, waving a Bible.

"Yes, I-I-I do," I stammer.

"Do you *really* love Jesus?" He looms over me, squeezing the Bible so tight his knuckles turn white.

"Yes, I *really* do," I say.

Eyebrows pinch tight, and he commands, "Read the Bible!"

"OK, OK. I will."

"But do you *love Jesus*?"

"Yes, I love Jesus! Now get the hell out of my face!"

None of this actually happened, but that is what it felt like during my childhood: adults pounding me with the Word of God, demanding that I accept Jesus into my heart. I did accept Jesus into my heart when I was three or four years old, but the adults kept questioning me, challenging me to love Jesus. I didn't understand. What was I supposed to do? Sit on a tree stump and write love letters to my Lord? Send the

Son of God valentines? Pray every minute of the day, assuring Jesus that I truly loved him, like reassuring a jealous lover? No one ever told me what to do with the love that I held in my heart. No one told me how to put that love into action and incorporate the Cosmic Christ into my daily life.

OK, so here is a weird leap: *text messages*. My wife and I and our two adult children constantly text one another as our primary means of communication, and at the end of each text we sign off with *Love you!* Now, with autocorrect and clumsy thumbs, I often text *Live you!* Live you! That got me thinking: I love Jesus by living him. *Live you!* I don't go through my day healing lepers or rubbing mud into blind men's eyes. And I am certainly not going to do what a few of my evangelical friends do—declare their love of Jesus constantly, loudly, incessantly.

"Hey, I picked up the frozen green beans you wanted."

"Praise the Lord!"

"Uh, the Lord didn't pick or freeze these green beans. Why are you dragging him into this?"

My born-again mother would answer the telephone, "Praise the Lord!" But within a few breaths, she would be ranting, "Do you know what that son of a bitch next door did? I told him to kiss my raw, naked ass!"

"Uh, Mom, back off a little. What would Jesus do?"

"He would tell that son of a bitch to kiss his holy ass."

"OK, Mom. Live you."

So how do I *live* Jesus? I don't know what works for you,

but here is what works for me: quietly and deliberately holding a sense of Jesus, the Cosmic Christ, in my heart. I imagine Christlike energy flowing through me, and I consciously pour that loving Christlike energy into everyone I meet. Even during a casual conversation on the sidewalks of New York, I bless the other person and imagine a white light surrounding them, blessing them.

I think we live Jesus when we are kind, patient, tolerant, and give others the benefit of the doubt, when we bless rather than judge, and when we take the time to look for and find a glimmer of divinity in the other person. I have found that if you look hard enough, there is usually something decent and praiseworthy in just about everyone. This may sound a little crazy, but when our FedEx driver comes to deliver a package, I raise my hand and say hello. But what I am actually doing is blessing the guy, sending him Christ's love. He always smiles and waves back, the Holy Spirit in action. Or maybe it's because I tip him really well at Christmastime. It doesn't matter. Live you!

38

FREAK

Every creature participates in some way
in the likeness of the Divine Essence.
—Thomas Aquinas

My son is part of a street ministry in Santa Monica, California. His buddy Sean McDermott recruited Fred to join him and preach on Sunday mornings. The two of them go around the neighborhood talking to the disenfranchised—alcoholics, drug addicts, homeless war vets—handing out snacks and inviting them to the service. The attendees gather in a semicircle on folding chairs in a park across the street from Saint Monica Catholic Church, the church where Fred was baptized. Sean and Fred read and discuss Bible verses, sing hymns, and pray for those gathered. Then they hand out shots of grape juice and crackers for Communion. It feels holy because it is so simple.

And yet friends and family members have called Fred a Jesus freak, a pejorative term for a seemingly overzealous believer who is high on the Lord, hugs incessantly, and flag-ellates you with *Christ's love!* That kind of behavior feels less like a disciple of Christ and more like a person with boundary issues. My son is not like that. Fred doesn't carry a wooden cross through the lanes of traffic on the 405 interstate singing the score to *Godspell*. He doesn't run around grocery stores grabbing shopping carts, praising Jesus, and baptizing unwary shoppers with hand sanitizer. Fred is gentle, sweet, and caring; he embodies the kind of love Jesus preached. Does that makes him a freak?

Even if you can't wrap your head around Jesus being the Son of God, God incarnate, let's look at the historical Jesus as an example. Here was a humble carpenter who played with children, hung out with fishermen, told interesting stories, encouraged folks to take care of widows, and visited people in prison. He threw swell picnics, serving barley loaves and fishes. He implored everyone to help the poor, feed the hungry, and be kind to strangers, even our enemies. Jesus was not a simpleton, but he was simple. The greatest minds have the ability to be simple. And that is what Jesus did: he made things simple. All the laws and rules and rituals were summed up in one commandment: love your God and love your neighbor as yourself. What a radical thought it was at the time and still is today.

One Sunday morning, Angelina and I attended Fred and Sean's service in the park. The usual collection of addicts and homeless were gathered. Sitting on one of the folding chairs was a skinny, grimy man. His clothes were covered in a greasy film and crusted dirt. He carried no backpack, no knapsack; his only possessions seemed to be the tattered clothes hanging on his skeletal body. And he stunk.

As Angelina and I approached our chairs, I graciously gestured for her to sit next to the crusty man. Being a germaphobe (and a bit of a hypocrite), I allowed my precious wife to sit next to this human oil slick while I kept a safe distance. I love humanity, but I sometimes have a problem with people, especially stinky ones.

The service continued with the usual shout-outs and interruptions from someone moved by the Spirit or the bearded guy with Tourette's. There was a Dunkin' Donuts box on a plastic folding chair next to Sean's empty foam coffee cup. Doughnuts are one of the perks of attending the outdoor service. In the middle of the lesson, the crusty man stood up, walked over to the doughnut box, and helped himself to a doughnut with vanilla icing and rainbow sprinkles. I shook my head and thought: *Of course, Mr. Stinky doesn't give a crap about the Word of God. He's only here for the doughnuts.* At that moment, I realized that I had become the type of Christian I vehemently criticize—self-righteous, intolerant, and judgmental.

Then the man did something astonishing. He wiggled his hand into his pants pocket, pulled out a crumpled dollar bill, and placed it in the empty cup. He then walked away, quietly, with great dignity, doughnut in hand. I wanted to chase after him, apologize, thank him, or give him a twenty-dollar bill. But all I could do was sit there and marvel at how each of us is part of the mystery that is Christ's love.

39
SOMETHING

God is an artist, and the universe
is God's work of art.
—THOMAS AQUINAS

"What? I can't hear you." I was on my cell phone, a finger plugging the other ear to shut out the sirens as I dodged pedestrians on the sidewalks of Manhattan. "What did you say?"

"I said I am worried about your father," Wayne, my father's partner, yelled into the phone.

"Why? Is he sick?" I asked.

"No, he's not sick, but he's not eating. All he does is mope around the house. He doesn't have any energy."

Dad had plunged into a soul-crushing depression. After years of slowly losing his eyesight to glaucoma, he was declared legally blind, which meant walking with a white cane and needing assistance to go anywhere, and, most discouraging of all, he could no longer create art.

My father was an award-winning amateur artist. He started drawing when he was three years old and continued to create throughout his life—charcoal sketches, pen and ink drawings, paintings, and clay sculptures. When I was a child, he would come home from the assembly line at Whirlpool, eat a quick dinner, feed the horses and guinea pigs, then go down to the basement and paint or sculpt until late in the night. Our home was always filled with noisy pets and raucous children, but Dad found a way to create. He couldn't afford expensive oils or canvas, so he stretched burlap and painted with leftover house paints. He painted majestic images on discarded pieces of plywood and framed the paintings with driftwood found by the river.

Dad rarely sold his work. He kept the pieces for his family. Although self-taught, he often won blue ribbons in competitions around the tristate area. After collecting a boxful of ribbons, my father decided to take an art class at the University of Evansville. He attended two classes, and the professor pulled my father aside and told him that he had nothing to teach him. He encouraged my father to save his money, forget classes, go home, and continue painting.

When creating, my father worked for hours without a break, lost in the creative process. Standing at his workbench one day, watching him mix paints in an old coffee can, I asked him, "Dad, how can you work that long without a break?"

"I don't know," he said. "I get an image in my mind. I see it clearly, every detail. And all I have to do is pull that image out of my mind and put it in the paint or the clay. It's like I go into a trance. Something takes over."

Now here is the thing: my father never called that something a muse, daemon, God, or divine spirit. He called it *something*. "Something takes over," he explained, "and it's not me doing the work. A lot of times, I look at a finished piece and I have no idea how I even did it."

But with glaucoma stealing away his sight, that something had vanished from my father's life. He was lost. I stepped off the noisy sidewalk into a coffee shop and asked Wayne to put my father on the phone.

"Hello, son," Dad whispered.

"Hey, Dad. Listen, I have an idea . . ." I offered to take him and Wayne to Florida to visit my sister, Beth. She and her husband, Rick, live in Palm City. I thought a little sunshine and time with family would cheer my father up.

"So, what do you think? You want to go to Florida?"

"Yeah, I guess so."

While we were visiting my sister, we went to an arts and crafts show. My father was still getting used to the cane, so he held my elbow for support as we stumbled our way along a sandy patch of lawn dotted with tents and display tables. A lot of the work was fairly amateurish. I mean, how many seashells can you hang on a piece of macramé? But then we came to a table filled with exquisite wood carvings. There were seabirds and lifelike pelicans and a few abstract pieces. Dad tapped the table leg with his cane and asked what was on display. I described the works—a pelican perched on a dock post, a flying egret suspended by a wire, and several colorful sea turtles.

Dad said, "Take this," and handed me his cane. He asked the artist behind the table for permission to touch the pieces. The artist, a beefy man with sunburned cheeks, was gracious and obliging. My father reached out his hands. His fingers found the wood. He ran his fingertips over the contours and curves of the egret. Then something happened. I watched a change come over my father. Energy seemed to vibrate and envelop him. Dad cocked his head as if listening to the wood, his fingertips tracing the carved grain. Then he turned to me. "I can do this."

We flew back to Evansville, and he started creating again—totally blind, except for one tiny peephole of sight glaucoma hadn't stolen. Dad had our neighbor help him rearrange and organize his workshop in the garage. They bought a carving kit, chisels, and knives. He even used kitchen knives, emery boards, and pecan picks to carve and shape the pieces. Dad would sketch the shape he saw in his imagination onto a piece of wood. The neighbor cut out the rough shape on a bandsaw. Dad had a body, a first draft to work with. Then he patiently and meticulously carved the wood with knives and chisels, feeling each contour and then sanding the grain to a fine sheen. Something had returned to his life.

The first piece he carved was a largemouth bass cut from a single wood plank and mounted on an oval stand. The fish is flat and two-dimensional, primitive and simple. But as Dad's confidence grew, the pieces became more complicated: two horses fighting, kicking, manes flying, a flurry of motion captured in the carved wood. His carvings started winning blue ribbons again at the local shows. One piece, titled *Drought*, depicts emaciated cattle searching for water on a dry riverbed. It won Best in Show. *Evansville Courier & Press* did a feature article about my father and photographed him at the workbench in his shop. A local news channel did a human-interest piece. My father became famous in Evansville and was invited to display his wood carvings and give lectures to Boy Scout troops, Kiwanis clubs, and retirement centers.

Dad continued to carve until his late eighties, when his body finally wore out and he didn't have the stamina to stand for three or four hours. He didn't have the strength to tap into and channel *something*, but he could feel it floating in the room. It was always there.

I have many of his wood carvings, paintings, and sculptures in my study. I more or less turned the room where I write into an art gallery, celebrating my father's creativity. Everywhere I look, I see his pieces. The horses fighting, the exposed ribs of the dying cattle at the dry waterhole, the eagle's head above my desk, each feather hand carved and glued into place by my father's hands. When I feel empty and need inspiration, I look around and always feel *something*.

40

BURNING RING OF FIRE

My mother lived out her final years in an "active senior citizen" community in Port Saint Lucie, Florida. It was a compound of prefab houses slapped up around a golf course and a man-made lake. Anyone who decided to move there got a free golf cart to drive. As far as I could tell, the primary activities of this place, besides golf, were day drinking, gossip, and infidelity. It was one of those neighborhoods where a wife dies and casseroles and sunbaked women wearing lipstick and push-up bras show up on the widower's porch. The day of the funeral. It was rumored that one resident, a retired plumber from New Jersey, rented a minivan once a month and brought a van full of hookers to his house so all the retired dentists, carpenters, and World War II vets could have a good time. Mother laughed, slapped her knee, and swore it was true. "I can always tell when the hooker van visits the neighborhood. The next day, all the old geezers zip by on their golf carts with smiles on their faces." She laughed so hard she had to wipe tears from her cheeks. "I'm telling you, this is a regular Peyton Place."

Here's the thing about my mother: she married and divorced or buried six husbands. She worked as a waitress and hairdresser and was a full-blown, fall-down, pass-out-in-the-car alcoholic for years. But one morning during her prayers, the Lord told her to stop drinking. And she did. She stopped cold on her own and didn't touch a drop of alcohol for decades. But when she turned eighty, she decided the Lord wouldn't mind if she had a Heineken or two. When my friends met my mother, they usually said, "She's a real pisser." I never wanted to imagine my mother urinating in her Bermuda shorts, but I knew what they meant: Mom was fun.

"Would you look at that?" Mom said, pointing out the window. We sat in her enclosed sunporch, a box with windows that looked out on a cul-de-sac with six other tiny houses. Mom gestured across the street toward a woman wearing a straw hat and pink sneakers, unloading the trunk of her Prius. "Look at that old bitch. That is her third trip to the store today. She went to Publix and Dillard's earlier, and now she has two bags from Sam's Club. She is always shopping. And where does she get her money?"

"Why don't you ask her?"

"I don't talk to her. She's a nosy gossip."

Now, I never knew if my mother was utterly oblivious or delighting in irony. Was she testing me? Trying to draw me into one of her serpentine arguments? I took the bait and asked, "How do you know she's nosy?"

"She always comes over and asks if I need anything

from the store."

"That's nice. That's a nice thing to do."

"She's not being nice. She comes over to see what I'm doing or to see if I have her husband hidden in the closet."

"Do you?"

"I don't know, go check. He may need water." She held up her empty bottle. "And while you're at it, grab me another Heineken."

I grabbed us Heinekens, and the conversation turned from neighborhood gossip to her favorite subject: Jesus Christ. I am not being flip, nor do I condescend. I was raised in the church and continue to be a follower of Jesus. But when it came to sin and salvation, my mother and I butted heads like two bighorn rams on a mountaintop. I recall this particular day vividly. The argument went something like this.

"Whoa, whoa, whoa, hold on. So you're saying that billions and billions of people will go to hell unless they believe in Jesus?"

"Yes. If you don't claim Jesus as your personal Lord and Savior and carry him in your heart, you will burn in hell."

"Forever?"

"Yes, forever. Don't give me that look. Are you saying it's not true?"

"I am not saying it's not true. It's just . . . OK, so what about a child, an innocent little girl, living in the jungles of Brazil, cut off from the modern world? Her tribe is isolated, but they're peaceful, and she is lovely. This little girl is kind to her baby brother and loves her parents. But one day, she has an accident, or an alligator eats her—"

"I don't think the Amazon has alligators."

"OK, fine. An anaconda swallows her. The point is she dies."

"She'll go to hell."

"Oh, come on."

"If she doesn't know and accept Jesus, she will burn in hell."

"But this child is innocent. She doesn't know about Jesus or—"

"That's why we need missionaries, to go out into the world and spread the good news."

I knew my mother believed in the efficacy of missionaries because she had supposedly given away half of her inheritance to Pat Robertson to build a TV station somewhere in Africa. She gave the other half to her second husband, Gene Hinton, to buy a bar in Marion, Illinois, the Grapevine.

"All right, so here's a hypothetical," I said. "There is a man. He's an atheist."

"Oh, Lord."

"He doesn't believe in God or Jesus or any religion, but he's a good man. He dedicates his life to helping others, working with Habitat for Humanity, and volunteering at food banks. He made money and gave it away to build a hospital for children. He dies. But he's an atheist."

"Straight to hell."

"But he has done good things. He helped people!"

"Doesn't matter. He didn't accept Jesus into his heart. Oh, look at that." My mother smiled and pointed out the window. A man with sunburned cheeks and a steel-gray flattop haircut drove past on his golf cart. "He is good looking. That is a good-looking man, right there." She sighed and shook her head. "His wife's still alive."

"You could pray she has a heart attack and drops dead so you can make your move."

"Don't be a smart-ass."

"Let me make up another hypothetical," I said.

"All right." Mom nodded and took a sip of beer.

"There's a rotten man. He lies, cheats, and steals. He beats his children and steals all the money his wife saved working two jobs so their kids could go to college. And he goes to Vegas, takes drugs, and gambles it all way."

"I know where you're going with this."

"He gets sick and is dying. But with his last breath, he confesses his sins and accepts Jesus into his heart."

"The man will go to heaven."

"That doesn't make sense!"

"Jesus died for his sins, so his sins are forgiven. We all fall short. My life has been a darn shitting mess, but I know Jesus died for my sins, and I'll see him in heaven."

"So I can be a rotten piece of crap my whole life, and just before I take my last breath, I call out and accept Jesus and *bam!*—I get into heaven?"

281

"But we don't know when that last breath is coming. It could be right now or ten years from now. Only the Lord knows."

"What about other religions? Judaism, Islam, Buddhism—"

"Burning ring of fire."

"Mom, come on."

"Hell is real."

"I don't know if I even believe in hell."

"What?"

"I don't know if I believe that hell is an actual place."

"You have been living in New York City too long. That is secular humanist thinking."

"The *concept* of hell has existed for ages. Look at the ancient Sumerians, Egyptians, Greeks, and Jewish mysticism. But I have a hard time believing we get cast down to an actual fiery pit to be tormented. Forever."

"God created a lake of fire as a place of punishment for Satan and demons, the fallen angels."

"I don't believe that. Burning lakes? I don't buy it."

"I know what I am getting you for Christmas."

"What?"

"A fire extinguisher." Mom laughed and took a sip of beer. "You'll need it when the flames of hell are licking your hind end, and the devil is poking you in the butt with his pitchfork."

"I don't believe any of that."

"You don't believe in the devil?"

"No, I know there's a devil. She lives in Port Saint Lucie and drinks Heinekens."

Mom slapped her knee and lowered her head, chuckling. "That's good. That was a good one."

The ferns outside her windows fluttered and bent over as rain droplets splashed and streaked the glass. It was one of those showers that roll through Florida most afternoons, lowering the temperature but raising the humidity. The windows steamed and started to blur.

"I think the concept of hell was created to manipulate the masses, scare the populous into submission so they would obey those in power," I said.

"Hell is mentioned throughout the Bible."

"I know."

"And did you know that Jesus preached more about hell than all the other Bible teachers, including Paul?"

"I didn't know that."

"*Gehenna* is the Greek word for a place of eternal torment. *Hades* is another Greek word for hell. You know I had to learn and read the original Greek when I got my master's degree."

"Yes, I know. And if I remember correctly, you got a B in that class."

"B-plus," she corrected me, waving a finger. "And that was a very tough course. I had to use flash cards." She sipped her beer. "After Jesus died on the cross, he descended into hell for three days to rescue the souls of the righteous."

"If they were righteous, what were they doing in hell in the first place?"

"What?"

"And you know this notion of death and resurrection didn't start with Jesus? There is Osiris, Dionysus, Adonis—"

"Heathen. My son is a damn heathen."

"Maybe hell is not a place."

"What are you talking about?"

"Maybe hell is eternal separation from God. Paul talks about our longing to leave this earthly tent and be in God's glory."

"Second Corinthians," she said with a smile.

"We long to return to God, to be a part of the Godhead. Perhaps we are separated, but we learn and grow through many lifetimes until we reach Brahma, the creator god."

"So now you're a Hindu?"

"The Hindu religion existed about two thousand years before Jesus came along."

"Just because something is old doesn't make it right."

"Look who's talking."

The phone rang. Mom snatched the portable receiver off the side table and answered. "Praise the Lord! What? No . . . I paid that bill. I most certainly did. . . . Well, tell him to kiss both cheeks of my ass. I'm not paying it again . . . I'm sitting here with Mark. Yeah, he's my sweetie . . . OK, sure." She hung up and leaned back in her chair. "Your sister can be a real bitch sometimes."

"Mom, Beth takes care of you. She makes sure you have groceries and the house is clean."

"She can do nice things and still be a bitch. Hey, I was thinking. You know, this senior-citizen community is for people fifty-five-plus, so you and Angelina are eligible. You two could get out of New York and move down here. You would get a free golf cart."

"I would rather swim naked through a lake of fire."

"Why? It's a nice place. Maybe what's-his-name will let you drive the hooker van." She winked and saluted me with her beer bottle.

"Let me ask you this. Why would a loving God, who knows all things, allow his children to burn in eternal torment? Would you like it if your children writhed in torment for eternity?"

"Maybe one of them. My oldest son, perhaps," she said, nodding in my direction. "So you don't believe in hell. Do you believe in heaven?"

"I don't believe in marble thrones, gold streets, and cherubs strumming harps. I believe heaven is God's energy, thought energy, the supreme mind that created and lives in all things."

"Panentheism."

"Yes. And when our spirit energy leaves our body, maybe it returns to the source and becomes part of the vibrant, electromagnetic field that is God's mind."

"Like a big ball of electricity."

"Something like that, but that energy is alive and sentient, creative and flowing. And maybe we check in with God to see how we're doing, discern what we need to work on, and come back down to live another life."

"So now you're what? A damn Buddhist? Should I shave your head and buy you a robe?"

"I'm open to the idea of reincarnation. I'm not saying I believe it or don't believe it. But think about it. Suppose, through many lifetimes, we learn and grow and experience every aspect of life so God can experience life through us, and we experience life through God. And we keep evolving until our minds and souls are as rich as God's mind and soul, and we finally transcend and remain in the presence of divine thought for eternity."

"So everyone goes to heaven?"

"Maybe. Eventually."

"That is called Universalism. You don't need Jesus. You don't need salvation. Everyone gets a free pass."

"I'm not saying I fully believe that, but I'm open to exploring other faiths and beliefs to see where they overlap and discover what all religions have in common."

"That sounds like a religious stew. Throw a bunch of beliefs into the pot and mix them all together. My honey, the gate is narrow, and the only way through that gate is to believe in Jesus Christ."

"Can't I accept Jesus as my Lord and Savior and still contemplate the possibility of karma or reincarnation?"

"No," she said, taking a swig of beer. "Speaking of alligators."

"When were we speaking about alligators?"

"The little Amazon girl."

"Oh, right."

"This happened a few months ago. A woman was walking her dog right here by the lake, and an alligator ate her dog. Right off the leash." Mom snapped her fingers and chuckled.

"Why are you laughing? I thought you liked dogs."

"I love dogs. Obviously alligators do too. They wrote about it in the newspapers. I guess little Fluffy ended up a tater tot for the gator."

"Do you think Fluffy went to hell?"

"Fluffy doesn't have a soul."

"How do you know? Maybe Fluffy reincarnated. Maybe Fluffy was one of your dead husbands come back to chew on your ankles and pee on your lawn."

"You are going straight to hell. Before you go, grab me another Heineken."

I headed toward the kitchen but noticed something outside. The rain had stopped. Through the foggy windows of the sunroom, I saw a figure approaching.

"Who is that?" I asked.

"I don't know," Mom said, pushing herself out of the chair. There was a knock. Mom opened the storm door. It was the lady with the straw hat and pink sneakers. She was holding a small cardboard box.

"Oh, I didn't know you had company," she said, peeking inside.

"It's my son Mark. He lives in New York." The sneaker lady gave me a little wave. "Do you want to come in?" Mom asked, opening the door wider.

"No, I've got to run. Here, I bought you this," she said, handing Mom the box. "It's a scented candle I picked up at Dillard's. Gardenia. I thought you might like it."

"Why, thank you. Are you sure you don't want to come in?"

"No, I've got to go pick up my husband." She gave a quick wave goodbye and crossed the street to her Prius.

"Well, that was very thoughtful," I said.

"She knew I had a man over here. The old bitch was spying on me." Mom pried open the top of the box and smelled the scented candle. "But that was a sweet thing to do."

41

JUNEAU

Blessed are the peacemakers.
—MATTHEW 5:9

I didn't move. I didn't say a word. I watched his eyes. I gripped the thick base of the beer mug in the palm of my hand. I thought if he took a swing, I would drive this glass mug into his face. Aim for the bridge of the nose, try to break it, or split his forehead open so the blood runs into his eyes and blinds him. Holy hell! Those were the thoughts running through my head. I am a card-carrying member of the AARP. I am on Medicare and collect Social Security, and here I was in a sports bar in Juneau strategizing how to win a bar fight.

I visited Alaska a few years ago for the first time. Angelina went to Juneau to perform in the world premiere of a new play, *With*, by Carter W. Lewis, at the Perseverance Theatre. I visited her a couple of times during the show's run because, after thirty-plus years together, I find it difficult to sleep at night without the rhythm of her breathing and the warmth of her body next to me. So I flew to Juneau, hung out at the hotel, read a bunch of books, took a few hikes, and went to bars.

While Angelina was performing, I decided to explore the town, have a drink, and find a place for dinner. Juneau is in a temperate rainforest. In November, it rains constantly, with a cold, blowing mist. It's a soggy world that time of year, a world of windshield wipers, hooded rain jackets, and waterproof boots. And of course, because it is Alaska, it gets dark early.

Every night, a murder of crows congregated above the hotel parking lot, perched on power lines, heads hunched into their wings, feathered shadows. This was a Friday night around six o'clock. I threw on an extra sweater and a rain jacket and headed to the downtown area of Juneau. The town booms with excitement in the summer when crowds disembark from the cruise ships crammed in the harbor. But on a November night the town is desolate, the sidewalks quiet and slick with rain. I passed a few stragglers and, oddly, a bearded man on a skateboard, smoking a cigarette, snaking his way down the empty street.

I found a sports bar off the main drag and went in for a beer. It was still early, so the crowd was sparse. Multiple television sets were suspended from the ceiling, muted and silent, playing basketball games, hockey replays, and highlights from football games. I found a stool at the far end of the bar, separate from the crowd. A short man with spiky blond hair took my order, a Stella draft. He thunked down the heavy mug, frosted with rime. I sipped my beer and scanned the crowd, my favorite pastime: people watching.

Everyone seemed relieved that it was Friday, the work-week over, a chance to let down. As I sipped my beer, a door banged behind me, and a burly guy with thick black hair and a scruffy mustache stumbled out of the dark hallway. I assumed he must have come out of the bathroom in the back. He walked past me, stopped and turned, then eyeballed me, an outsider, a stranger, an interloper. I didn't look like someone from New York City, someone sophisticated or fancy. I had on scuffed-up boots, blue jeans, a sweater, and an unzipped rain jacket, like everyone else in the bar.

The guy wobbled a little, still staring at me, then waved his hand back and forth in front of his face. "Whew, some-thing smells in here," he said, loud enough for everyone at the bar to hear. "And it's you!"

He growled and poked his finger at my face. That is when I cupped the beer mug in my palm, my weapon. He kept glaring at me. I noticed the paint stains on his clothes; small Jackson Pollock–like splatters on his work pants and shirt. Housepainter. He was blowing off steam, loosening up in the bar, before driving home to sleep it off. I understood. He probably had a long week. But I was prepared to defend myself.

The guy didn't swing. He teetered a little, then turned and walked over to his cluster of friends, two women and three men huddled at the bar. He clapped two men on the back and whispered something to the group. They all laughed and turned their heads, grinning at me. I was still holding the bottom of the mug. There are three responses in moments of danger: fight, flight, or freeze. I was frozen. I didn't move. Finally, after a few more snarky chuckles, the painter and his gang forgot about me and returned to their conversation below the flickering TV screens.

I am not going to leave until I finish my beer. I will not be intimidated. The spiky-haired blond bartender approached me. "Something to eat?"

"No, I am fine," I said, forcing a smile. "I'm good." He left. I finished my beer, zipped up my jacket, and headed toward the door.

Just before I grabbed the metal handle, I heard a booming voice. "Hey, good to see you," the painter yelled, his voice dripping with sarcasm. "Don't bother to come back."

An explosion of laughter filled the bar. That hit a nerve. I stood at the door, my hand on the handle, and thought: *I'm going to go back there and beat the living hell out of that obnoxious piece of shit.* In quick jump cuts, I imagined myself striding back to the bar, punching the guy in the face, his friends scrambling, him shoving me, me grabbing a barstool and beating him in the head until his face was a bloody stew. All this flashed through my mind in a matter of seconds. I heard more laughter from the bar, a couple of drunken whoops. I knew the civilized thing to do would be to turn around, walk straight up to the guy, sincerely ask him why he had a problem with me, and offer to buy him a beer. That or punch him in the face and walk out. I cracked the door open a bit. The cold, damp air of Juneau brought me back to reality. I knew what to do.

I stepped out the door and walked in the drizzling rain, trying to calm myself. I was still creating fantasies of going back into the bar and beating the man senseless. My amygdala was fired up, supercharged, and all cognitive reasoning was gone. I was in pure atavistic animal mode. It took almost an hour to calm down enough to have dinner.

Of course, I found a place near the water and ordered salmon because, hey, it was Alaska. As I waited for my meal, I tried to calm my rage. Jung referred to this dark, primitive force deep within us as the shadow, the irrational and instinctive part of the mind. I had been in psychotherapy for twenty-plus years, so I knew not to ignore or repress these emotions. It was unhealthy.

The food came, and while I tore a piece of bread, I thought about Jesus. He was humiliated, beaten, and eventually executed without ever fighting back. He took it. Is that what I was supposed to do, take it? Now, I am not comparing my little hiccup of public embarrassment to Christ's flogging and execution. During his torments, Jesus never retaliated. He could have channeled his father's superpowers and flash-fried all of his persecutors, but he didn't. I wondered if I could do that. Could I pray hard enough to send a bolt of lightning crackling down into the sports bar and fry the housepainter's miserable ass? Probably not what Jesus would do. Jesus absorbed the brutality. He suffered. Even with his dying breath, Jesus didn't curse his persecutors; he asked his father to forgive them, for they knew not what they were doing. The opposite of angrily smiting and destroying his enemies. And then I realized Christianity is about opposites—at least, the Christianity the historic Jesus preached.

Jesus said, "But if anyone slaps you on the right cheek, turn to him the other also." He goes on to say, "And if anyone would sue you and take your tunic, let him have your cloak as well."[1] Talk about opposites. Instead of prancing around in gold-laced garments, Jesus wore sandals and traveling clothes. Instead of sitting on a throne, he knelt and washed dirty feet. Jesus did precisely the opposite of what people expected. If you flip an angry impulse and do the opposite, the impulse is usually Christlike. In his letter to the Colossians, Saint Paul did an excellent job of summing all of this up: "Put on then, as God's chosen ones, holy and beloved, compassionate hearts, kindness, humility, meekness, and patience."[2] Could I do that, put on meekness, humble myself, and forget my anger?

I finished my meal and asked for the check. As I left the restaurant, I noticed the drizzle had turned to snow flurries, moths flickering under the streetlights. I flipped up the hood of my jacket and walked the damp sidewalk, my shadow skimming along the pavement. As I walked, I said a silent

---

[1] Matthew 5:39–40.
[2] Colossians 3:12.

prayer. I thanked God for quelling my agitation and calming my spirit. I asked God to bless the housepainter and help him find peace in his heart. I think I meant it. I headed toward the hotel. As I left the lighted sidewalk and stepped into the darkness of the hotel's parking lot, my shadow disappeared.

42
CHECKING IN

Nova was out of control. Walking her on a leash was a comedy of errors. She would chase a squirrel and yank me across the yard or suddenly stop to sniff the curb, and I would trip over her. She ran laps around my ankles, hog-tying my legs with the leash. She wasn't being mean or disobedient; she was a puppy. It wasn't her fault. I was too gentle. Nova is so sweet. I didn't want to be aggressive and traumatize her puppy psyche. But I needed help, so I hired a dog trainer.

Amber is a diminutive woman with the commanding presence of General George S. Patton. When she approaches, dogs snap to attention and salute. The first time Nova met Amber, I swear she raised her paw to her eyebrow. I quickly learned that this commander wasn't training Nova. She was training me.

Amber taught me how to hold the leash, keep the dog to my left side, and make commands simple: Heel. Sit. Stay. Amber's authority was so definitive and unwavering that when she said "Sit," I bent my legs but caught myself before my butt hit the grass. Amber explained that the key to training a dog is forming a relationship, bonding, and staying energetically connected to your pet. She taught me there is an energy exchange between the dog's owner and the dog. Stay connected. And to do that, the dog should check in with the owner. With every voice command or while transitioning from one command to the next, the dog should check in to get permission and ensure it is in sync with the owner.

The training worked. All of those weeks in the ice and snow paid off because now I can walk Nova through the trails around our farm without a leash. She checks in with me. Nova dashes through the woods or scurries up the path, but then she stops, looks over her shoulder, and silently asks, "We good? Am I on the right path?" I nod assurance and say "Good girl," and she romps away. Nova stops and checks in if we come to a fork in the woods. I don't have to say anything. I gesture left or right, and she follows the silent command.

I realized praying is a form of checking in with God. We can pray for help, forgiveness, or guidance, offer thanks, or sit quietly and savor the sweet presence of God. But checking in is also essential. While I rush through my busy days, it is crucial for me to stop and check in with Spirit. "We good? Am I on the right path? Am I doing what you need to be done?" Several times a day, I say a quick prayer and then wait for the silent nudge from Spirit. It feels like a release in my solar plexus, a psychological click that assures, "All good." I do this several times a day, especially when making a decision or going into a meeting or the classroom. I want to keep an energetic connection with God to ensure that the relationship is intact and that I am on the right track. God doesn't pop a dog treat into my mouth, but occasionally I feel a holy pat on the head.

43

STILL POINT

Stillness reveals the secrets of eternity.
—Lao-tzu

"Dad, it was incredible," Fred said, pouring almond milk on his Raisin Bran.

"What?" I asked, setting a plate of scrambled eggs next to my coffee cup and sitting across from him.

"This one kid, during recess . . ." Fred smiled and shook his head. "It was *so* LA."

I was spending a couple of days with my son in California. Fred had recently completed his master's degree in psychology and was supporting himself by working part-time as a substitute teacher. As we ate our breakfast, he told me this story.

Fred was substituting at The Wesley School, a private school in the San Fernando Valley. It was a warm, bright Southern California day. Children squealed and raced around the playground. Fred supervised recess while two first graders crawled up his body and hung from his biceps like spider monkeys. Fred heard yelling and saw a gaggle of six- and seven-year-olds gathered around two boys in an altercation. An argument had erupted over a soccer ball, and one boy was in tears, fists clenched, and quivering with rage. Fred stepped in, took away the soccer ball, and demanded apologies. He settled the dispute and led the crying six-year-old aside. The child was red-faced, wiping tears, unable to take a full breath.

Fred knelt, held the boy by his arms, and said, "You need to calm yourself, so we can talk about this. I want you to take a few deep breaths—slow, deep breaths—and relax." The child looked up and screamed, "I hate mindfulness!"

I sometimes think the childish part of our adult nature is like that young boy. We hate mindfulness. We hurry and scurry through the day to complete our to-do list, compete, conquer, acquire, and glorify ourselves on social media. We are addicted to stress. We mistake frantic activity for productivity; our minds are so filled with the monkey chatter of the day we can't hear ourselves think. We are never still.

In her insightful book *Liturgy of the Ordinary*, Tish Harrison Warren references a study done at the University of Virginia in 2014. Psychologist Timothy Wilson conducted an experiment in which individuals were asked to sit in a room quietly, with no technology, no stimulus, for fifteen minutes. The participants were alone with their private thoughts. If they sought stimulation, they could push a small button that would administer a low-voltage electrical shock. Something like 65 percent of the men and 25 percent of the women could not sit still for fifteen minutes. They pushed the button and electrocuted themselves rather than sit in silence. Think about that: fifteen minutes of silence is intolerable for many people. And yet, throughout the ages, Jesus and the prophets, sages, and saints have encouraged stillness.

Jesus withdrew from the crowds to spend time alone, in the desert, in a garden, in prayer, to seek oneness with God. Psalm 46:10 reads: "Be still, and know that I am God." Muslims believe silence is the language of God. The Jewish tradition is the Sabbath, a day of rest. Australian Aboriginals embrace the healing power of stillness by practicing *dadirri*, a deep listening, an intentional stillness. Native Americans seek the peace of all sound as a way to connect to Wakan Tanka, the Great Spirit. The Greek church fathers called this silence *hesychia*, the starting point and the final destination of prayer.

Meister Eckhart said, "Nothing in nature is so like God as stillness." Silence, or quietness, is how we access divinity. I imagine it's easier to do if you are a hermit on a mountaintop or a Benedictine monk in a monastery. But we live in a fast-paced, feverish, energized world. How do we maintain that sacred stillness as we go about daily life? How do we stay connected to Spirit when confronting constant challenges?

I learned to do it during the most challenging period of my life, the first season of *Roseanne*. I created that television program, but there was a battle for control from the very beginning. The lovely and talented Roseanne Barr was—how do I say this nicely?—Satan's sassy sister. Every day was a head-on collision. I was a first-time showrunner, so I was overwhelmed and exhausted. To survive, I needed to find a way to stay centered and connected to Spirit. So I developed a technique.

As I drove to the studio in the mornings, I prayed until I found the still point that lived inside me. Then I imagined a white light surrounding me, protecting me. It was an invisible shield, a spiritual cylinder that encompassed me so that when Roseanne went off on a tirade, cursing and screaming, I could stand inside that white light and watch her hateful words bounce off the shield and ricochet across the room. It worked. I waited until Roseanne exhausted herself, then I would say, "OK, let's get back to the scene." I protected myself instead of engaging in the tumult as she wanted.

Through the years, I have imagined that cylinder of light surrounding me during arguments with my wife, in heated political discussions with friends, or while navigating the frantic streets of New York City. Most of the time, my imaginary shield is impenetrable. But fatigue, negativity, and self-doubt crack that protective barrier, and I lose my center, my connection to Spirit.

Thomas Aquinas said, "Angels are announcers of divine silence." Angels do their best work when we are still. These days, when I feel spiritually unmoored, I go for a walk in the woods on our farm. There is a path leading to a small concrete bench near a creek. An engraved stone rests in front of the bench that reads: *Listen carefully. You can hear the angels laughing.* I don't hear cherubs giggling or the rustle of gossamer wings. But I have found that if I sit on that bench and practice what the Quakers call expectant waiting, I usually hear God's voice whispering in my heart.

44
WOLF

Angelina and I had just finished a late lunch at Hudson Clearwater and strolled down Barrow Street. I felt amorous so I wrapped my arm around Angelina's waist and flirted with my wife. She laughed and hip checked me. We turned the corner onto Commerce and saw a friend (I will call her Sheryl) and her fiancé standing in front of the Cherry Lane Theatre. Angelina took one look and said, "Something is wrong."

Angelina rushed over to them. "Are you all right? What is it? What's wrong?"

"I'm fine. I'm OK," Sheryl said, clawing her fingers through her hair. She seemed dazed but wasn't crying. Her muscles trembled, adrenaline surging through her body. Between breaths, she managed to tell us what had happened: She was taking her dog Dougan for his afternoon walk. She didn't see the man coming toward her. Dougan was sniffing along the curb, so her hands were wrapped around the leash, keeping the dog out of the street. Before she could react, the man grabbed her. He groped her breasts and ran his hands down the front of her body, assaulting her on a sun-filled street in the West Village. Sheryl screamed for help. The man ran away. Confused pedestrians stopped, unsure what had happened.

Angelina pulled Sheryl into a tight hug, mumbling into her hair, "Oh, my God. I am so sorry."

"Is there anything we can do?" I asked. Sheryl assured us she was OK. Her fiancé explained they were going to the police station to file a report.

"Do you want us to come with you?" Angelina asked.

"No, we're fine," Sheryl said. "I'm OK. Really." Her fiancé wrapped his arm around her, and they headed to the Sixth Precinct.

Angelina had a meeting at the theater, so I gave her a distracted hug and started walking. I realized that I couldn't go home and write. I needed to walk. I walked to Washington Square Park, wandered around the buildings of NYU, then turned south toward SoHo. As I walked, I thought about Sheryl, who is always smiling. She is petite and intelligent, and she possesses a sweet spirit. And yet this man felt free enough to molest her in broad daylight. I picked up my pace. My visceral reaction to Sheryl's assault was to find a baseball bat, hunt down the pervert, and break every bone in his body. Not very Christlike, I know, but I couldn't control it. The animal inside me had been unleashed. The wolf was howling. He wanted blood.

And then, in my imagination, the angel appeared. She

swept down in front of the wolf. The wolf bared his fangs and lunged at the angel. She fanned her wings and ascended, the wolf snapping at her ankles. With slashes of fur, the flutter of wings, growls, and explosions of light, the angel eventually drove the wolf back into the cave, the dark crevices of my soul that serve as his den. I slowed my pace, stopped walking, and looked around. I was standing at the corner of Houston and Greene Street. I couldn't remember how I got there. The angel had calmed me and brought me back to my senses, so I headed home.

By the time I got to the house, Angelina had finished her meeting at the theater and checked on Sheryl. While at the police station, Sheryl learned the same man had molested other women within the same hour in the same neighborhood. She identified him in a lineup. He was arrested. Sheryl was safe. But I was still troubled. Why did I have such a violent reaction? Why this howling rage? I needed to understand. The way I process my feelings is by writing, so I pulled out a yellow pad. But nothing came. Why was I still so livid? The man had been arrested. And then I looked down at the yellow pad and realized I had written my son's name: *Fred*. I circled his name several times, and memories came flooding back.

We were living on the Upper West Side at the time. I had left my office in Midtown and walked through Central Park to our apartment. I got home early that day and unpacked my briefcase when I heard keys rattling and someone at the door.

"Hello?" I called out.

Pounding. The door shook. "Dad! Dad! Open the door!" I rushed over, opened the door, and there was my fourteen-year-old son, holding his house key, trembling. His hand shook so badly he couldn't get the key into the keyhole. He was crying.

I reached out to him. "Oh, my God. Honey, what is it? What's wrong?"

Fred stumbled inside the apartment, dropping his backpack on the floor. "I was at the subway stop near school," Fred said between shaky breaths, "and these three guys came up from behind me. I didn't see them . . ."

"Fred, calm down. Come on, sit. Sit." I led him to the couch. He crumpled onto the sofa. I kneeled in front of him. "Take a breath. Breathe." Fred took a deep breath and calmed a little. I pushed the hair off his forehead. "What happened?"

Fred rocked back and forth, arms folded across his chest. "I was in the subway by the school, getting the metro card out of my wallet. They pushed me. Slammed me against the wall. They wanted my wallet. I didn't fight. I didn't turn around. I gave them the wallet and my metro card. I held up my hands to show them I wasn't going to fight. And the big guy punched me, punched me in the back of the head, as hard as he could."

"Come here, let me see. Lean forward." I ran my hands through my son's hair, feeling the scalp. "There's no blood. You're not bleeding. You're OK."

Fred looked up at me and asked, "How can someone do that?"

The wolf leaped out of the cave, threw back his head, and howled. I stood up and screamed, "Those mother*fuckers*! God damn them!" I ran through the apartment going through every closet and slamming doors. I was looking for a baseball bat, a club, an iron bar, or any kind of weapon. I wanted to see their brains on the sidewalk. I found an umbrella. It wasn't very big. But it had a wooden handle.

"Dad, what are—"

"Come on," I said.

"What are you doing?"

"Come with me," I demanded, dragging Fred out of the apartment. We took the subway to the stop near his school and started walking. The angel inside me was nowhere in sight. The wolf was in control, driving me along the sidewalk. I stalked the streets, determined to hunt down those deviant fuckers. We circled the blocks by Fred's school. I held the umbrella by the metal point, swinging it like a club, aiming it at young men on the street. "Is that them?"

"No."

"Is that the guy?"

"I don't know."

We approached several teens leaning against the chain-link fence of a playground. "What about them?" I asked.

"Dad, I really didn't see—"

"What about him?"

"Dad!" Fred yelled and stopped walking. "I never actually saw them. I was facing the wall. They hit me before I could turn around."

"All right. OK," I mumbled. "Let's keep walking."

Fred and I walked. And we walked. And we walked. We covered the entire Upper West Side. We walked for almost two hours before the angel appeared. She confronted the wolf, circling him, fanning waves of light, driving him back into his cave. Fred and I slowed our pace. We didn't say a word for the last twenty minutes or so. Then I stopped and turned to my son. "Fred?"

"Yes."

"I want you to know that everything I am doing is wrong. It's wrong." I held up the umbrella. "This is not the answer. Do you understand?" I put my hand on his shoulder. "This is not right. But I had to do something. I couldn't just shrug and say, 'Hey, this is how the world is.' As your father, I had to do something. But this is not the answer. Do you understand?"

Fred nodded. "Let's go home."

We walked back to the apartment. I encouraged Fred to take a shower and change his clothes. Angelina and Matisse were not home yet, so I poured myself a glass of wine and started cooking dinner. As I pulled food out of the refrigerator, I remembered Tennessee Williams once said that the only unforgivable sin is deliberate cruelty. I'm not so sure. I believe even that can be forgiven. But what I find difficult to forgive is when an act of deliberate cruelty destroys innocence.

Staring at the yellow pad, I realized why I responded so strongly to the assault on Sheryl. I wrote her name on the pad and underlined it, then wrote *innocence* beside her name. Sheryl is a bright light, a tender soul. Her innocence had been violated. That's why the wolf charged out of the cave, ready to rip and tear.

I was ashamed that I didn't have more control over the animal inside me, but then I realized: I did. I didn't do anything rash or criminal. I didn't act on the violent impulses surging inside me. The angel kept the animal in check.

I strive to keep the wolf hidden from others. I don't want anyone to know that an angry beast lives inside me. I gladly parade my angel persona before the public and take great pride in being a compassionate human being. But the wolf . . .

I undoubtedly cannot unleash the beast because that would be too destructive. I also cannot ignore the wolf or pretend he doesn't exist. I have many friends, religious and nonreligious, who won't admit they have a wolf living inside them. They don't want to acknowledge or give energy to that kind of darkness. So they ignore the animal hidden in the shadows of their soul, hoping it will disappear. But if you don't acknowledge the wolf, he will find a way to break free and wreak havoc.

Now that I am in the last third of my life, I have accepted the beast. I acknowledge that the wolf gives me drive and energy, the energy I need to create. When the wolf is prowling and restless, he inspires me to keep searching, learning, and growing. The wolf energy is as much a part of my life force as the angel energy. The wolf roars, ready to destroy and protect; the angel calms, transforming destructive impulses into creativity and compassion. The two live in paradoxical tension, each depending on the other, a symbiotic relationship. It is a dance of light and shadow, compassion and rage, love and loathing, fangs and celestial feathers. It is a dance that will continue until I draw my last breath.

45

LEGACY

When my father-in-law was in the hospital in Michigan, leukemia stealing minutes from his final days, my wife and her two sisters did something extraordinary. They taped up photographs of their father's life on the blank wall directly across from his hospital bed. There were baptisms and first Communions, weddings and holiday feasts, and one of Stefano Fiordellisi leaning on his new car, a Cadillac. There were the faces of his grandchildren smiling back at Nonno as he grew weaker in body but brighter in spirit. And there were drawings, children's drawings of flowers and rainbows and get-well wishes. A faded photograph of a handsome soccer player strolling down a cobblestone street in Baiano, Italy, with his new bride on his arm. A few pictures from the honeymoon, Stefano and Caterina leaning on a railing in Capri, pointing to the Blue Grotto. They looked skinny and happy and innocent.

What was not taped on the wall were his awards and certifications from General Motors, where Stefano Fiordellisi worked as a designer and draftsman for more than thirty years. No framed first dollar earned, no college diplomas or newspaper clippings. From the wall, his legacy stared back at him—a loving wife, four kind and generous children, and a gaggle of grandkids. Nonno grew weaker by the hour, he could barely lift his head, but his eyes scanned those taped-up images, remembering, his soul recording the faces he was about to take with him on his journey.

He died with his wife and four children at his bedside. They held his hands, rubbed lotion on his feet, and dabbed a napkin soaked in red wine on his lips. Angelina said that right before he died, her father opened his eyes, ran fingers through his hair, and looked at the gathered faces. He closed his eyes, and a few minutes later, he was gone. In my mind, it was the perfect send-off to the other side. As I approach my final years, and the end becomes an actuality, I ask myself, *Which photographs do I want to be taped to the wall for my journey?*

46

NASHVILLE

To be kind is the greatest measure of human happiness.
—Francis Hutchinson

I stood at the open door, one leg on the pavement, the other inside the gray Nissan, struggling to get my mask on without knocking off my glasses.

"Just get in," the Uber driver snapped.

"I don't have my mask—"

"Don't worry about the mask. Get in. Get in the car."

I crawled into the back seat, fumbling to get the straps over my ears, as my brother slid in from the street side and slammed the door. The Uber driver gunned the Nissan up Fifth Avenue South, tossing us around in the back seat, driving us from the Omni Hotel out toward Belle Meade. In the rearview mirror, I watched the driver's eyebrows pinch together as he weaved through traffic. To cut the tension, I asked him, "You from Nashville?" The driver shook his head without speaking.

"Where are you from originally?" I asked.

"Chicago." He merged with the traffic on I-40 W.

"I like Chicago. It's one of my favorite cities, except for the cold," I said.

There was silence. I looked at my brother, who shrugged *What the hell?* We settled back for the ride. After a few moments, the driver said, "I ended up in Nashville because of my stepfather." The driver glanced in the mirror to see if we were listening. We were. So he told us his story.

"You see, I was raised by my mama, a single parent, no father around. This was on the South Side of Chicago. I was in constant trouble, running the streets. I was going to end up in jail or dead. That was for sure. Then my stepfather called me. My mother married the man and moved to Nashville a few years before. When he called, my stepfather told me he was dying, and he needed my help. He asked me to please come down. He sent me money. So I came down. When I got here to Nashville, he was dying all right, but he didn't need me. He had everything in order, all his papers, insurance, the will. He was an organized man. And I realized he didn't need my help. He just wanted to get me out of Chicago. It was his way of getting me out of my messed-up life."

The Uber driver swung the car onto I-65 S and headed toward Hillsboro Pike. The pinch between his eyebrows softened, and his shoulders sagged a little. He continued his story.

"He died, my stepfather, and I stayed with my mother for a while, but then I got restless and went back to Chicago.

And something happened. I saw that place with different eyes, you know. I had an epiphany. That's the only word for it, an epiphany. I couldn't stay there. So I turned around and moved to Nashville and have been living here pretty close to thirty years. I'm still renting, but I'm trying to save enough to buy a house. Put some money on a down payment. I got a good wife, two daughters, a son, and six grandchildren. Christmas is coming, so I haven't slept much, putting in extra hours so the grandbabies have gifts under the tree. They are something else, those kids. I got to tell you, I've been a drinker, and I have taken every drug out there, but when I held my first grandchild, when they placed that baby girl in my arms, it was the greatest high I have ever known. They say you love your grandbabies more than your own children. I don't know if that is true. But a grandchild opens your heart to the magnitude of life. Those babies inspire a deeper kind of love."

The driver pulled into the parking lot of a strip mall, and there was the world-famous Bluebird Cafe, wedged between a dry cleaner and a barbershop. The driver slowed to a stop, parked the car, and sat there. His mind was not in the car. Bradley and I waited. I watched the driver's mask expand and contract with each breath, like a heartbeat. He shook his head slightly, looked at us in the rearview mirror, and said, "I wouldn't have experienced any of this goodness if it weren't for that dying man. He knew exactly what he was doing."

We sat in silence for a moment, then I pulled several bills from my pocket, handed them to the driver, and said,

"For your grandchildren. Their Christmas." The driver hesitated, then took the tip. "Thank you. Much appreciated."

Bradley and I crawled out of the Nissan, and he pulled away. I said, "You know, maybe we didn't come to Nashville to hear music. Maybe we came to hear that Uber driver's story."

"Maybe." Bradley smiled.

47

GOSSAMER WINGS

Flying home from Nashville triggered a memory. When I first moved to New York City in the 1970s and was a starving artist, I tried desperately to earn a living doing anything other than waiting tables. So I decided to compose lyrics for country and western songs. Now, keep in mind that I was not a musician. I didn't play an instrument, and I couldn't read music. I could barely carry a tune. Yet I convinced myself I could make a small fortune writing the lyrics for bestselling country songs heard on radios across the country.

I sat in my tiny studio apartment at the wobbly-legged table and scratched out lyrics for weeks and weeks. I had a folder filled with surefire hits. I could imagine musicians in Nashville getting into arguments, or even fistfights, battling over who would get the opportunity to put melodies to my poetry.

I wrote a story song about a waitress at a truck stop in Tulsa who got stabbed and died in the arms of her forbidden lover. I wrote about the terrors of going on a blind date with a marginally sane woman who drank too much and wrecked my new Impala. I wrote about bluetick hounds asleep under a rusted pickup truck, beer brawls, and the lonely prairie where I buried my sweet, dear wife.

I was convinced I would make wheelbarrows full of money so I could afford to live in NYC and pursue my dreams of becoming a theater artist. I mailed the bundle of master-pieces to every publishing house in Nashville, and I waited for the accolades and money to roll in.

Every single publisher, manager, and musician rejected my lyric poems. They returned the envelope with a red stamp: NO SOLICITATIONS. Some institutions didn't even bother responding.

Except for Tom T. Hall, God bless his soul. He actually took the time to send me a letter gently suggesting that I seek another line of work. His response was not a form letter. It was typed on a piece of stationery and at the bottom was Tom T. Hall's signature and a handwritten scribble: *Good luck!* I lost the letter years ago, but I still remember the man's kindness.

Of all the corny stories and sappy lyrics that I wrote, one line still lingers in my memory: *Wrapped in the gossamer wings of grace.*

I think that line is pretty darn good. If a country singer or composer is reading this book, I offer that line up to you: *Wrapped in the gossamer wings of grace.* I would love to hear that sung on the radio.

48

WIND DANCER

The closer one approaches to God, the simpler one becomes.
—TERESA OF AVILA

"Can you explain something to me, like the name?" The executive was in his midthirties, wearing baggy jeans and a blazer with pronounced shoulder pads, one unfortunate fashion trend of the late 1980s. He turned to the female executive sitting next to him. She wore a power suit and sported fluffy curls with Farrah Fawcett bangs.

"We'd like to know why you named your production company Wind Dancer?" They held pens over pads, waiting for my answer.

"Wind represents the breath of God, the Holy Spirit," I explained, "and dancing is a celebration of that Spirit. I was inspired by Native American culture, the cloud dancer, the Lakota sun dance, and the concept of the Great Spirit, Wanka Tanka. I knew that if I ever formed a production company, it would be named Wind Dancer."

There were a few nods and notes scratched onto pads. The Wind Dancer team was gathered around an oval-shaped conference table at the Walt Disney Studios in Burbank. I sat across from the two executives from an advertising agency we'd hired to help us brand the company and create an animated logo. Animated logos appear at the beginning of films or the end of television programs and serve as a signature, a visual and auditory expression of a company's spiritual essence.

"And what are you really about?" the Farrah Fawcett–hair executive asked.

"We are about telling stories," I said.

"We know you write and produce television shows. But what are you, ultimately, about? Can you say it in a word or two?"

"Creativity," I said. "I want this company to celebrate the creative spirit, the force that inspires all art and animates all life." As I explained the concept, I got excited and stood up. Having been a mediocre actor, I still had enough ham juice running through my veins to prompt a performance, so I acted out the images I saw flickering in my imagination.

I raised one hand high above my head. "Think of it this way—artists metaphorically reach up to the heavens to gather God-light, creative energy, and that energy surges through their very being and pours out onto the page, the pigment on a canvas, the chisel sculpting stone, the dancer's body, the seven notes on a composer's sheet music! Artists make the invisible visible. The Wind Dancer logo should reflect that dynamic, explosive, ineffable process."

Blank faces. The ad executives stared at me as if I were standing there naked except for wearing a dead armadillo as a loincloth. Nothing. No nods. No notes.

"OK, look," I said, taking my seat. "It's about the creative process. Three writers own this company. What writers do is mysterious. We go into a shaman-like trance and live in the ether of our imagination where ideas, images, concepts, and characters come to life. Then we assign words to what we see in our imagination, and those words, squiggly black or blue markings, are put onto a page. Then a collection of artists—actors, directors, designers, composers, wardrobe, hair, and makeup departments—read and interpret those scribbles and bring what the writer imagined to life on stages and screens around the world. There is something sacred about that. About the process of writing."

The room was silent for a few seconds. Then, luckily, a roundtable discussion began about how to capture that sacred process, those ineffable feelings in a moving image. Ideas were kicked around, and everyone weighed in, sharing opinions. The advertising team asked for a couple of weeks to conceptualize and come back to us with sketches and storyboards.

When the team returned, they seemed nervous but excited as they laid the storyboards on the conference table. I took one look at the sketches, and my heart dropped into my stomach. Dreadful. Simply dreadful. Every idea was awful. One illustration showed a hairy man with his arm extended above his head, holding a ball of light. I asked the advertising team why the guy was so fuzzy, and the executive with the Farrah Fawcett bangs explained that it wasn't hair, it was energy coming off the man's body. Really? When I acted out the concept for the team, I must have looked like a Neanderthal holding a snow globe.

They quickly moved to another sketch. It was an abstract drawing of wispy clouds. When animated, the clouds would flutter to life, stretch out, and wrap around a tall, willowy figure. I thought it looked like witch fingers strangling a baby giraffe. My stunned expression inspired them to move to another concept.

This one also had puffy, bulbous clouds and wind blowing trees sideways. Or was it candles? I turned the sketch around, trying to see the creative spirit in action, but all I saw was a baboon's butt blowing out birthday candles with a fart.

After some polite lies—"This is an excellent start. I think you are on to something. Let us think about it, and we will get back to you"—the agency was paid, and we never saw them again. But we still needed a logo. I didn't want to waste money and countless hours with other agencies, so we found an unexpected creator in-house.

Jim Praytor started working with me as an intern during the first season of *Roseanne*. Jim was prompt, polite, and cheerful. The other interns slid foam-boxed lunches across the table and tossed cellophane-wrapped plastic utensils at the writers. Jim served the writers their lunches on plates with a cloth napkin and actual flatware. He was attentive. So when I made an overall deal with Disney Studios, Jim came along.

He worked his way up from intern to segment producer. He conceived, designed, and executed the animated transitions in *Home Improvement*. It was Jim's idea to cut scenes in half with a saw and fall away or have a riding lawnmower mow the screen and transition from one scene to the next. Jim was brilliant. So we asked him to create the Wind Dancer logo.

What he designed was simple, and simple is always best. It was a drawn line that morphed into a dove as the name Wind Dancer appeared, underscored by a few graceful notes. Jim had captured the writer's process—Spirit coming to life in words. Something about the logo felt innocent.

We used that animated logo for years, but when the company expanded and started developing motion pictures, we wanted an image that seemed more corporate, so we created another logo.

Since writers owned the company, we used a quill pen as the main feature. The pen dropped from the heavens and touched a pool of water that rippled to life. It was a little more sophisticated, but beautiful.

But then something terrible happened. I caught the all-too-common Hollywood disease: mogulitis. My raging ego and competitive drive kicked into hypergear. I forced the company to develop more television projects and feature films, and commission theater projects. Wind Dancer grew, and as the company grew, I struggled more and more to stay focused on the creative aspects and not get entangled in the business of the business.

Writers think of stories as art. The industry thinks of stories as products. Big difference. I had inadvertently fallen into the mogul trap. Instead of creating stories from instinct and passion and discerning where they fit in the marketplace, the company started conceiving stories as products, something to sell. Projects were no longer birthed from a single vision; it was art by committee. Somewhere in the early nineties, marketing became king. The left-brainers—lawyers, MBAs, and marketing executives—began telling the right-brain creatives what they could and could not create. It was ass-backward. The tail wagging the dog. Here's an example.

I was attached to direct a feature film for Twentieth Century Fox, a raucous family comedy. Fox had created a one-sheet (the movie poster), devised a marketing plan, chosen dates for the opening weekend, and secured over three thousand screens across the country—but they didn't have a completed screenplay. They had a marketing plan but no script. It didn't matter. The project had "pre-awareness." The studio had a product they knew they could sell. Tail wagging the dog.

Eventually, I dropped out of the project. But the left-brainers had brainwashed me. Instead of sitting alone and daydreaming like a child and spending time in the creative ether, I was in a constant stream of meetings conceiving products for the marketplace. I was running myself ragged in the hamster wheel of Hollywood. More, more, more. Bigger,

bigger, bigger. The company I founded to celebrate creativity had transformed into a factory. And quality took a back seat to quantity.

One day, I heard a phrase floating around the office: "Sell it, don't smell it."

I realized that Wind Dancer was developing projects I would never watch at home or buy tickets to see in a movie theater. Creatively, I was drying up. Unlike the caveman with the snow globe, I no longer reached up to the heavens, channeling creative spirit through the right side of my brain onto the page. It was all left brain, stats, demographics, and spreadsheets, and all the crap I hated but felt compelled to do to keep the company growing. And again, we needed a new logo to reflect the changing company's spirit.

It wasn't until I wrote this essay that I realized the final Wind Dancer logo I had unconsciously created reflected my inner struggle at the time. The logo was an eagle chained to a parched landscape. The eagle flaps its wings, desperately trying to break free, fly away, and soar, but the heavy chain keeps the majestic bird grounded, a prisoner. When conceiving this image, I imagined that each chain link represented the forces that keep artists shackled—fear, doubt, anxiety, and insecurity. And in the animated version of the new logo, as the eagle strains to break free, we see one link start to break, the eagle on the verge of escaping and flying away.

Carl Sandburg said, "Poetry is the journal of the sea animal, living on land, wanting to fly in the air." But it's not just poets. It's all of us. Somewhere deep inside our souls, we know that we can fly, ascend, and transform. But I was chained to the company. There was no escape. I exhausted myself trying to break free and become an artist again. Then, one day, I had an epiphany in a conference room at Lionsgate.

I was sitting on one side of a conference table, and the left-brain decision-makers from the studio sat on the other, along with two salespeople. Those two men had nothing to do with the creative process. Their job was to sell existing programs to television stations around the globe. This was before the phenomenon of streaming services. Those two executives were like vacuum salesmen, going door to door selling products. I was there to pitch a new idea for a half-hour television comedy.

The male lead was a single father raising a teenage daughter. A painter moves into the apartment next door, becoming a surrogate mother to the teenage girl, causing friction with the father. But the painter and single father have chemistry, and a flirtatious relationship develops. As I pitched the ten-episode arc, I stood up, acted out the two lead characters, and explained how they would have their first kiss in the tenth episode. And one of the salesmen—I will call him Murray—jumped up, crossed his arms, and slashed them repeatedly, yelling, "No! No! No! *No!*"

"Excuse me?" I asked.

"They can't kiss," Murray said, still slashing his arms.

"Why not?"

"No way. No kiss."

I started to explain how I envisioned the scene. I would write it so the kiss would be charming, almost accidental. But instead, I asked the obvious question, "Wait, so . . . why can't they kiss?"

"Because . . ." Murray went into a lengthy tirade about a comedy on the Fox network in which two lead characters kissed and the show lost viewership in the key demographic. His sales data had shown the kiss led to a drop in share points, and viewership diminished.

Kablam! My head exploded. I saw my brains splatter all over the conference room and drip down the walls. This sales-person, a man born without curiosity or creativity, was now determining creative content. At that moment, I had a divine nudge. No, it was more like a spiritual punch in the gut. The spirit voice inside me said emphatically: *Done. Finished. You're out of here.*

We quickly wrapped up the meeting, and I drove to the Wind Dancer offices in Hollywood. I asked my partner, David McFadzean, to come into my office and told him we were shutting down the company. I no longer wanted to do this because the inmates had taken over the asylum. Creativity was crushed. Sales data ruled. I realized the logo, the spiritual essence of the company, had transformed from an innocent dove to a shackled bird of prey. I had been seduced by Hollywood and lost my way. I had abandoned the creative impulse that started the company.

It took months, actually a couple of years, but I eventually shuttered Wind Dancer, retreated to the country, and decided to try my hand at writing prose. So instead of attending marketing meetings and sales pitches, I sit alone in my study and daydream.

I don't need an animated logo for that. But if I did, it would look something like this: An old gray-haired geezer sits humped over a yellow pad, staring at the blank page. The sunlight from the window morphs into a hairy Neanderthal, who walks over and bonks the gray-haired geezer on the head with a snow globe, and the writer begins to write.

49
YELLOW PADS

I love yellow pads. They excite me, thrill me, and actually set my heart aflutter. My nerdy pulse quickens when I pull a fresh yellow pad out of the desk drawer because yellow pads represent a new beginning, birth, creation, infinite possibilities, and a blank canvas on which to dream.

I scribble my prayers, creative musings, and daydreams onto those pads. I explore new worlds, create characters, confess my sins, and reveal my most intimate thoughts and fears. And here is the beautiful part: no one will ever read, photocopy, or record anything I scribble on those yellow pages. They are private, only for me—and Spirit.

After I closed my production company and moved to our farm a few years ago, I realized the prayer journal I kept on one yellow pad and the creative journal I kept on another pad were starting to blend. For most of my career, I kept my work time and prayer time separated—two different yellow pads. But now the creative pad and the prayer pad have become one. Intuition inspires writing; divine nudges turn into scribbles on a page; ineffable feelings become tangible concepts when put into words. Thought and energy flow through the body into the pen and onto the page: spirit and matter coalesce, giving birth to new ideas.

It is humbling. It is thrilling. It brings joy. When I pray, I create; when I create, I pray.

Flannery O'Connor said all of this in five words: "The artist prays by creating."

50

NUGGET

The reality is a nightmare, the nightmare a world of pickup trucks and vans parked in a gravel lot, voices barking orders, echoing inside a cavernous barn, where wranglers stab prods and bang aluminum poles, driving horses through a narrow chute into holding pens without food or water. Dust and fear float in the air. The healthier horses, if they can be called that, are shipped to slaughterhouses across the borders into Mexico or Canada, the meat sold for human consumption in foreign countries. The horses that are too far gone—the blind, lame, emaciated—are purchased and sold to canning companies, then turned into dog food. This is the nightmare reality of a kill auction.

Kill auctions are local events across the United States where abused, neglected, or abandoned horses are sold. Small crowds gather to bid on the damaged animals. Sometimes families attend, looking to purchase an inexpensive pet, but the primary bidders are kill buyers. Kill buyers are brokers, middlemen, who come with checkbooks or wads of cash in hand, prepared to outbid competitors, buying the horses cheap and then selling them to slaughterhouses for a profit. Horse rescues, nonprofit organizations, raise money and send representatives to the auctions to bid against the kill buyers, hoping to rescue horses that have a chance of surviving.

"Imagine a horse," Sharon said, "only twelve hands high, forty-eight inches, weighing about five hundred pounds. That's Nugget."

February winds whipped shards of ice, chapping our faces and numbing our fingers as we stumbled over the frozen ground. Hunched against the cold, Matisse and I followed Sharon, who runs a horse rescue in western Connecticut, as she led us between the paddocks.

Sharon held her hat in place and yelled back over her shoulder, "A kill buyer purchased Nugget and carted him to a feedlot. Horses are sold to slaughterhouses by the pound, so the kill buyers fatten them up before shipping them off."

Sharon had arrived at the feedlot with an envelope of donated cash, scanned the ragtag herd, and spotted Nugget. His black-and-white coat was matted with mud and feces, but Sharon sensed there was a healthy horse under all that filth.

"I decided the little Hackney was the horse to save," Sharon said. She rescued Nugget the day before he was to be sold to the slaughterhouse.

I turned to Matisse. "You know this is a little crazy?"

"I know." Matisse grinned.

Matisse was looking to acquire rescue horses for equine

therapy, a specialized form of healing called family constellation therapy. *Why?* Why buy a crippled or emotionally damaged horse? Why purchase problems? On the drive to Connecticut, Matisse had explained that rescue horses, horses that have experienced trauma, are highly sensitized and best suited for constellation therapy. I recalled *trauma* as the Greek word for *wound*. My daughter was purposefully buying *wounded animals*, physically or emotionally damaged horses, which seemed a little insane to me.

Sharon rolled the door open, and we stepped inside the barn, which smelled of sweet hay and horses. We followed her to a corner stall, where we met Nugget. When I first laid eyes on the horse, I almost laughed because Nugget looked like a plush toy, as if a full-size horse had been thrown into a clothes dryer and shrunk down to a pint-size toy. The word *sprite* came to mind.

"Easy, easy," Sharon whispered as she opened the stall door. A year of nurturing had transformed Nugget into a postcard-perfect pony. His black-and-white spotted coat was sleek and beautiful. Sharon stroked Nugget's head and explained, "Nugget is a Morgan cart horse, also known as a Hackney pony. The breed is known for its alert spirit and high-stepping trot when pulling a cart."

I watched my daughter, who took one look at the little horse and fell in love. But when I stepped into the stall, Nugget reared up and backed away, slamming into the other horse, a small, chestnut Arabian.

"Easy now, easy," Sharon said. "This one's name is Obie. He's partially blind and has a neurological condition, but he's adorable."

Nugget backed away from me. His fear was palpable, filling the space, causing Obie to walk obsessively in a tight circle. Matisse took off a glove and ran her hand along Obie's hide as he circled past.

Sharon explained, "These two bonded months ago. They're inseparable."

Without hesitating, Matisse agreed to take them both. Again, I worried my daughter was buying a world of trouble, setting herself up for heartache. Before I could say anything, Matisse asked to see the other horses.

Sharon led us to a grooming area near the tack room, where we met the superstar of the farm, a sorrel racehorse named Gigi. Gigi had run three professional races before tendon damage ended her career. She was discovered in an abandoned dirt lot, skeletal, mange eating away her hide, but her spirit was still fierce. Gigi was graceful and sassy and not very friendly. She kept swinging her head to the side as if to bite us.

I stepped back. Matisse stepped up. She stroked Gigi's neck, looked into her eyes, and said, "She's perfect." A price was negotiated, and arrangements were made to have Nugget, Obie, and Gigi transported to our farm in the Hudson Valley in early April.

The spring breeze still had a winter's bite when the horses arrived. The trailer backed up to the corral, the loading chute banged open, and all three horses stumbled out of the trailer. Nugget broke into a canter, circling the pasture, skittish and frightened. Physically, Nugget was the healthiest of the three horses but was the most psychologically damaged. According to the paperwork, Nugget was a seven-year-old gelding from New Holland, Pennsylvania. He was well bred but possessed a stubborn streak, which is probably why he was beaten by a man my size. Nugget threw his head back and flattened his ears whenever I approached the corral. If I stepped toward Nugget, he whinnied in fear and trotted away.

Horses are prey animals; they have a flight instinct, and that instinct is exacerbated when an animal has been abused or traumatized. They also have acute hearing and smell; horses spend their lives avoiding pain and escaping predators. Their brains are wired for fear—like a father's brain. I feared for Matisse. Every time she stepped into the corral to clean a hoof or brush a mane, I held my breath. Matisse's heart was in the right place, but she was not an experienced horseperson. She was unguarded and took risks.

One afternoon, Matisse bent down to check Gigi's hind hoof, and my stomach tightened, knowing one quick kick could crush her skull or break ribs. But Matisse was fearless, or maybe just naive.

In May, the earth warmed, and the pastures morphed into lush green carpets. Matisse decided to turn out the horses to graze for a few hours, so I helped her slip halters on Gigi and Obie, but Nugget refused the halter. Matisse walked up to Nugget, and he backed up. She waited and approached the animal again. The horse trotted away. Matisse coaxed Nugget with a soothing voice, assuring him everything was fine, but the horse snorted and turned his back.

I got anxious and had to leave the paddock because rescue horses pick up on the emotions of other creatures—two- and four-legged. I leaned on the corral gate and watched as my daughter, halter in hand, approached Nugget again and again. Each time, Nugget scurried away. This went on for over an hour. Matisse never lost patience; she was gentle and tenacious. Finally, Nugget tired and stood still. Matisse inched up. Nugget raised his head. Matisse slipped the halter on.

Later that summer, Matisse decided to expand the herd from three rescue horses to five. She acquired Oakley, a majestic hunter-jumper, who was high-strung and emotionally unstable. The last horse Matisse adopted was Goliath, the gentle giant, a solid-white draft horse, seventeen and a half hands high, weighing over two thousand pounds. Goliath has an arched neck with a flowing mane and a massive head that he rests on your shoulder when you nuzzle his neck. He looks like a horse a knight or a princess would ride in a fairy tale.

Goliath was abandoned in west Texas, cut up and crippled. When he arrived in Garrison, Matisse noticed the horse trembled and had difficulty lowering his head to eat. She called the veterinarian, who ran tests, and we learned the horse suffers from shivers, a degenerative neuromuscular disease that slowly cripples the animal, similar to ALS in humans.

The condition worsens if an animal experiences fear or stress. And there was a lot of stress because the horses were fighting.

For horses to become a herd, they must establish a pecking order. Horses taunt and challenge until a hierarchy is established, usually with a dominant mare leading the pack. In this case, it was the racehorse, Gigi. She kicked, bit, and intimated the other horses, eventually ruling the herd. Nugget and Obie were relegated to the lowest position and separated from the other horses. Goliath and Oakley competed for Gigi's affection. Oakley unleashed his rage on Goliath, attacking and driving him away from Gigi. I didn't say anything to Matisse, but I thought there was no way these animals would ever become a herd. One of them, or Matisse, was going to get hurt. And what I feared, happened.

Matisse went out one morning to toss hay to the horses and discovered a deep gash on Goliath's chest, above the right leg. Oakley had kicked him. The wound got infected and filled with pus. The vet came and administered medication, but the wound needed constant attention. Matisse squeezed out the pus three times a day, washed the wound, and applied an anti-septic ointment. Later that week, a storm blew in over Storm King Mountain, whipping through the Hudson Valley, bending trees, and slashing rain sideways across the corrals. Nugget panicked and huddled with Obie in the run-in shed. Oakley trotted wildly around the corral, his mane flying. Goliath was anxious and unmanageable. Matisse couldn't hold him in place and clean the wound, so she called my cell phone and asked me to help. I threw on a rain slicker and headed out.

The wind had died down by the time I got to the corral, but a steady rain pounded the paddock, forming ankle-deep puddles. I held the lead line while Matisse tended to Goliath. The wound was tender. Every time Matisse touched it, Goliath backed away. She stroked his muscular neck, whispering in his ear until Goliath finally relaxed and rested his head on my shoulder. Matisse knelt in the mud and cleaned the wound. One of my favorite Bible verses floated into my consciousness as I watched my daughter, rain soaked, water dripping off her cowboy hat. It's from 1 John 4:18: "There is no fear in love, but perfect love casts out fear."

Elisabeth Kübler-Ross wrote, "Deep down, at our cores, there are only two emotions: love and fear." Love and fear are the two primary emotions of rescue horses and humans. These two feelings drive us, motivate us. Every decision we make and how we react to life comes from a place of love or fear. Love comes from a place of openness and acceptance and moves us toward something we desire. Fear comes from a place of resistance and suspicion and moves us away from something we want to avoid. Love is proactive and engenders empathy. Fear is reactive and engenders separateness. Love and fear cannot be experienced simultaneously, and the surest way to eradicate fear is to love: love conquers fear.

Goliath eventually healed. Over the dark winter months, the herd slowly settled into a community, a functioning family. The horses grew healthier and more trusting.

NUGGET

The following spring, Nugget was still wary of me, but if I was calm and moved slowly, he allowed me to scratch his neck. One afternoon, Matisse strode over to the corral, a rope halter slung over her shoulder. I stepped back and watched as she swung the gate open and called out to Nugget. The little horse trotted over and stopped in front of her. Matisse held up the halter, and Nugget stepped forward and bowed his head.

51

GARDEN HOSE

If I trip over that damn hose one more time, I will throw it in the trash, burn it, or strangle someone with it. We have a green garden hose that has a life of its own. It writhes and wiggles and finds places to hide. And it loves to get tangled up, knotted, and twisted, which takes a herculean effort to uncoil the thing. It's like wrestling an anaconda. I usually win the battle, but sometimes the hose wins, and I end up on the ground, huffing and puffing, out of breath, surrendering to the green monster that makes my life miserable.

Why have a hose? Well, water flows through it. You can aim water at plants and trees, your wife's azaleas in the pot on the back porch, or your wife when she's not looking. Hoses channel and direct the water that gives life—*living waters*.

To me water represents fertility, purity, divine wisdom, and the Holy Spirit. Jesus was baptized with water. He walked on water. He turned water into wine. Jesus said that if we drink the living waters, we would never be thirsty again. Water is mentioned 772 times in the Bible. In religions and mythologies worldwide, sprites, spirits, and deities dwell in the waters of lakes, streams, rivers, and oceans. Water is life.

But for a hose to be useful, it has to be unkinked, with no knots or twists. While wrestling the green monster the other day, I realized sin is like knots in a hose. Sin stops the flow. When I am bitter, judgmental, or hurtful, knots form in the hose. When I am selfish and put myself before others, the knots tighten, blocking the water. A tangled hose is useless; no water can flow through it. In the same way Spirit cannot flow through us when we are twisted and knotted. So how do I untangle my knots? Here is what I have found works best: we pray, ask God for forgiveness, be humble and patient, and carefully untangle each knot to become instruments for God so that living waters can flow through us.

52
PREDATORS

"Did you hear that?" I asked.

"What?" Angelina whispered.

"Shh, listen. You hear?"

"Yes."

It was around two thirty in the morning. The night was warm, but a light breeze blew off the Hudson River, so Angelina and I slept with our bedroom windows open. I was jolted awake by barking, loud yips, and triumphant howls. The coyotes had killed and were celebrating with song.

The pack had been hunting in the woods all summer, prowling the property, and tormenting our farm animals. Angelina and I have a small farm in the Hudson Valley that we share with our daughter, Matisse. She keeps miniature horses inherited from my father and rescue horses she uses for equine therapy. We have chickens, turkeys, and a small flock of sheep: prey that attract the predators. We had found scat and seen paw prints in the ravine near the marsh. There was a den hidden in the craggy rocks near the edge of our property.

The pack of predators would slink out of the ravine at night and sniff around the barn, circling the corrals.

They were not coyotes; they were coydogs. Feral dogs had mingled and bred with the coyote pack. Coydogs are larger than coyotes, about the size of a German shepherd, and have a predator's instinct. They eat anything from small rodents to deer, and they can be more dangerous than coyotes because they are not afraid of humans. Coydogs are incredibly adaptable, cunning, and lethal. Three summers ago, one aging male skirted the edge of the woods, hovering near the house for days. He was a loner, mangy and starving. My wife's teacup terrier, Pico, slipped out of the mudroom door and headed across the field up toward the barn. It was only a few minutes before we realized the dog was gone, but it was too late. He disappeared. There's little doubt what happened. We saw the tracks but never found the carcass.

The coydogs would leave, sometimes for months, but they always returned. One spring, we were away from the farm for the day. When we got home that evening, the sheep pasture looked as if someone had torn a mattress apart and scattered clumps of cotton. A pack of coydogs had broken through the electric wire that runs between the corral boards and killed two ewes. We found hooves and hide, eviscerated. One bold male kept returning, stalking the newborn lambs. He was brazen and would charge the corrals in broad daylight, probing and poking, looking for an opening. We chased him off, but within minutes he would return, back hunched, hair raised, snarling.

The scent of birth and the bleating of lambs were too enticing. We set humane traps, but they didn't work. Finally, we had a neighbor shoot him. I regretted destroying the animal, but it was only a matter of time before he killed the baby lambs. And tonight, the coydogs were back, an even bigger pack.

Hearing the howls through the open window, I jumped out of bed, dressing as I stumbled down the stairs, and grabbed a hickory walking stick as I ran out the door. Thinking back to that moment, it was probably a pathetic sight: a gray-haired old guy running around in the dark, half-dressed, waving a stick. But I was ready to protect the flock, fight off the predators, and kill them if necessary. I heard crashing through the woods. My wild ranting had scared the coydogs away. I checked the barn, the chicken coop, and the horses. The sheep were gathered in a tight, protective cluster in the middle of the corral, frightened but safe. I headed back to the house and crawled into bed.

I stretched out on top of the sheet with my jeans and shirt on, shoes nearby, in case I had to run outside again. There were no more howls; the predators were gone for the night. I heard the sound of crickets and tree frogs, the occasional small animal scurrying through the brush.

As I lay there, I remembered a poster that hung on Mr. Theil's Sunday School class wall. When my seven-year-old mind got bored with the lesson, I would study the poster. It was a painting of Jesus carrying a shepherd's crook, leading a flock of sheep. At the bottom of the poster was the quote from John 10:11: "I am the good shepherd."

I always thought that was a quaint, bucolic notion, but I finally understood the metaphor. A shepherd loves and protects the sheep and keeps a vigilant eye over the animals. A shepherd is willing to die for his flock. I am not a shepherd and certainly not Christlike, but I worry about the flock. The chickens and turkeys are protected inside a coop, the horses are safe because of their size, but the sheep are vulnerable.

When I travel or even go into the city for the day, a part of my mind is up on the farm, worrying about the sheep. Are they safe? Are the gates locked? Is the electric fence on? Are predators circling the corral? Constant worry. Something I learned from my father.

My father, his entire life, raised animals, everything from guinea pigs to miniature horses to pigeons and pygmy goats. He fussed over them, fed and groomed them. He showed them in competitions, usually winning the blue ribbons. When I was growing up, it wasn't unusual to find a sick or abandoned animal in a cardboard box in the corner of the kitchen.

The first time I brought Angelina to my father's house was to announce our engagement. It was a bitterly cold December evening. There was a newborn goat in the kitchen, curled up on a dish towel inside a cardboard box by the heating vent. The mother had died giving birth, so Dad took over the mothering. He bottle-fed the goat every three hours throughout the night.

But now my father is too old to care for animals. That's why he gave his miniature horses to Matisse. So instead of worrying about animals, Dad worries about his four adult children—every day, day and night, anticipating every possible accident, every danger, imagining every horrible scenario. I am a senior citizen, and my ninety-one-year-old father still worries about me. On our weekly phone call, my father always says "Be safe" before hanging up.

"I will, Dad."

"Don't ride in any airplanes."

"There's a pandemic raging. I won't be getting on a plane."

"You know, you should always drive with your headlights on."

"I know, Dad."

"Even in the daytime."

"Got it, yes. I understand."

When he knows I'm going into New York City, Dad warns, "Make sure you look both ways before you cross the street."

"Dad, come on."

"Those people in that city are a little crazy."

"OK, OK . . ."

"Especially the taxi drivers."

I silently scream, *Agggh, Dad! Stop! Seriously. You are driving me insane!* Instead, I say, "Bye, Dad, I love you."

"Love you," he says. "Be safe." And he hangs up.

You see, my father equates worry with love; the more you worry, the more you love. I don't believe that. Fear is corrosive; it steals happiness, destroys peace of mind, and ruins the moment's joy.

I'm afraid I have to disagree with my father, and yet I do the same thing. I have a worry worm wiggling inside my brain: Where are Matisse and Fred? Are they safe? Who are they with? Are they traveling? Fred is out in California. Was there an earthquake? Fires? Mudslides? Is Matisse working with the horses? Is she alone?

I know all of this worry is wasted energy, but I can't help it. It's inculcated into my very being. Does God worry and fret about us? Does God have a worry worm inside her head? Does she wring her hands and wonder if we are wearing seat belts, or whether we will make it home safely before curfew? I imagine not, since God knows everything. God doesn't worry. She loves.

One day I had to drive into the city for a meeting. Matisse, hair in a ponytail, sweat streaking her face, stomped the horse manure off her boots and walked me to the car.

"Get someone to help you with Oakley when the vet comes," I said.

"I will," she assured me.

"Don't handle him by yourself."

"OK."

"I mean it, get some help."

"I will."

"OK. I'll see you tonight."

Matisse hugged me goodbye. I tossed my computer onto the passenger seat, climbed in, and started the Jeep. As I drove away, Matisse waved and said "Be safe" as she walked back to her horses through the sunlight.

53
EULOGY

My father died peacefully at his home on March 13, 2021, at the age of ninety-one years. He was buried at Sunset Memorial Cemetery in Evansville, Indiana, on March 17, 2021. His passing inspired many memories to come to mind. Plus, I was tasked with giving the eulogy.

As I thought about my dad, I was struck by the one characteristic that defined him throughout his life: his kindness. Mark Twain said, "Kindness is a language that the deaf can hear and the blind can see." I found this quote interesting, bordering on the ironic, since my father was legally blind and almost completely deaf. Glaucoma took his eyesight and ninety-one years of life had diminished his hearing.

I knew well that my father was not a perfect man, but he was a kind man. He was not a learned man, by no means a scholar, but he was kind. He was a gifted artist, working in different mediums his entire life—drawing, painting, sculpting, woodcarving—winning numerous awards, but that really didn't define him. What defined Fredrick Golden

Williams was his kindness.

When I was growing up, it seemed to me there was always a sick or newborn animal in the house, usually in a cardboard box by the heat register in the kitchen. Every three or four hours, throughout the night, Dad would get up to bottle-feed a baby goat, or give a guinea pig medicine, or check the broken wing of a pigeon. He poured his love and gentle spirit into his animals and his children.

When I was four years old, I was convinced that Dracula lived in the armoire in my bedroom. My baby brother Randy would sleep through the night, but I would lie in bed, rigid with fright, the sheet pulled up to my nose, eyes peeking out, staring at the armoire, waiting for Dracula to throw open the doors, sweep across the room, and suck all the blood out of my body. This terror of a goofy-looking monster with jet-black hair and a flowing red cape was real. I kept my parents up, screaming each time I saw the armoire door crack open, or when I heard a diabolical giggle coming from inside of that piece of furniture. I was terrified every single night. But Dad found a solution: He pulled an old canvas cot out of the garage and set it up next to the bed. He would lie on the cot and hold my hand until I fell asleep.

The last months of his life, my father started to blend his dream life, his imagination, and reality. What he dreamed was real, what was real felt like a dream, and his imagination carried him back to his earliest childhood, wisps of memories floating like clouds. Often he saw children in his room, three or four young kids playing on the floor of his bedroom or looking at his woodcarvings on the dresser. One Sunday morning during my weekly phone call, he told me about the three children who had spent the night in his room. He knew that I had sent them to his house to stay the night before catching a train the next morning. He explained that he was up until dawn entertaining them: He told them stories, got them cookies from the kitchen, and showed them how to draw. He gave each of them pads of paper and pencils and taught them how to draw trees and horses, puppies, and barns with chickens in the yard. He told me the kids were well behaved and very polite. When morning came, the children left his room to catch their train. Even in his dementia, my father was kind.

Two weeks before his passing, Dad was admitted to the emergency room at Deaconess Hospital. He was hallucinating. His dreams, imagination, and reality had merged, creating a cloud of confusion. I stood at his bedside as nurses took his vitals, and Dad pointed at a turtle and her two babies crawling across the sheet of his hospital bed. When the emergency room doctor came to give me the results of the tests she had run, Dad petted an imaginary puppy and introduced the dog to the doctor. My father was in the hospital for three days before going home, and during that time every nurse, technician, and doctor said the same thing: "He is so sweet."

One afternoon, as Dad was floating back to reality, he kept reaching across the hospital bed and plucking at something. I asked him, "Dad, what are you doing?" He said, "I'm picking these yellow flowers. See? They're so beautiful." For a brief moment, I wished that I had a canvas cot so I could set it up next to the bed and hold his hand.

Here is what I learned from my father: At the end of life, it's not about the ribbons won or the trophies lined up on the bookshelf; it's not about accolades or your photo in the newspaper. It's about life partners, family, and friends, and all the lives you touch with your kindness.

54

BIOLOGY

*The day of my spiritual awakening was the day I saw and knew
I saw all things in God and God in all things.*
—MECHTHILD OF MAGDEBURG

Angelina had a couple of friends up from the city for a visit. I will call them Martin and Edith. Martin is an avid reader and spends every waking hour on his computer. He is someone who googles on his phone to fact-check everything you say: "Actually, if all the ice caps melt, the sea level would rise *230* feet, not *200* feet." After lunch, Martin and I walked in the woods around our farm. Sunlight dappled the trails. A light breeze blew off the Hudson River, teasing the sugar maples.

Martin asked, "What are you working on these days?"

"I am writing personal essays and spiritual musings that I hope to turn into a book."

"Spiritual musings? What is that?"

I knew Martin was a devout atheist, so I hesitated to say anything. I didn't want to ruin a pleasant hike with a theological debate, so I kept walking. But Martin was insistent.

"You really believe all this God stuff?"

"Yes, I do."

He shook his head. "It doesn't make sense to me."

"It shouldn't make sense. God is a mystery," I said. "If we understood the mystery, God would stop being God."

"I don't believe in God, and I don't trust religions."

"God and organized religion are two different things."

"You realize more atrocities have been committed in the name of God than by all the terrorist groups throughout history?"

"I can't argue with that."

"And praying to a magical person floating up in the clouds. Really?"

"I don't think of God as a person."

"Don't you Christians pray, 'Our Father, who art in heaven . . .'?"

"Yes, but the 'Father' is metaphorical. God is without gender. No white beard. No goddess gown or leaves in her hair. Those are images humans impose on an ineffable mystery."

"How do you know that mystery exists?"

I stopped walking and gestured. "Look around. Look at the trees and sunlight. All the teeming life, the vibrating energy of this woods."

Martin put his hands on his hips and studied the trees. "I appreciate nature. I do. Especially getting out of Manhattan into the fresh air. But this isn't God."

I had to decide: Do I engage and risk a heated debate or keep walking? I couldn't help myself. I engaged. "Think of it this way. God is not 'out there.' I believe God is *in here*," I said, pointing to my chest. "I am convinced the spirit that lives inside me is the same life force inside you and these trees. And everything that exists. There are many labels for this spiritual force, but let's call it divine intelligence."

"OK," Martin agreed.

"Divine intelligence speaks to our souls. It is the intelligence that guides salmons to migrate from the ocean to the same riverbed year after year to spawn or teaches gray whales to swim twelve thousand miles round trip from the Arctic to give birth in the warm waters of Baja and return with their newborns to the same frigid waters for a summer of feeding."

"That is biology," Martin said.

"Look up in that tree. See the robin's nest? Did you know every robin's nest is made of twigs and grass and is the same uniform design, like a cupped hand, and the same size? Does divine intelligence instruct robins on how to build nests?"

"Biology," Martin repeated.

"Over in our orchard, we have a sapling, a baby tree. What informs that tree on how to draw nutrients from the soil and absorb sunshine and rain to create an apple? I believe God is divine intelligence, the creative force that makes and lives within all things. It constantly communicates so life throughout the universe can continue to evolve and transform."

Matin pulled out his cell phone to fact-check me. As

he scrolled through his phone, he mumbled, "High school biology." He punched and swiped and scanned an article: "Osmosis. Fertilization. Pollination. The flower buds open, the petals fall off, and the base transforms into—"

"It does what?" I teased.

"It *transforms* by the cells dividing again and again and eventually it becomes an apple."

Spirit must have been working overtime that day because, as Martin studied his phone, explaining osmosis, a butterfly flew out of the bushes and landed on my right forearm. It sat there, pulsating with life. I could see the delicate antennae, the brush of red powder coating the wings, and the two yellow-and-blue eyes painted on each wing. I raised my arm, and Martin leaned in for a closer look, his nose almost touching the butterfly. He whispered, "Beautiful."

Then the butterfly broke the moment, caught the breeze, and fluttered away. We watched as it ascended among the branches.

"What was that?" Martin asked.

I smiled and said, "Biology."

55

TEA WITH ADRI

I dragged my soul along the cracked sidewalk, bumping it over the curb through the bits of litter that lined the gutters of the West Village in Manhattan. I hadn't slept for three days. Blackbirds of despair had built a nest in my heart. And laid rotten eggs. I had closed my production company and moved back to New York City to pursue my first passion— writing plays.

I had written a new play, *Actually, We're F**ked*, that had its world premiere at the Cherry Lane Theatre. It was a comedy about four millennials deciding whether to have children when the planet is dying. According to many scientists, the earth has entered the extinction phase. Denial, indifference, corporate greed, and anthropocentrism are destroying the planet. So why give birth? If the earth is doomed, why procreate? Is it even moral to bring children into a dying world?

I intended to write a funny play about a grave existential issue. The production was excellent. We had a fine director, John Pasquin, a fantastic cast, creative designers, and my wife, Angelina Fiordellisi, who produced and shepherded the production. Audiences responded well to the play, but the reviewer from the *New York Times* gutted me.

After forty years working in the entertainment industry, I was used to bad reviews and usually ignored them. After all, it was only one person's opinion. But this review was exceptionally vicious and felt like a personal attack. I received emails and phone calls from friends who asked what I had done to piss off this woman. Did I poison her dog? Puke on her baby? Angelina mentioned to Adriana Trigiani that I had been walking around the house like a zombie, bumping into walls, mumbling to myself. So Adri called and told me to come to her home for tea.

For those of you who don't know, Adriana Trigiani is a *New York Times* bestselling author of twenty books, a television writer, a film director, a producer, and a popular podcast host. She's a wife and mother, and simply extraordinary. The name of her production company is The Glory of Everything. That gives you an idea of the woman's soul.

When I arrived at Adriana's townhouse, I walked up the stoop, and she gave me a big hug. When Adri hugs you, sunshine cascades through your body, and you hear bubbly brooks in forests filled with birdsong. Cool breezes blow down a mountain, across valleys, and rustle golden stalks of corn. She is an earth mother, mother of the earth—Gaia in sweater and slacks.

Adri's kitchen smelled of freshly baked biscotti and cut

flowers. I sat at her table sipping my tea, and we talked for more than an hour about our families, writing, critics, and life. Then the conversation veered toward the existential question: Are we, indeed, fucked? There are close to eight billion people. The planet is cluttered and contaminated. The earth is suffocating, fighting for every breath. Is it too late? Are we already doomed?

Adri set her teacup aside, leaving a half-moon lipstick stain on the rim. She clasped her hands together and said, "We have to wake people up. That's what artists do—wake people up and force them to pay attention."

I knew she was right. I teach my students at Columbia that writing is like holding a spotlight and shining it on a subject. Metaphorically, the writer says to the audience, "Look at this. Pay attention. This is important." Flesh-and-blood characters are created to embody the concept being explored. Then I had an epiphany.

If the earth is sentient, alive, with a soul—which I believe it is—then perhaps we should treat Mother Earth the way one would treat a beloved friend, such as Adriana Trigiani. Instead of thinking of our planet as a piece of rock spinning in cold space, what if we gave the world a face? What if we laminated Adriana Trigiani's face onto the planet? If the earth had an actual human face, we might treat it better and be a little kinder. Imagine Mother Earth as Mother Adri. The spinning blue ball would have a shock of wild curly hair, bright red lipstick, and a touch of mascara.

Would you want to hurt someone that adorable? Would you smudge Mother Earth's lipstick? Would you dump tons of plastic on her? Would you drill holes looking for oil, frack her veins for natural gas, destroy rainforests, contaminate rivers and streams with toxic chemicals, and decimate rainforests? Why would you want to kill a loving mother who feeds, nurtures, and gives life? What if we invited world leaders, politicians, influencers, and the CEOs of corporations to sit down and have tea with Adri? Could we stop the ecocide and save the planet?

As we finished our tea, Adri flipped a cluster of curls off her forehead and said, "Fuck the reviewers. Keep writing. You're a good writer. Cut back on the wine and go to bed early. You'll be fine."

Adri escorted me to the door and gave me a final hug. As I walked away, she yelled, "Be kind to yourself."

As I walked home, the sidewalks didn't seem as cracked and broken. I noticed there was less trash in the gutter. Did the street cleaner sweep the pavement while I was having tea? Then I saw a sycamore tree. It was planted in a square of dirt at the edge of the sidewalk and surrounded by a wrought iron fence built many years ago. Over the years, the tree had grown and expanded and defeated the artificial confines. The trunk absorbed the metal rods into its flesh as the branches stretched to the sky, reaching for the sun.

56

OLD POPS

People who dwell in God dwell in the eternal now.
There, people can never grow old.
There, everything is present, and everything is new.
—MEISTER ECKHART

I'm one of those guys who stands in front of the mirror and sucks in his stomach. After a shower, with a towel wrapped around my waist, I check to see if I have gained any weight, then strike a few muscle poses. Yeah, the pecs are still good, and arms are not too bad for a seventy-year-old.

The mirror nods and reluctantly agrees, *OK, yeah. Your triceps still bulge a little.*

"Damn right," I say to the mirror as I flex my arm.

You are pathetic.

"What?" I yell, grabbing the cuticle scissors, pretending to trim my eyebrows. "What are you talking about?"

Angelina stands in the doorway, shaking her head. "You are so vain."

"I'm not vain," I insist.

"Oh, no, not at all."

"I'm not."

"You work out two hours a day."

"I want to stay healthy."

"Six days a week."

"I need to sweat out toxins. It clears my head. When I am writing, I need a clear head."

"So doing deep squats with a dumbbell clears your head?"

"Yes."

"You realize that you spend more time in front of the mirror than I do."

"No, I don't."

Angelina walks away, mumbling something about mirrors and magnets and how I'm a piece of steel.

Am I vain? I was an actor a hundred years ago, so I guess I still have an actor's ego. When someone touches my arm, I instinctively flex my bicep just to make sure they feel the density and strength. I admit that when I stand in front of the mirror, I pinch the roll of fat around my waist, my love handles, to make sure they haven't moved from two fingers of fat to a handful. I take pride in my appearance. I don't want to be one of those old men with hair growing out of my ears, missing belt loops, or leaving the house with one blue and one black sock.

We used to live on the Upper West Side in New York.

One warm spring morning, I was walking down Central Park West to a breakfast meeting when I noticed an older gentleman standing at a bus stop, holding a briefcase. His hair was oiled and perfectly parted. He wore a brown tweed sports coat, crisp white shirt, and a blue tie with a paisley print. His wingtips were buffed to a high sheen, but he wasn't wearing pants. His boxer undershorts hit about midthigh. Socks. Shoes. No pants. He was gazing at the trees in the park, watching a squirrel jump from limb to limb, oblivious to the fact that he was only half-dressed.

I thought, *What happened?* Had the doorman at his building not said anything? Was the uniformed man holding the door open too shocked to respond? Was it too embarrassing? I stood there, unsure what to do. Should I say something? Help him home? Call someone? He seemed fine, except for his exposed knobby knees. I glanced at my watch and realized I was late for my meeting, so I left him there on the sidewalk.

I don't want to leave the house without my pants. That is why I fight geezerhood.

You see, no one teaches you how to grow old. No class trains you how to age. We are taught how to read and write, add and subtract, drive a car, and fill out our taxes, but no one teaches us about decrepitude. There are plenty of classes about *anti*aging and plenty of products to help you maintain a youthful appearance. But if you are lucky enough to make it to the last third of your life, as I have, you sort of stumble and bumble your way into your twilight years. You accept the sags and wrinkles and the paunch, the creaky knees, and death. Katharine Hepburn said, "There's a certain melancholy watching oneself rot." I think it was Katharine who said that. I could be making it up.

One day my son asked, "Dad, how old do you feel?"

"Thirty-two," I said without thinking. Because, inside, that is how old I feel. I stopped aging at thirty-two. Inside I am young and vibrant, a bit of a stud, with a headful of thick brown hair. Then I look in the mirror. Yikes! I study my reflection and whisper, "I can't be that old."

Yeah, get real, says the mirror, rolling its eyes.

"Inside, I'm thirty-two."

Like hell you are.

"No, really. I am vibrant, alert, and alive."

Not for long.

I gaze into the mirror and repeat my mantra: "I have the wisdom of old age and the vitality of youth."

Wow, I didn't know you were so woo-woo, says the mirror.

"It's not woo-woo. It's a positive affirmation."

Well, affirm away because your ass is getting old.

"Shut up."

Seriously, turn around. The cheeks of your butt look like two undercooked pancakes.

"Why are you so mean to me?" I ask.

Hey, I'm just holding up the mirror.

"But I work out. I eat right, exercise."

Time is not kind. The mirror smirks, a snarky glare coming off the glass.

"Well, say what you want, I am going to rage against the dying of the light."

And the mirror starts singing Cole Porter: *Don't you know, little fool, you never can win. Use your mentality. Wake up to reality.*

I strike back and sing that Lesley Gore classic. "You don't own me. I'm not just one of your many toys!"

"Matt?"

Oh, shit! I hear footsteps and hurry out of the bathroom. I don't want Angelina to find me arguing with the mirror. I have a sneaking suspicion that she is looking for an excuse to have me committed.

"Hey," I say.

"Hey."

I give her a hug, trying to distract her. And that's when I see her gray hair, the creases around her eyes, the windows of her soul, reflecting the divine spark inside her that is ageless and eternal. I kiss her and go to the closet to dress.

"Were you singing to the mirror?"

I pretend I don't hear her. I squeeze into my tight metro-sexual jeans. No baggy old-man pants for me. I slip on my "club fit" shirt, hugging my not-so-saggy body. I'm feeling good. I'm feeling thirty-two again. I even have designer sneakers. No wingtips for this guy. And then I remember the comedy club.

Our nephew Stefano Lewin came to New York to visit and hang out. I told him, "Hey, it's a nice night. What would you like to do?" I could almost hear his twenty-four-year-old brain spinning. He told me he wanted to go to Artichoke Basille's Pizza on MacDougal Street and then a comedy club. "Let's go," I said. And we hit the street, a sweet, shaggy-haired kid and his really cool uncle, who was wearing hip sneakers.

I ate three slices of artichoke pizza, loaded with artichoke hearts, cream sauce, spinach, mozzarella, and Pecorino Romano cheese. It was about eight thousand calories. The mirror is not going to be happy. I can already see that smart-ass shaking his head at me, tiny shards of light flickering around the room. We finished the pizza and went down the street and into a cellar to hear some up-and-coming comedians. The place was tiny and dank. There were about nine people in the audience, all in their twenties or thirties. It was a weeknight, so I understand why the crowd was sparse.

The emcee for the night grabbed the microphone. He was a skinny, twitchy kid with a mean mouth and an irritating voice. Every time he opened his mouth, it was like being stabbed in the face with a lobster fork.

But Stefano was excited, so we ordered beers, kicked back, and watched the acts. One very young comedian dressed in a toga did a rambling fifteen-minute monologue about chariots and a drunken Caesar. It was simply terrible. I thought, *I have a shower curtain that is funnier than you.* I felt awful judging the guy, so I said a quick prayer, *God, help the man in the toga. Please bonk him on the head with your comedy stick.*

Then the twitchy MC introduced a dark-haired comedian in her late twenties, who kept running her hand through her curly hair and shrugging her shoulders. Her entire act was about being neurotic. I found myself smiling because she was telling the world that she was basically a hot mess. OK, I can relate.

Then the twitchy MC leaped back up on the stage and started his routine. I pretended to listen because the place was so tiny. I didn't want to be rude. Finally, the MC said something funny. I don't remember the joke, but it surprised me, and I laughed.

The MC stopped his act, turned, pointed at me, and said, "Hey, old pops liked that one." *Old pops? I'm going to jump up on that stage and bitch-slap that little creep across the room.* But my back hurt, and I was getting tired. After all, it was eleven o'clock, two hours past my bedtime.

57

DESIRE

I hear the shower running and Angelina humming as I slide the razor over my face. Scraping away the white foam under my chin, I notice the little turkey wattle, the bags under my eyes, and the new crevice that has formed on my forehead.

The shower shuts off, but Angelina continues to hum. I grab a towel off the rack, spread it open, and wait for her to step into its warmth. Gravity has won; parts sag. The creases on her face create parentheses for her smile. Gray damp ringlets kiss my wife's forehead. In her eyes, I glimpse the part of her that will never die. I rub the towel over her back, patting the water droplets dry, and realize: desire doesn't age.

58

DANCING WITH
THE STARS

My wife and I were in Kauai, Hawaii, escaping the cold and taking a needed break. One afternoon, I passed one of those shops that sells inexpensive jewelry and trinkets, and in the window was a star-shaped stained-glass ornament suspended by a string. It was twirling. When the breeze blew, the star twisted and spun, throwing light and a multitude of colors on the glass and the surrounding walls. This little star filled the space with dancing energy. Is this what it looks like when God dances? Light shimmering in space.

It struck me that I had seen the swirling kaleidoscope of colors before, but I wasn't sure where.

I pondered the colors in the store's window for a couple of days, then went online to the NASA website and pulled up images from the Hubble Space Telescope. There it was: the colors I saw in the store window resembled those found in the Antennae galaxies—rose-red and rust-colored clouds, pink swirls, dots of white, and periwinkle-blue splashes.

GLIMPSES

With each click on the computer, I realized all the spirals and ellipticals of light, the gas clouds, and the tendrils of cosmic dirt seemed to be dancing. I searched for other galaxies. The Pillars of Creation appeared stately and foxtrotting. Star clusters were break-dancing. Spiral galaxies were whirling dervishes. The Orion Nebula was definitely doing the twist. And perhaps the most beautiful of all was the Crab Nebula, a galaxy that exploded in AD 1054 but continues to dance in the darkness. Galaxy upon galaxy upon galaxy moving molecules in space and throwing off energy, light, and what appears to be joy.

Perhaps the cosmos is God dancing.

59

PRECIOUS

"Do you know where you are?"

"Yes."

"Do you know why we are here?" Beth asked, setting the suitcase on the floor at the foot of the bed. Mom looked around the room: a single bed, beige bedspread, a wooden nightstand with a lamp, two forest-green upholstered chairs, and a door to the bathroom. The linoleum floor was polished. The room smelled of disinfectant.

"Mom, do you know why we are here?"

"Yeah, sure I do," Mom said, struggling to get her breath. Walking the corridors of the hospice had tired her. She leaned against the wall, sucking in small puffs of air. Her eighty-four-year-old lungs were withered and stressed. She would suck in a small burst of air, pucker her lips, blow out, usually three times, and then draw the next breath.

"Mom, you understand?"

"What?"

"You're in hospice. We're going to put you down."

Beth was never one to mince words.

"Good," Mom said.

"We brought you here because we are going to take you out. This is it. You're not leaving here."

"Fine. That's fine with me." Mom took a labored breath and smiled.

Fifty-plus years of smoking cigarettes had ravaged her lungs. The COPD had progressed to the final stages: emphysema, chronic bronchitis, fatigue, and weight loss. I still associate the smell of cigarettes with my mother. As a child, it seemed there was always a cigarette dangling in her mouth. She would puff on a cigarette, eyes squinting against the smoke, as she changed my baby brother's diaper. A cup of coffee was never poured without a cigarette. The cigarette lighter came out as soon as she turned the key in the car's ignition. Mom smoked Salems. I remember the tagline for that particular brand: *Take a puff . . . it is springtime.*

Mom sat on the bed, holding a small gray-and-white stuffed bunny rabbit. It had been a decoration in an Easter basket, but now Mom carried it everywhere, her talisman. Beth unpacked the suitcase, putting panties, a couple of bras, and three nightgowns in the top drawer of the nightstand. She set Mom's house slippers under the bed and hung a terry-cloth bathrobe and one sundress in the closet across from the bathroom. I noticed Mom staring at the only decoration in the room: a framed poster on the wall. It was a single white lily resting in a painted vase. The flower looked elegant and lonely. Lily was my mother's nickname, along with Lil and Lily Belle. Her full legal name was Lillian Marie Schmitt, though the last one changed often, first to Williams, then Hinton, Crowe, Wilke, Bull, and Mullin. I knew we could never fit all of that on a headstone. We would have to shorten her name, but to what? Which of her husbands' names would get tossed and which would be memorialized in a cemetery?

"Mom?" Beth said, setting the inhaler on the nightstand. Mom continued to stare at the poster, clutching the stuffed rabbit.

"Mom?" Beth tapped the inhaler against the top of the nightstand.

"What?"

"Right here. Do you see this? Here is your inhaler."

Mom nodded, stroking the rabbit's fur with her thumb.

"I am putting it on the nightstand. Do you hear me? Hey, listen to me," Beth demanded.

My mother rolled her eyes, shaking her head. "She's such a bitch."

"Don't start," Beth said.

"She is a total bitch," Mom said, grinning.

Beth ran her fingers through her hair and shot me a look. "It's good you're here because I would kill her if you weren't." My sister wrapped her fingers around our mother's neck. "You can't imagine how many times I have thought about strangling you in your sleep."

"You should have," Mom said, "it would have saved us

from coming to hospice."

Beth laughed and pointed at the inhaler. "It's right there."

"I know. I see it," Mom said.

"OK, I am out of here. She's all yours," Beth said, gathering her things.

A nurse knocked on the door and stepped into the room. "Good morning. I'm here to take her vitals."

Beth gestured toward our mother. "If she doesn't behave, just smack her in the head." The nurse hesitated, not sure how to respond. Beth shrugged. "Sometimes you have to get her attention." With a frozen smile, the nurse went about her business and wrapped the blood pressure cuff around my mother's arm.

Beth pulled me aside. "You'll be OK. Mom is tired. So she'll probably sleep." Beth kissed me on the cheek. "Love you. Call me if you need anything."

She slung her purse over her shoulder and left. I realized that, over the years, the mother and daughter roles had reversed. The daughter now mothered the mother. With my sister gone, all the energy and life seemed to drain out of Mom. She looked frail and gaunt. The room grew quiet. I heard the buzz of fluorescent lights—something metallic ticked inside the wall.

"I'm finished. Thank you," the nurse said and hurried out of the room. Mom nuzzled her head into the pillow, clutching the stuffed rabbit in her right hand, and closed her eyes. "I think I'll rest my eyes," she said. "Only for a little while."

"OK, I'll be here," I said and settled into one of the green upholstered chairs. Within seconds, Mom was asleep.

I listened to her wheeze and watched her chest quiver with each breath. I thought about switching roles and how the masculine and feminine roles were flipped in our family. The anima and animus traded places. My father never touched a cigarette. My mother chain-smoked. Dad's idea of a mixed drink was to pour a shot of Mogen David wine into a tumbler of 7Up. After a few sips, he claimed he felt "loopy." My mother drank straight shots of whiskey. My father rarely went to church; nature was his cathedral. Mother dragged her children to church every Sunday morning, even with a blinding hangover. Dad built tree houses and taught his sons how to ride horses while my mother ran the household. My father was my hero. My mother handled all the finances and paid the bills. For her, Dad was like having a fifth child. She gave my father an allowance of $1.50 a week so that he could purchase snacks from the vending machine at Whirlpool. Mom took the station wagon in for repairs. Dad taught us how to make animal-shaped pancakes. Dad was intuitive. Mom was intelligent.

I joke that my brain is German, but my soul is Irish. And to a certain extent, that is true. I have threads of melancholy running through my soul like Irish lace. I inherited my mother's dogged determination and her sense of humor. When Dad told a story, you cried. When Mom told a story, you laughed.

"You're still here?" my mother said, fluttering her hand through her hair. She looked around the room, disoriented.

"Yes, I am. I'm right here."

"Good." She tried to sit up but was too weak. I reached under both arms and lifted her to a sitting position. She dropped the stuffed rabbit. I picked it off the floor and placed it in her hand.

"You don't have to sit here, sweetie. You can go. Have lunch or something. I'm fine."

"No, I'm staying here. Do you want to listen to the radio, or I can read to you?" She wrinkled her eyebrows and shook her head. "Do you want me to tell you jokes? I can do impersonations for you like I did when I was little."

That brought a smile to her face. I launched into an impersonation of my great-aunt Mouse. I mimed holding a cigarette, twitched my right eye, jerked my head to the side, and stammered the way Aunt Mouse did when pissed off. "D-d-damn them. They'd never get me into hospice. I would k-k-kick all their asses."

Mom laughed, which triggered a coughing fit. I patted her back, ran to the bathroom, and filled a clear plastic cup with tap water. I held the cup to her lips. She took a sip and sighed. "Oh, shit. Don't make me laugh. It hurts too much."

"All r-r-right, dammit. I w-w-won't!" I said, jerking my head and twitching my eye, which caused her to laugh again, triggering another coughing fit. I settled on the edge of the bed and rubbed her back, feeling the cord of bones in her spine.

Laughter is how we survived the chaos, our parents' divorce, the arguments and accusations, and years of separation.

I made a living writing comedy, but I am the least funny of all my siblings. Randy, Beth, and Bradley are jokesters and terrific storytellers. Stories get expanded and pushed to the extreme to enhance the humor. My wife calls it Williams' exaggeration. Anytime one of the Williams tells a story, Angelina suggests that you cut it in half and then cut it in half again, and you may get close to the truth. Through the years, laughter was the glue that held our broken family together.

Mom and I laughed and told stories the rest of the afternoon. We rehashed all the craziness of living in the country on Park Road: Baby getting loose and living in our telephone, me sneaking cigarettes and catching the couch on fire up in the hayloft, my brother and I shooting each other with arrows or playing tag with steak knives.

"I ran one of you kids to the emergency room every other week," Mom said. "Somebody was always bleeding. No wonder I had a nervous breakdown."

"Three nervous breakdowns," I reminded her.

Mom waved her hand. "Two, three . . . who's counting?"

Our stories carried us back to Read Street and tales of the winos that lived next door. Gladys, Dale, and Herb would get drunk, yell and argue, and throw wine bottles that landed in our tiny backyard. "I remember you hanging clothes on the line. Herb always sauntered over, took off his hat, and leaned on the fence to talk with you."

"I wore a halter top and shorts to get a suntan. When I reached up to clip clothes on the line, I'd catch the old fart staring at my titties."

"No, he didn't."

"Sure did. He gawked. I was a looker."

"Still are."

"Really, it was kind of flattering. Oh, and those damn monkeys in the basement."

For some reason, our father thought it would be a good idea to mail order eight squirrel monkeys from South America and keep them in an iron cage in our basement. The monkeys were petite and adorable and screeched and fought and threw feces at us every time we walked into the basement. One cute little bastard broke a stick off the climbing branch and figured out how to flip the latch on the cage. All eight monkeys escaped. They raced through the house, crawled into air vents, and scratched their way along air ducts and crawl spaces stuffed with insulation. They scampered over furniture, knocked over lamps, and climbed on top of the refrigerator, screeching at my mother. My mother screeched back. It took Dad and two winos most of the night to catch the monkeys in burlap bags and wrestle them back into the cage.

"I should have shoved every last one of those monkeys up your father's ass. One at a time." She threw back her head and laughed. And at that moment, I didn't see a withered woman dying in a hospice. I glimpsed a teenager wearing bobby socks and saddle oxfords swing dancing with my father to Frank Sinatra. I imagined them at the National Guard armory, 1949, two seniors in high school, moving to the music, never realizing what joy and heartache lay ahead.

Anyone who has experienced hospice knows it is like entering an alternate universe. Time becomes abstract—days and nights blend. People drifted in and out of the room: Beth's husband, Rick, grandchildren, and friends from church. Beth and I traded off caring for our mother as the morphine floated through her veins and carried her to distant places. Different nurses came and went, checking vitals and offering iced water from a sippy cup. Angelina flew to Florida to be with us for the last few days. It was a comfort to have her there, but I felt restless. I wanted to do something, but I wasn't sure what. I asked Angelina, "What should I do? Is there something I need to do?"

"Sit here," she said. "That's all you need to do." My wife understood that sometimes sitting quietly with someone is the most profound expression of love. My mother's breathing slowed. She stopped taking food and drink. There were long pauses between breaths. I heard a rattle in her chest. One night, the nurse on duty checked my mother's vitals and informed us it would not be too long, probably less than twenty-four hours. She suggested that Angelina and I rest and assured us that she would call us if things changed.

Angelina kissed my mother's cheek and whispered, "Love you, Lil."

I kissed Mom's forehead and told her that I loved her. Her eyes fluttered open, and she looked at me for several seconds, then raised her hand and touched my face.

"You are so precious," she said and closed her eyes.

Angelina and I returned to the hotel and waited for the call.

My mother died around 2:00 a.m. on April 20, 2016, two days after my sixty-fifth birthday. It happened so quickly that the nurse only had time to call Beth and tell her our mother had passed. Beth didn't want to disturb Angelina and me, so she let us sleep. We learned about my mother's death the following morning. Beth made arrangements for a memorial service at Treasure Coast Seawinds Funeral Home and Crematory in Stuart, Florida. Before they closed the coffin, Beth placed the stuffed rabbit in our mother's hand. The body was flown to Evansville, Indiana, for burial.

We buried our mother in Oak Hill Cemetery next to her mother, Hedwig Schmitt, Momo. The name we chose for her headstone was Mom's maiden name: Lillian Marie Schmitt. The service was unadorned and straightforward. I didn't cry. There was no reason for tears. All past hurts and differences dissipated when she touched my cheek and said her last words to me, "You are so precious." That was her benediction. As the Lutheran minister spoke about ashes and dust, I recalled something my mother said the afternoon in the hospice when we laughed and traded stories.

I asked, "Mom, are you afraid?"

"Not at all. I'm ready to be with Jesus."

And then she said something that stopped me. I didn't know whether it was an original thought or something she had read in a devotional or heard at church. She smiled and said, "My last breath on earth will be my first breath in heaven."

60

PASTOR'S HEART

The creative process has a feminine quality,
and the creative work arises from unconscious depths—
we might say, from the realms of the mothers.
—CARL JUNG

When a writer dies, what happens to the untold stories? Do the tales die with the teller? Do the unshared narratives float up, join the cosmic ether, and live there waiting for another storyteller to snag a word, a phrase, a character, or a concept and channel those stories onto the page?

I had closed my production company, Wind Dancer, jumped out of the Hollywood hamster wheel, and moved to our farm in the Hudson Valley. It was the first time I wasn't in production on a play, film, or television program in almost forty years. I retired. I joked that I had been turned out to pasture on our farm. But I still had stories to tell. How could I tell them?

There were no production schedules, rewrites, casting

sessions, or meetings with the networks and studios. I was lost, unmoored, and unsure what to do. I sensed the ferret of depression slinking around my study, waiting to burrow into my soul and build a nest. But why? I have a beautiful home, a great marriage, loving children, and my health. From the outside, I am sure someone would think: *What is that guy's problem? His ass is in ice cream.* I could teach, of course, volunteer, or help family and friends with projects. But was my creative life over? I didn't want to die with all of these stories living inside me.

One night I couldn't sleep. It was around three o'clock in the morning. I went downstairs to my study and clicked on the reading light. I opened the top drawer of the desk and grabbed my Bible, the one Momo had given me for my confirmation. The duct tape holding it together was starting to peel. The gold embossing had faded, but my name and the year were still legible: Mark Allen Williams 1965.

I keep old letters and birthday cards in the front of it. When I opened the cover, a faded letter fell out. It was from my mother, written years before her death. It was her perfect cursive, straight lines with poetic loops, and in the upper right-hand corner she had written the date 10-29-97. It was one of my mother's many letters asking my forgiveness for the tumultuous breakup of the family and our years of estrangement.

There was nothing to forgive. My mother and I made our peace in the end. Lying in a hospice bed, my mother touched my cheek and said her last words to me, "You are so precious."

We closed the door on the past pain. I felt at peace. But as I scanned the letter, I stopped when I saw a sentence at the bottom of the page: "I feel you especially got hurt because, I believe my mother was right, you have a pastor's heart." *Pastor's heart.* I had not thought about that phrase for years. Momo wanted me to become a Lutheran minister. That was her dream.

I read my mother's other letters, each imploring my forgiveness and declaring her love. I spread the letters on my desk next to the Bible, and as I touched each letter, I got chills. Goose bumps rippled up my arms. I felt my grandmother's presence. Please understand that I didn't see a wispy gray ghost. There wasn't some shimmering specter floating around the room. It may have been my writer's imagination, but it didn't matter. The energy in the room shifted. I felt *something*.

I was afraid to move because I didn't want this feeling to disappear. I took slow, deep breaths, and as I did, my grandmother's presence grew stronger. I didn't know what to do, but I desperately wanted to talk to her. And then I sensed she knew what I was feeling and could hear my thoughts. Our thoughts became a conversation, a conversation not with spoken words but from our hearts.

I was twenty-three years old when my grandmother died. And so much had happened over the years that I didn't know where to begin. So in my heart, I asked, *Are you surprised your grandson has gray hair and wrinkles?* I imagined her smiling.

Then I thought, *I'm so glad you are here with me.* I felt she was glad also, so I continued.

I have the Bible you gave me. It's a little beat up, but I still use it. She seemed to know. *I never fulfilled your dream and became a pastor,* I said in my thoughts. *But I told stories on stages and screens. Did you know I was a big deal in Hollywood for a few years? But that faded, like all things in life.*

In my mind's eye, I saw her holding the tattered tissue she always carried, the miracle tissue that never wore out and was never discarded. I didn't know how long this feeling, this connection with her, would last, so I pushed on. I had so much I wanted to tell her.

I read somewhere that sometimes a dream skips a generation. And that may have happened with your dream for me because my son, Fred, has a street ministry. He preaches. And he sings in his church choir and plays the bass guitar. He is a good man with a tender heart who is married to a wonderful woman, Hanna, who teaches fourth graders. I wish you could meet them, if only for a moment. They are trying to start a family. And if God blesses them, their offspring will be your great-great-grandchildren.

I relaxed a little. This intuitive talking felt less awkward. *And Matisse, my daughter, has a brilliant mind, is deeply spiritual, and is a healer. She has rescue horses and runs an equine therapy program. I sometimes see glimpses of you in my daughter's profile. Matisse has a sharp nose and the same eye color as you. And Angelina, my wife, my life partner, you would like her. She doesn't sing me to sleep with German lullabies the way you did, but she growls out Motown and sings Neapolitan love songs when she cooks pasta. Angelina is strong and tender and fierce. And she loves her family as deeply as you did yours.*

The wind blew off the Hudson, rustling the wisteria outside my study. The morning was coming. I sensed I was running out of time. *If I could rewind time, I would sit on the front porch swing with you and help you snap green beans and tell you funny stories like I did when I was a child. I would cut your grass and stay to eat ice cream and berries with you. If I could rewind time, I would attend your funeral.*

A wave of sadness washed over me. I had waited almost fifty years to say these words: *I am so sorry I didn't come to your funeral. I'm sorry I wasn't there to honor you. I never said goodbye. The last time I saw you, you were standing on the back porch steps, holding a cup filled with raspberries. You wanted me to stay, but I was too busy. I had to go. You knew, didn't you? You knew we would never see each other again. I left for graduate school completely self-absorbed and distracted. I didn't even call you in the last months of your life.*

I fought back my guilt and tears and finally confessed to her, *It took me almost fifty years to realize that the thumbprints on my heart are yours. When I was young and malleable, like fresh clay, you gently shaped and molded my heart. It was you who showed me how to love. It was you who embodied Christ's tender nature. You never called attention to yourself. You lived in service to others. When I imagine God's pure love, it is your face that I see. But I wasn't there for the end of your life. Please forgive me. Forgive my selfishness. Please know the thumbprints are still there.*

And then something inside me shifted. The tear in the fabric of my soul was sealed. The wound healed.

I didn't know how many hours had passed, but the sky outside began to brighten. I listened to the birds singing their wake-up songs. Our heart talk was coming to an end. I thanked Momo for coming and spending time with me, for healing me. Before leaving the room, I said aloud, "I love you." I clicked off the light and went to bed.

The following day, I poured a cup of coffee and went into my study. She was gone. I couldn't sense or feel my grandmother's presence. Everything was as it had been. I picked up the worn letters, placed them back inside the front cover of the Bible, and returned them to the desk drawer. I took out a yellow pad and started writing. I had no idea where the words would lead me or what stories would evolve. I had no idea that what I scribbled on the pad that morning was the beginning of this book. The beginning of a new journey as a storyteller. One with a pastor's heart.

EPILOGUE

While finishing the first draft of this book, Putin's armies invaded Ukraine. As I proofread and polished the essays encouraging kindness and compassion, I recalled news reports showing the bombing of the Mariupol Maternity Hospital. Is there a more profound example of evil than destroying mothers as they bring new life into the world? Russian planes bombed a theater filled with civilians, even though the word *Children* was chalked on the sidewalk for the pilots to see from their fighter jets. Yet the bombs fell. Missiles rained down on innocent civilians in Bucha. Articles on my cell phone showed images of bodies splayed in the street, covered with coats or old blankets, waiting for burial. And the horrors of this senseless war rippled across the globe, dividing nations, fomenting rage, creating food shortages in Africa, and sword-rattling with China.

I had nightmares. I'd jolt awake in the middle of the night and discover my face was wet from crying. I shut down. How could I publish a book about finding glimpses of charity and goodness? How could I encourage compassion with all the carnage? Writing about grace, mercy, and hope made me feel naive and foolish. It seemed absurd to look for glimpses of God when the world had grown so dark and cold.

And then Spirit intervened.

I had lunch with Ariel Curry, one of the editors working with me on this book. She and her husband, Joshua, had visited friends in Maine and were passing through New York City on their way home to Tennessee. Angelina joined us in my favorite Italian restaurant in the West Village. The four of us got to know one another by telling stories, and then Ariel and I discussed the marketing of this book. Who would read it? How could I get it out into the world? My intention was simple: raise money for neglected, abandoned, or abused children. All of my profits from the sale of *Glimpses*, public readings, and speaking engagements would be donated to charities that support children in need around the globe. But was I fooling myself? Was this book an exercise in futility? I didn't say it at lunch, but I thought perhaps *Glimpses* should be shoved in a drawer and forgotten.

Throughout most of the lunch, Ariel's husband was quiet. Joshua is warm, congenial, and solidly built, like a baseball player or a farmhand who tosses bales of hay onto the back of a truck. As we waited for the check, I asked Joshua, "So, what do you do?"

He explained that on his way home he was meeting people in Washington, DC, before flying to Ukraine. *What? He was flying into a war zone?* Then Joshua told me of the incredible path he had chosen. He and a couple of other ex-servicemen had created a mission: to provide first-aid kits to soldiers and civilians on the front line. Joshua smiled. "We started out pretty simple. On our first trip, we packed suitcases full of medical kits and flew to Poland, then drove into Ukraine. We hand out the kits and teach the soldiers and civilians about battlefield triage."

And there was the glimpse.

Hearing Joshua's story, I got chills. For weeks, I had been fretting and worrying about the war, searching for ways to help, but here was someone doing something tangible. Here was a young man putting himself in harm's way to help those suffering. I learned that Joshua was one of the founders of Task Force Yankee (TFY), along with Harrison Jozefowicz and Jeremy Wiggins, all veterans who felt inspired to help.

TFY was not military. Their missions were purely humanitarian. Since the start of the war, the organization had expanded its operations to include evacuating refugees from combat zones, providing food to isolated communities, as well as working with refugees on the next step of their lives. This wasn't a glimpse; it was a shining example of goodness, kindness, and compassion.

I want to believe we are not doomed. I want to celebrate the good that still exists in the world. The embers of hope may be dim and buried under ash, but what if we can ignite hope by blowing on those embers and feed the divine spark, the God part that lives in all of us. I believe Spirit connects us. As you know by now, I believe we are all connected to the same creative spiritual force regardless of what label we slap on divinity or image we impose on God. Irrespective of how we pray or worship, we are connected to the mystery, infinite intelligence, divine love.

I left the lunch inspired. Rather than shelve *Glimpses*, I was more motivated than ever to share stories that encouraged readers to look for and find glimpses of goodness in our troubled world.

Every thought we think creates energy, and we put that energy out into the world with our words, and words inspire actions. Can we all pray for peace, love, goodness, mercy, and grace? Can we think these concepts, say affirming words, and bring about positive change? Can we live out these ideals? Can we change the world with our thoughts, words, prayers, and kind actions? I believe we can.

ACKNOWLEDGMENTS

I always wondered why acknowledgments at the back of books were so long. Now I understand; it takes a large cast of characters to bring a book to life. I will try to keep this brief without ignoring anyone who encouraged me, cheered me on, propped me up, or spent hours giving me valuable feedback. So here goes . . .

First, I must thank my wife, my lover, my partner, and the mother of our children, Angelina Fiordellisi. Without her, I would be lost. Thanks to our children, Matisse Elizabeth Williams and Fredrick Emerson Stefan Williams. Matisse is my muse and most enthusiastic cheerleader. Her encouragement helped me flick that little demon of self-doubt off my shoulder and keep clicking away at the computer keys. Fredrick is my best buddy and the voice of truth. After reading some of the early essays, my son said, "Dad, stop writing like Matt Williams, the Hollywood guy, and start writing like Mark Williams, the blue-collar kid from Indiana." Invaluable advice that shifted the voice of the book.

I have infinite gratitude to Matthew McLachlan, my remarkable assistant, who helped me shape the stories, added humor, and spent countless hours on the floor with me, arranging and rearranging the chapters to find an unorthodox but satisfying structure. Adriana Trigiani, my dear friend, bestselling author, and wonder woman of the publishing world, sent an email telling me to stop fretting and enjoy the ride because the book works. James Manos Jr., a good friend and brilliant writer, read early drafts and convinced me I wasn't insane attempting to write a faith-based book. Jeff Sparks and Oley Sassone, long-time friends, also read a few of the early essays and urged me to keep writing.

Ashley Abercrombie and Ariel Currie read an early draft of the book and gave me specific and perceptive feedback. Not only are they two of the kindest people on the planet, Ashley and Ariel may be two of the smartest. Forefront Books assigned Michael "Mickey" Maudlin to edit the book; our pairing could not have been better. As an editor, Mickey brought insight and clarity without imposing his voice. I am sincerely grateful for his work. Billie Brownell was so gracious and gentle throughout the copyedit and proofing that it didn't feel like work.

Caitlin O'Shaughnessy was like my corner man in a boxing match. When I felt beaten and bruised, I retreated to her corner, where she wiped away the sweat, gave me a swig of water, and offered up strategy. She kept me fighting. Kenny Morgan and his team at Goodstory built a social media presence from scratch so I could brand and promote the book. David Zayas Jr. and Adonis Bello recorded my *Glimpses* podcasts and followed me around with a camera and a microphone so I could provide content to the insatiable beast—social media. Natalie Martin and David Martin at Heed Public Relations worked overtime to get the name *Glimpses* out in the world.

Finally, a big shout-out to the wonderful folks at Forefront Books: Justin Batt, Jennifer Gingerich, Lauren Ward, and Jonathan Merkh. I couldn't ask for a better team.

In many ways, this book is a record of my life and the spiritual journey I have taken. In the early years of that journey, I traveled with my two brothers, Randy and Bradley, and my sister, Beth. It was a journey filled with unimaginable heartbreak and moments of ineffable joy. I am so grateful for their constant love and fabulous sense of humor. Recalling them, I immediately smile.

And finally, I thank God, the Divine Creator, who keeps nudging me back onto the lighted path.